Tolley's
Simplified Assessing

by

Janek Matthews MA(Cantab), FCA,
Barrister of Pump Court Tax Chambers

Nigel Eastaway FCA, FCCA, FCMA, FCIS,
FTII, FHKSA, FTIHK, FOI, TEP, AITP
of Moores Rowland, Chartered Accountants

Tolley Publishing Company Ltd
A UNITED NEWSPAPERS PUBLICATION

Published by
Tolley Publishing Company Limited
Tolley House
2 Addiscombe Road
Croydon
Surrey
CR9 5AF
081–686 9141

Typeset in Great Britain by
Phoenix Photosetting, Chatham, Kent

Printed in Great Britain by
BPC Wheatons Ltd, Exeter

ISBN 0 85459 925–8

Preface

'He never wants anything but what's right and fair; only when you come to settle what's right and fair, its everything that he wants and nothing that you want. And that is his idea of a compromise. Give me the Brown compromise when I'm on his side.'

Thomas Hughes – *Tom Brown's Schooldays*

Like the JH Shorthouse's *Church of England*, *Simplified Assessing* is no doubt a compromise; between simplicity and comprehensibility on the one hand and watertight tax gathering on the other. The authors consider that, not unnaturally, the Inland Revenue won the Brown Compromise with a pronounced phobia for possible avoidance which belies the name given to probably the most fundamental change in the tax system in the last 70 years.

However we would like to thank all who contributed to the meetings of the Simplified Assessing Consultative Committee, both from the ranks of the Revenue and what now appear to be called the customers' representatives.

We would also like to thank our colleagues at Pump Court Tax Chambers and Moores Rowland for their help and advice, and in particular Paula Higgleton ATII, ATT for checking the manuscript and to Celia Duncan for typing it and coping with our voluminous amendments and indecipherable handwriting.

Inland Revenue texts are Crown copyright and are reproduced by kind permission of the Controller of Her Majesty's Stationery Office.

The law and practice is stated up to the date of the *Finance Act 1994*.

Jan Matthews
Nigel Eastaway

Contents

Contents

Contents

Contents

Contents

Table of Cases

Table of Statutes

Table of Statutes

Chapter 1

Introduction

Background, consultative documents and consultation process

1.1   On 14 August 1991 the Inland Revenue published their first Consultation Paper 'A Simpler System for Taxing the Self Employed', seeking views on proposals for simplifying and streamlining the way the self-employed were taxed. This followed the new corporation tax system under 'Pay and File'. The expressed main objectives were to:

(*a*)   make it easier for taxpayers to understand;

(*b*)   make it simpler and more efficient to administer;

(*c*)   make it possible for the Revenue normally to accept the tax return and accounts without further correspondence;

(*d*)   make it possible for taxpayers normally to pay the right amount of tax at the right time without Revenue intervention by a self-assessment system; and

(*e*)   open up the way to further reforms to simplify and improve the personal tax system.

1.2   The preceding year ('PY') basis of assessment for the self-employed had been part of the UK tax system for 70 years following the recommendations of the 1920 Royal Commission. It was open to the criticism that the total profits assessed over the life of a business were not in general the same as the profits earned. Moreover, taxpayers frequently found the rules difficult to understand and to apply, which led to a lack of confidence in the fairness of the system, and put burdens upon taxpayers, their advisers and the Revenue in trying to apply the rules correctly.

1.3   The Consultation Paper put forward two alternative proposals to replace the PY basis of assessment for the self-employed. The first was a current year ('CY') basis, whereby tax would continue to be calculated and paid for income tax years, but it would be based upon the profits for the accounts ending in a particular year rather than the preceding year, leaving the taxpayer free to choose his own accounting period. The second was an accounting period ('AP') basis, whereby larger businesses could continue to choose their accounting periods and pay tax by reference to those accounting periods, similar to corporation tax for companies. Smaller businesses would have to make up accounts to a date close to the tax year end, and pay tax by reference to the actual profit earned in a fiscal year.

1.4   This Consultation Paper attracted a wide response, with most accepting the need for reform, and more than two out of three in broad agreement with the proposals for the CY basis and for self-assessment. A subsequent Consultative Document 'A Simpler System for Assessing Personal Tax' was then issued in November 1992. This document developed the idea that the new system should extend beyond the self-employed, to cover employees who paid tax by assessment and those who received investment income. Under the revised proposals:

(*a*)   all income would be taxed on a CY basis; and

(*b*)   taxpayers who were sent tax returns could choose whether to self-assess or to continue to allow the Revenue to work out their liability. In the latter case returns would have to be filed with the Revenue earlier to enable the Revenue to work out the tax.

1.5   Those who had responded to the previous discussion document generally preferred the CY basis to the AP basis, although the latter was considered to be simpler in some aspects. The later discussion document took the CY basis further forward. It also assumed that all income taxed by assessment would be included in the new system, and that the schedular machinery of assessment would be done away with. Partners would also be assessed separately rather than on a joint basis. But there was no intention to make any radical changes for employees, most of whom were not sent tax returns and for whom PAYE worked out the correct tax liability.

1.6   Following these two Consultative Documents, and the representations made to the Revenue, in early 1993 the Revenue established committees with representative bodies for the taxpayer. A series of discussion papers were prepared dealing with different topics, and the issues were debated in subsequent committee meetings during 1993, which also considered the earlier drafts of the legislation. The authors participated in these proceedings on behalf of the Institute of Taxation.

1.7   This is the first time in the history of tax legislation that there has been such a lengthy dialogue between the Revenue and representatives of the body of taxpayers before the introduction of the relevant legislation. It reflected acceptance by the Revenue that such a radical change could not simply be imposed upon taxpayers without a full consultation process, and without the co-operation of the taxpayer's professional advisers. Clearly the Revenue were also mindful of a possible fall in tax revenue during the transitional period in the event that the system did not work properly, and were concerned that it might break down unless it received an element of consensus.

1.8 Many of the representations made by the taxpayer bodies were accepted by the Revenue and incorporated in the subsequent legislation. To this extent the consultation procedure had positive results. In particular, the Revenue were persuaded not to impose fiscal accounting, and to remove some of the more draconian aspects of the surcharges and penalty provisions. Other representations were noted by the Revenue but regrettably not accepted. Sadly, what was perhaps the major concern of the representative bodies, that the changes appeared to do little to achieve the principal objective of simplification for the average taxpayer, has been little heeded. This is a criticism perhaps to be levelled more at the Parliamentary draftsman than the Revenue. But the Revenue's concern with tax avoidance has always been present, and must have contributed to the length and complexity of the legislation.

Finance Act 1994 and timing for introduction of Simplified Assessing

1.9 The primary legislation introducing the new system, described as 'Simplified Assessing' is contained in the *Finance Act 1994*. The changes are largely implemented by amending *TMA 1970* and *TA 1988*. The change from the PY to CY basis takes effect for new businesses commencing after 5 April 1994. For existing businesses, 1996/97 is a transitional year with its own rules, whilst the full CY basis comes into force in 1997/98. Self-assessment comes into force from 1996/97.

1.10 There is to be a second tranche of legislation in *FA 1995*, which will cover the remaining aspects of the new system, notably the details for employers and employees. There will also be a number of practice statements and codes of practice setting out the Revenue's policy for dealing with specific aspects of the legislation.

Current year basis

1.11 Under the CY system, self-employed persons will generally be charged on the profits made in the accounting period which ends in the year of assessment. So where accounts are made up annually to 30 June, the liability for 1998/99 will be based on the profits in the accounts for the year to 30 June 1998. In the year of commencement the profits assessed will be those which actually arise from the date of commencement to the following 5 April. Hence where a business commences on 1 July 1996 and makes up its accounts to 30 June 1997, the assessment for 1996/97 will be based upon three-quarters of the profits shown in the accounts for the year to 30 June 1997.

1.12 In the year of cessation the profits will be those from the end of the basis period assessed in the preceding year to the cessation date. So assuming that a business which has made up accounts to 30 September ceases on 30 June 2000, the profits assessed in 2000/2001 will be those between 30 September 1999 and 30 June 2000. However, the expressed objective of the new rules is to tax the actual profits which are generated by a business during its lifetime. Accordingly any profits which are taken into account more than once will be eligible for 'overlap relief', either when the business ends, or for an earlier period for which the basis period is longer than a year. So in this example, the profits of the final period may be adjusted to take into account any available overlap relief. There are also special rules where a business changes its accounting date, the general principle being to tax at least twelve months profits in a year.

Transitional arrangements

1.13   For businesses which are in existence on 5 April 1994 there are special rules in the transitional year 1996/97. In the usual case, where accounts are made up to the same date, the profits assessed to tax will be 50 per cent of those for the two years ending in 1996/97. Thus a business which makes up its accounts to 30 June will be assessable in 1995/96 on the profits of the year ending on 30 June 1994. For 1996/97, the profits for the two years to 30 June 1995 and 30 June 1996 will be aggregated, and tax payable on half of the total sum. There are to be anti-avoidance provisions in *FA 1995* to counter attempts to take advantage of these transitional rules.

Partnerships

1.14   From 1997/98 there will no longer be a joint assessment, but each partner will be assessed individually on his or her share of the partnership profits. This share will be allocated by reference to the period of account rather than the year of assessment. A change of partner, where at least one partner carries on the business before and after the change, is not regarded as a cessation.

Losses

1.15   As part of the introduction of a CY basis, there are a number of consequential amendments to the provisions regarding losses. In particular relief for trading losses is to be given against other income of the year of the loss, or the preceding year (rather than the following year).

Capital allowances

1.16   From 1997/98 capital allowances are generally to be treated as trading expenses, and balancing charges as trading receipts, similar to corporation tax.

Self-assessment

1.17 At the heart of the new system is self-assessment for individuals and trustees. The present tax return is to be altered to dovetail in with self-assessment, and its format is currently being determined. The tax return, together with a self-assessment of the taxpayer's income tax and CGT liability, is generally to be filed by 31 January following the end of the tax year. Provision is made for the possibility of the Revenue correcting any obvious errors or mistakes, known as 'repairs'. The taxpayer who submits his return on time also has a year from the filing date to make any amendments to the return, which corresponds with the period during which the Revenue can give notice of its intention to audit the return. Thereafter, subject to certain Revenue powers of discovery and the taxpayer's ability to make a claim for relief for error or mistake, the return and the tax liability becomes final and conclusive.

1.18 However, those not wishing to self-assess can leave the calculation of their tax liability and the raising of the assessment to the Revenue, but the return must then generally be filed by 30 September following the end of the tax year. Moreover, in those cases where the filing date has passed without the return and self-assessment having being submitted, the Revenue are empowered to make their own determination of the tax due. The tax so determined then becomes payable, but the determination is superseded if the return and self-assessment are later filed.

Revenue audit and data retention

1.19 Policing of the self-assessment system is implemented by giving the Revenue wide powers of enquiring into returns, with the ability to call for documents, accounts and other information. This right of 'random audit' generally expires once twelve months have elapsed from the filing date.

1.20 To assist the Revenue in such enquiries, taxpayers are required to maintain comprehensive records for possible review, generally for five years after the filing date for those engaged in a business, and for twelve months in other cases.

Discovery and finality

1.21 After the twelve-month period has elapsed during which Revenue enquiries can be raised, a taxpayer's liability can only be increased if the Revenue 'discover' that there has been an under-assessment. The existing rules for discovery are based upon a mixture of statute, case law and Revenue practice. Under the new statutory provisions, the Revenue can generally only make a discovery assessment if there has been fraud or neglect by the taxpayer, or inadequate disclosure was made.

Payment of tax

1.22   Payments on account of income tax, described as interim payments, are to be made by 31 January in the year of assessment and 31 July immediately following the year of assessment. These are normally based on the liability of the preceding year, with each payment amounting to 50 per cent thereof. The taxpayer has the right to reduce the interim payments if he considers that his actual liability will be less. Interim payments will also not be required where substantially all of the taxpayer's liability is deducted at source, for example under PAYE.

1.23   Payment of the balance of the taxpayer's income tax liability, together with the whole of any CGT liability, is then to be made by 31 January following the end of the year of assessment, i.e. when the taxpayer's return and self-assessment is to be filed.

Surcharges and interest for late payment

1.24   In the event that payment of the final instalment is more than 28 days late, there is an automatic 5 per cent surcharge. There is a further 5 per cent surcharge if payment has not been made by the end of the following six months. In addition interest runs if the interim payments or the final payment are made after the due dates.

Penalties

1.25   If a tax return is submitted late, there is an automatic £100 penalty, which is increased by a further £100 after six months. However both of these penalties are limited to the amount of tax due for the period. After a year's default, the penalty can be as much as the tax liability itself. The Revenue can also apply to the Commissioners for the imposition of further penalties up to £60 per day.

Appeals

1.26   The present procedure for appeals to the General or Special Commissioners is preserved for cases where assessments are made by the Revenue, or where the Revenue seek to amend the taxpayer's self-assessment.

References

1.27   The *Finance Act 1994* makes numerous amendments to existing legislation, particularly in the *Taxes Management Act 1970* and the *Taxes Act 1988*.

References are to the legislation as amended unless otherwise specified. Where it would be helpful for clarity reference is made to 'amended' or 'substituted' *sections*, meaning as amended or substituted by the provisions of the *Finance Act 1994* or to 'original enactment' referring to the legislation prior to the *Finance Act 1994*.

Chapter 2

New Rules of Assessment under Schedule D, Cases I and II

Accounting issues

2.1 The change to Simplified Assessing does not of itself affect the way in which a business keeps its books or makes up its accounts. The business is still free to make up its accounts to any date within the fiscal year, and as long as these accounts are prepared on a consistent basis in accordance with generally accepted accounting principles they will form the starting point for the taxable profits.

Under the current year basis rules any reference to a trade includes a reference to a profession, vocation, employment or office, under *FA 1994, s 218(2)*. Appendix B sets out SSAP2, the statement of the ICAEW relating to accounting policies.

2.2 The Revenue pronouncements on the circumstances in which a cash or conventional (rather than an earnings) basis will be acceptable remain applicable, such as SP A27 'Accounts on a cash basis' which provides as follows:

'A company, whether limited or unlimited, is normally required to prepare accounts for tax purposes on an earnings basis, as defined in *TA 1988, s 110(3)*. An individual or a partnership carrying on a trade is similarly required to prepare accounts on an earnings basis, but in the circumstances set out below, accounts prepared on a cash basis, or on a conventional basis such as bills issued or work completed which is neither full "earnings" nor pure "cash", may be accepted from an individual or partnership carrying on a profession or vocation.

Where a profession or vocation is newly set up, or is treated as new for tax purposes under *TA 1988, s 113(1)*, the profits of the first three years from the date of setting up or of the change to which *TA 1988, s 113(1)* applies, are required to be computed on the earnings basis (as defined in *TA 1988, s 110(3)*) in determining all tax liabilities affected by the profits of these years.

The computation of subsequent profits will continue on the earnings basis until the taxpayer asks to change to a cash or other conventional basis. Such a change will be accepted if the new basis seems likely to

provide a reasonable measure of the taxpayer's profit. This is interpreted as meaning that the profits computed on the new basis will not,
taking one year with another, differ materially from the profits
computed on the earnings basis.

The change must also be a complete one. For example, receipts after
the change for work done before the change must be brought into the
computation of profits on the cash basis notwithstanding that they have
already been brought into account in the computation on the earnings
basis; similarly, expenses accrued due but unpaid which were debited
in the accounts on the earnings basis may again be debited in the subsequent accounts on the cash basis when they are paid.

A further condition is that the taxpayer wishing to make such a change
is required to give a written undertaking that he will issue bills for
services rendered or work done (that is in the normal way, completed
work but also including work in progress where interim payments or
payments on account are contemplated by the terms of the contract or
are customary) at regular and frequent intervals. The intervals may be
chosen by the taxpayer but they should be quarterly or more often, and
they should be specified in the undertaking.

Attention is drawn to the possibility of liability under *TA 1988, s 104*,
wherever accounts are prepared on a basis other than earnings: in
computing such liability there is no provision for any relief in respect of
any profits which may have been brought into the computation twice
when the change from the earnings basis was made.

Where accounts are prepared on a cash or other conventional basis and
it is desired to change to an earnings basis, no objection will be raised
but attention is again drawn to the liability that will arise under *TA
1988, s 104*. A subsequent claim to revert to a conventional basis
would not be accepted.'

2.3   This practice statement is not applicable to barristers, to whom
the provisions of SP A/3 apply, which continues unchanged and basically
allows barristers to be assessed on a cash basis from commencement.

2.4   Businesses already on a cash basis or bills delivered basis may
continue to be so taxed and the post-cessation receipts provisions in *TA
1988, ss 103–110* continue in force.

Adjustments to accounts

2.5   The profits as shown by the accounts will, as at present, require
adjustment for tax purposes by adding back expenses shown in the
accounts that are disallowed for tax purposes or dealt with as annual
payments, and excluding income assessed under other heads such as rents
received under Schedule A, untaxed interest under Schedule D, Case III,
income from foreign securities or possessions under Schedule D, Cases IV

and V, furnished lettings and other sundry sources of income under Schedule D, Case VI, income from offices or employments taxed under Schedule E, investment income subject to tax at source, or capital profits subject to capital gains tax. The only substantive change will be that capital allowances under Simplified Assessing are to be deducted as trading expenses instead of being subject to separate claims. The capital allowances changes are dealt with in Chapter 5.

2.6   Normally only Schedule D, Cases I and II income is chargeable on a current accounting year basis, with other forms of income and chargeable gains charged on a strict fiscal year basis. The exceptions are partnership income which includes peripheral income, considered in Chapter 7, and income from overseas trades and professions which, although assessed under Schedule D, Case V, is charged on the current accounting year basis applicable to Schedule D, Cases I and II (see Chapter 3).

Introduction to the current year basis

2.7   The fundamental principles behind the current year basis are that the adjusted profits of a business should, over its life, equate with the amount on which it is taxed, and that at least twelve months profits should be assessed in each full fiscal year during which a business is in existence. It was also a requirement that there should be no loss to the Exchequer on the change from the preceding year basis of assessment to the current year basis.

2.8   The effect is that the system is a lot more complex than originally envisaged in the Consultative Papers. It results in some of the profits being assessed twice on commencement, or on a change of accounting date to a date ending earlier in the fiscal year. The preceding year basis applicable to existing businesses also resulted in a multiple assessment on the opening period profits. To compensate for such 'double' assessments there is a relief on cessation for what are described as 'overlap profits', and partial relief on a change of accounting date to a date later in the fiscal year, which involves charging to tax profits for a period in excess of twelve months.

2.9   As well as adjusting for the overlap the new rules have to cater for the transition from the preceding year basis for existing businesses. This is done through a transitional year in 1996/97, which broadly is taxed on half the combined profits of the two years ending with the accounting year ending in 1996/97, with the interval to 5 April 1997 being an additional overlap period. The averaging of profits in this way gives rise to an apparent opportunity for saving tax by maximising the profits in the transitional period. This potential is clearly recognised by the Revenue, who have issued a statement setting out their anti-avoidance proposals. The detailed provisions are to be contained in the *Finance Act 1995*. Planning and anti-avoidance is dealt with in Chapter 16.

2.10   A further complication is that the double charging of profits requires the double allowance of foreign tax credits in the opening period. The transitional arrangements require foreign tax credits to be abated under the averaging provisions. This makes the calculation of any excess credit on cessation a complex matter which is dealt with in Chapter 6. Moreover, not all businesses are profitable all the time and losses have to be catered for. The double counting of profits on commencement and on a change to an accounting period ending earlier in the fiscal year in turn requires amendment to prevent the double allowance of the same loss. Furthermore the transitional provisions have to provide that losses do not go unrelieved. These provisions are dealt with in Chapter 4.

2.11   A study of the legislation so far enacted and the anti-avoidance measures still to come suggest that the generic title used by the Revenue of 'Simplified Assessing' is somewhat of a misnomer. In the explanations which follow there are a series of continuing examples which set out the rules for determining the basis periods on commencement and subsequent years. These are set out initially in narrative form, then with fully worked figures after 2.23 and 2.35 below. Moreover, there is a flow chart in Appendix A 'Hunt the Basis Period' which is designed to assist taxpayers and their advisers in their quest for the basis period for any year of assessment.

Definitions

2.12   For the purpose of the new provisions there are a number of definitions as follows.

'Accounting date' is defined as the date in a year of assessment to which accounts are made up; or where there are two or more such dates because a set of accounts is produced for a short period, and both periods end in the same fiscal year; the latest of those dates. The 'commencement date' and the 'commencement year' are also defined respectively as the date on which, and the fiscal year in which, the trade, profession or vocation is set up and commenced. [*TA 1988, s 60(5); FA 1994, s 200*].

The profits which are included in the computations of two successive years of assessment are known as 'overlap profits' and the 'overlap period' means the number of days in the period in which the overlap profit arose, i.e. those days included in more than one basis period. [*TA 1988, s 63A(5); FA 1994, s 205*].

Commencement

First year of assessment

2.13   The current year basis applies to a new business commencing on or after 6 April 1994, or deemed to commence on a partnership change on or after that date where an election for continuation is not made under *TA 1988, s 113(2)*. [*FA 1994, s 218(1)*]. The profits or gains for the first year of assessment are charged for the period from commencement to the following 5 April. So the position is the same as under the existing preceding year basis rules. [*TA 1988, s 61(1); FA 1994, s 201*]. Accounts are split on a time basis as necessary to arrive at the profits for this period [*FA 1994, s 201; TA 1988, ss 72, 834(4)*] unless apportionment on some other basis, for example by reference to specific deals falling in each period, would produce a more accurate method of apportioning profits to each period, *Marshall Hus & Partners Ltd v Bolton* [*1981*] *STC 18*. It is unlikely that the Revenue will use anything other than a time basis unless the circumstances are exceptional.

Examples 1–3 (continuing)

Mr Mil started business on 1 August 1998 and produced accounts to 5 April 1999. These form the basis period for 1998/99. (*Example 1*)

Mr Molniya started business on 1 August 1998 and produced accounts to 31 July 1999. The (time apportioned) period to 5 April 1999 (8/12) forms the basis period for 1998/99. (*Example 2*)

Mr Moscvich started business on 1 August 1998 and produced accounts to 31 December 1998 and annually thereafter. His basis period for 1998/99 is 1.8.98 to 31.12.98 plus 3/12 of the year to 31 December 1999, i.e. from commencement to the following 5 April. (*Example 3*)

Strictly, apportionment should be by months and fractions of months in the respective periods [*TA 1988, s 72(2)*] although in practice apportionment in months or days is usually accepted.

Second year of assessment

Where there is a twelve-month accounting period ending in year

2.14   If an accounting period ends in the second year of assessment and the accounting date is twelve months or more from the commencement, the assessment is based on the profits for the twelve-month period ending with that accounting date. [*TA 1988, s 60(3)(a); FA 1994, s 200*]. This will be the most typical case. Note that the accounting date is not necessarily the first accounting date but the first accounting date that falls twelve months or more after commencement.

Examples 1–3 and 5 (continuing)

Mr Mil who started business on 1 August 1988 and produced his first accounts to 5 April 1999 makes up his annual accounts in the second year to 5 April 2000. They end more than twelve months from commencement and so form the basis period for 1999/2000. (*Example 1*)

Mr. Molniya started business on 1 August 1998 and produced accounts to 31 July 1999, i.e. for a period of twelve months. The basis period for 1999/2000 is the year ended 31 July 1999, i.e. the first (twelve-month) accounting date ending in the second year of assessment. (*Example 2*)

Mr Moscvich who started business on 1 August 1998 produced accounts to 31 December 1998. He makes up his annual accounts to the same date in the second year, i.e. 31 December 1999, which forms the basis period for 1999/2000. (*Example 3*)

Mr Nesterov started business on 1 August 1998 and produced accounts to 31 December 1999, i.e., for a period of more than twelve months. The basis period for 1999/2000 is the year ended 31 December 1999, i.e. 12/17 of the period 1.8.1998 to 31.12.1999. (*Example 5*)

Where there is no twelve-month accounting period ending in year

2.15   If there is not a twelve-month accounting date ending in the second year of assessment the basis period is the twelve months from commencement [*TA 1988, s 61(2)(a); FA 1994, s 201*] save where the unusual circumstances in 2.19 apply. This preserves the principle that at least twelve months profits are to be assessed in a year of assessment.

Example 4 (continuing)

Mr Nikitin started business on 1 August 1998 and produced accounts to 30 June 1999, i.e. for a period of less than twelve months ending in the second year of assessment. The basis period for 1999/2000 is the year ended 31 July 1999 (being the first twelve months from commencement) computed as the profits for the period from 1.8.1998 to 30.6.1999 and 1/12 of the profits for the year ended 30.6.2000.

Where no accounting period in year and a change of accounting date in third year

2.16   If there is a change of accounting date in the third year of assessment, with accounts made up to a date different from the accounting date in the first year of assessment, and there is no accounting date ending in the second year of assessment, the accounting date change is deemed under the change of accounting date rules (see 2.24 *et seq.* below) to have taken place twelve months before the actual change. This may give a deemed accounting date in the second fiscal year less than twelve months from commencement, in which case the profits for the second fiscal year are charged by reference to the twelve months from commencement. [*TA 1988, s 61(2)(b); FA 1994, s 201*].

Example 7 (continuing)

Mr Moskalev started business on 1 August 1998 and produced accounts to 5 April 1999 and then to 30 June 2000, i.e. a change of accounting date. There is no accounting period ending in 1999/2000. Therefore under the change of accounting date rules the change to the new accounting date of 30 June is deemed to take place one year earlier, i.e. 30 June 1999. This is less than twelve months from commencement so the basis period for the second year is the twelve months from commencement, i.e. 1.8.1998 to 5.4.1999 plus 4/15 of the period 6.4.1999 to 30.6.2000.

Where there is a change in accounting date less than 12 months from commencement

2.17 If there is a change of accounting date in the second year of assessment, i.e. accounts are made up for a date different from the accounting date in the first year of assessment, but for a period ending less than twelve months from commencement, the basis period for the second year is the profits for the first twelve months. [*TA 1988, s 61(2)(b); FA 1994, s 201*].

Example 8 (continuing)

Mr Bakshayev started business on 1 August 1998 and produced accounts to 31 December 1998 and then to 30 April 1999 and annually thereafter. The basis period for 1999/2000 is the period 1.8.1998 to 31.12.1998, plus 1.1.1999 to 30.4.1999, plus 1.5.1999 to 31.7.1999, i.e. 3/12 of year ended 30.4.2000; that is the profits for the first twelve months.

Where there is a change in accounting date more than twelve months from commencement

2.18 If the accounting date change is more than twelve months from commencement, the second year basis period is the year to the new accounting date. [*TA 1988, s 60(3)(a); FA 1994, s 200*].

15

Example 9 (continuing)

Mr Gudkov started business on 1 August 1998 and produced accounts to 31 December 1998 and then to 30 September 1999 and annually thereafter. The new accounting date of 30 September 1999 is more than twelve months from commencement, therefore the basis period is the twelve months ending on the new accounting date; i.e. 3/5 of the five-month period to 31 December 1998 plus the nine months to 30 September 1999.

Where there is no accounting date in first or second year

2.19   If there is no accounting date in either the first or second fiscal years (perhaps because the business commenced towards the end of a fiscal year) and accounts are made for a long period to an accounting date early in the third fiscal year, the basis period for the second year is the fiscal year itself. [*TA 1988, s 60(1); FA 1994, s 200*]. This sub-section always applies where no other provisions give an alternative basis period for a year of assessment.

Example 6 (continuing)

Mr Lisunov started business on 1 August 1998 and produced accounts to 30 June 2000, i.e. for a period of more than twelve months ending in the third fiscal year. As there is not an accounting period in 1999/2000, no change of accounting date and no other provisions apply, the basis period for the second fiscal year, 1999/2000, is the fiscal year ended 5 April 2000; i.e. 12/23 of the period 1.8.1998 to 30.6.2000.

Third year of assessment

Where first twelve-month accounting period is in third year

2.20   In the third fiscal year the basis period will be the twelve months ending with the accounting date if this is the first accounting date ending twelve months or more after commencement, i.e. ignoring any accounting dates less than twelve months from commencement. [*TA 1988, s 60(3)(a); FA 1994, s 200*].

Example 6 (continuing)

Mr Lisunov started business on 1 August 1998 and produced accounts to 30 June 2000 and annually thereafter. The basis period for the third fiscal year, 2000/01, is the twelve months to 30 June 2000, i.e. 12/23 of the period 1.8.1998 to 30.6.2000.

Where first twelve-month accounting period is in second year

2.21   If the first accounting date ending twelve months or more after commencement fell in the second fiscal year, the basis period for the third fiscal year is the period of twelve months beginning immediately after the end of the basis period in the second year of assessment. If accounts are made up on an annual basis this would be the accounts for the year ending in the third fiscal year, which would be the normal position. [*TA 1988, s 60(3)(b); FA 1994, s 200*].

Example 1–3 (continuing)

Mr Mil started business on 1 August 1998 and produced accounts to 5 April 1999 and annually thereafter. The basis period for 2000/01 is the year ended 5 April 2001, the accounting year ending in the fiscal year. (*Example 1*)

Mr Molniya started business on 1 August 1998 and produced accounts to 31 July 1999 and annually thereafter. The basis period for 2000/01 is the year ended 31 July 2000, the accounting year ending in the fiscal year. (*Example 2*)

Mr Moscvich started business on 1 August 1998 and produced accounts to 31 December 1998 and annually thereafter. The basis period for 2000/01 is the year ended 31 December 2000, the accounting year ending in the fiscal year. (*Example 3*)

Subsequent years of assessment

2.22   In the fourth and subsequent fiscal years the basis period continues to be the period of twelve months after the end of the basis period for the preceding year of assessment. Again, so long as accounts are made up for a twelve-month period, this will normally result in the accounts for the year ending in the fiscal year forming the basis period for that year. [*TA 1988, s 60(3)(b); FA 1994, s 200*].

Examples 2 and 3 (continuing)

Mr Molniya started business on 1 August 1998 and produced accounts to 31 July 1999 and annually thereafter. The basis period for 2001/02 is the year ended 31 July 2001, the accounting year ending in the fiscal year. (*Example 2*)

Mr Moscvich started business on 1 August 1998 and produced accounts to 31 December 1998 and annually thereafter. The basis period for 2001/02 is the year ended 31 December 2001, the accounting year ending in the fiscal year. (*Example 3*)

2.23 This basic rule can be displaced on a change of accounting date under the rules dealt with in 2.24 to 2.34 below. The fall back basis period of the fiscal year (see 2.19) does not apply since these latter rules fix an alternative basis period applicable to the fiscal year. [*TA 1988, s 60(1)(2); FA 1994, s 200*].

Example 1

Fiscal year accounting

Mr Mil started business on 1 August 1998 and produced accounts to 5 April 1999, i.e. to the end of the fiscal year, and annually thereafter.

Profits (as adjusted for tax purposes)

1.8.98 to 5.4.99		£8,000
y/e 5.4.2000		£18,000
y/e 5.4.2001		£24,000
y/e 5.4.2002		£30,000

Taxable

1998/99	1.8.98 to 5.4.99	£8,000	(*a*)
1999/00	y/e 5.4.2000	£18,000	(*b*)
2000/01	y/e 5.4.2001	£24,000	(*c*)
2001/02	y/e 5.4.2002	£30,000	(*d*)

Notes

(*a*) *TA 1988, s 61(1); FA 1994, s 201*, commencement to 5 April.

(*b*) *TA 1988, s 61(2); FA 1994, s 201* is inapplicable, as period from commencement, 1.8.1998 to accounting date, 5.4.2000 is not less than twelve months. Therefore, *TA 1988, s 60(3)(a); FA 1994, s 200* applies as this is the first year of assessment in which the accounting date falls not less than twelve months after commencement.

(*c*) *TA 1988, s 60(3)(b); FA 1994, s 200*.

(*d*) *TA 1988, s 60(3)(b); FA 1994, s 200*.

Example 2

First accounts for twelve months

Mr Molniya started business on 1 August 1998 and produced accounts to 31 July 1999, i.e. for a period of twelve months, and annually thereafter.

Profits (as adjusted for tax purposes)
y/e 31.7.1999	£14,000
y/e 31.7.2000	£20,000
y/e 31.7.2001	£26,000

Taxable
1998/99	(1.8.98 to 5.4.99 8/12 × £14,000)	£9,333	(a)
1999/00	y/e 31.7.1999	£14,000	(b)
2000/01	y/e 31.7.2000	£20,000	(c)
2001/02	y/e 31.7.2001	£26,000	(d)

Notes

(a)   *TA 1988, s 61(1); FA 1994, s 201*, commencement to 5 April.

(b)   *TA 1988, s 61(2); FA 1994, s 201* inapplicable as period from commencement 1.8.98 to accounting date 31.7.99 is not less than twelve months. [*TA 1988, s 61(2)(a); FA 1994, s 201*]. Therefore, the basis period for the first year of assessment in which there is an accounting period under *TA 1988, s 60(3)(a); FA 1994, s 200* is the year ended 31.7.99.

(c)   *TA 1988, s 60(3)(b); FA 1994, s 200.*

(d)   *TA 1988, s 60(3)(b); FA 1994, s 200.*

The period from commencement on 1.8.98 to 5.4.99 is taxed both for 1998/99 and 1999/00 and is therefore an overlap period relievable under *TA 1988, s 63A; FA 1994, s 205* resulting in overlap profits of £9,333 (see 2.37 *et seq.* below).

Example 3

First accounts for less than twelve months ending in first fiscal year

Mr Moscvich started business on 1 August 1998 and produced accounts to 31 December 1998, i.e. for a period of less than twelve months ending in the fiscal year of commencement, and annually thereafter.

Profits (as adjusted for tax purposes)

1.8.98 to 31.12.98	£5,000
y/e 31.12.1999	£16,500
y/e 31.12.2000	£22,500
y/e 31.12.2001	£28,500

Taxable

1998/99	1.8.98 to 5.4.99		
	£5,000 + (3/12 × £16,500)	£9,125	(a)
1999/00	y/e 31.12.99	£16,500	(b)
2000/01	y/e 31.12.00	£22,500	(c)
2001/02	y/e 31.12.01	£28,500	(d)

Notes

(a) *TA 1988, s 61(1); FA 1994, s 201* commencement to 5 April.

(b) *TA 1988, s 61(2); FA 1994, s 201* does not apply, although the second year of assessment, as the period from commencement 1.8.98 to the accounting date given by *TA 1988, s 60(5); FA 1994, s 200* of 31.12.99, is not less than twelve months. Therefore, this is the first year of assessment in which there is an accounting date which falls not less than twelve months after the commencement date and the basis period is fixed by *TA 1988, s 60(3)(a); FA 1994, s 200*.

(c) *TA 1988, s 60(3)(b); FA 1994, s 200.*

(d) *TA 1988, s 60(3)(b); FA 1994, s 200.*

The period from 1.1.1999 to 5.4.99 is taxed both for 1998/99 and 1999/00 and is therefore an overlap period relievable under *TA 1988, s 63A; FA 1994, s 205* resulting in overlap profits of £4,125 (3/12 × £16,500).

Example 4

First accounts for less than twelve months ending in second fiscal year

Mr Nikitin started business on 1 August 1998 and produced accounts to 30 June 1999, i.e. for a period of less than twelve months ending in the fiscal year following that of commencement, and annually thereafter.

Profits (as adjusted for tax purposes)

1.8.98 to 30.6.99	£12,500
y/e 30.6.2000	£19,500
y/e 30.6.2001	£25,500

Taxable

1998/99	1.8.98 to 5.4.99		
	(8/11 × £12,500)	£9,090	(a)
1999/00	1.8.98 to 31.7.99		
	£12,500 + (1/12 × £19,500)	£14,125	(b)

2000/01	y/e 30.6.2000	£19,500	(c)
2001/02	y/e 30.6.2001	£25,500	(d)

Notes

(a)   *TA 1988, s 61(1); FA 1994, s 201*, commencement to 5 April.

(b)   *TA 1988, s 61(2)(a); FA 1994, s 201* does apply on the second year of assessment, because the period from commencement 1.8.98 to the accounting date is less than twelve months. The basis period given by *TA 1988, s 61(2)(a); FA 1994, s 201* is the twelve months from commencement i.e. 1.8.98 to 31.7.99. This conforms to the requirement for at least twelve months profits to be taxed in every year other than that of commencement or cessation.

(c)   *TA 1988, s 60(3)(a); FA 1994, s 200* applies as 30.6.2000 is the first accounting date which falls not less than twelve months after commencement.

(d)   *TA 1988, s 60(3)(b); FA 1994, s 200*.

The period from commencement on 1.8.98 to 5.4.99 is taxed both in 1998/99 and 1999/00 and is therefore an overlap period relieved under *TA 1988, s 63A; FA 1994, s 205* with overlap profits of £9,090. The period from 1.7.99 to 31.7.99 is taxed both in 1999/00 and 2000/01 and is therefore an overlap period relievable under *TA 1988, s 63A; FA 1994, s 205* resulting in overlap profits of £1,625 (1/12 × £19,500) increasing the overlap profits to £10,715.

Example 5

First accounts for more than twelve months ending in second fiscal year

Mr Nesterov started business on 1 August 1998 and produced accounts to 31 December 1999, i.e. for a period of more than twelve months ending in the fiscal year following that of commencement, and annually thereafter.

Profits (as adjusted for tax purposes)

1.8.98 to 31.12.99		£21,500
y/e 31.12.2000		£22,500
y/e 31.12.2001		£28,500

Taxable

1998/99	1.8.98 to 5.4.99		
	(8/17 × £21,500)	£10,117	(a)
1999/00	1.1.99 to 31.12.99		
	(12/17 × £21,500)	£15,176	(b)
2000/01	y/e 31.12.2000	£22,500	(c)
2001/02	y/e 31.12.2001	£28,500	(d)

Notes

(a)   *TA 1988, s 61(1); FA 1994, s 201* commencement to 5 April.

(b)   *TA 1988, s 60(3)(a); FA 1994, s 200* applies, twelve months to first accounting date. *TA 1988, s 61(2); FA 1994, s 201* does not apply as the accounting period is not less than twelve months.

(c)   *TA 1988, s 60(3)(b); FA 1994, s 200.*

(d)   *TA 1988, s 60(3)(b); FA 1994, s 200.*

The period from 1.1.99 to 5.4.99 is taxed both in 1998/99 and 1999/00 and is therefore an overlap period relievable under *TA 1988, s 63A; FA 1994, s 205* resulting in overlap profits of £3,794 (3/17 × £21,500).

Example 6

First accounts for more than twelve months ending in third fiscal year

Mr Lisunov started business on 1 August 1998 and produced accounts to 30 June 2000, i.e. for a period of more than twelve months ending in the second fiscal year following the year of commencement, and annually thereafter.

Profits (as adjusted for tax purposes)
1.8.1998 to 30.6.2000	£32,000	
y/e 30.6.2001	£25,500	

Taxable
1998/99	1.8.98 to 5.4.99		
	(8/23 × £32,000)	£11,130	(a)
1999/00	6.4.99 to 5.4.00		
	(12/23 × £32,000)	£16,696	(b)
2000/01	1.7.99 to 30.6.00		
	(12/23 × £32,000)	£16,696	(c)
2001/02	y/e 30.6.2001	£25,500	(d)

Notes

(a)   *TA 1988, s 61(1); FA 1994, s 201* commencement to 5 April.

(b)   *TA 1988, s 60(1); FA 1994, s 200* applies on the fiscal year basis as there is no accounting period ending in the second year of assessment, therefore *TA 1988, s 60(3); FA 1994, s 200* cannot apply, and therefore *TA 1988, s 61; FA 1994, s 201* cannot apply either in view of *TA 1988, s 61(2)(a); FA 1994, s 201.*

(c)   *TA 1988, s 60(3)(a); FA 1994, s 200* applies, twelve months to first accounting date. *TA 1988, s 61(2); FA 1994, s 201* does not apply as it is the third year of assessment, nor does *TA 1988, s 60(3)(b); FA 1994, s 200* as *TA 1988, s 60(3)(a); FA 1994, s 200* applies.

(*d*)   *TA 1988, s 60(3)(b); FA 1994, s 200.*

The period from 1.7.99 to 5.4.00 is taxed in both 1999/00 and 2000/01 and is therefore an overlap period relievable under *TA 1988, s 63A; FA 1994, s 205* resulting in overlap profits of £12,521 (9/23 × £32,000).

Example 7

Change of accounting date in third year

Mr Moskalev started business on 1 August 1998 and produced accounts to 5 April 1999 and then to 30 June 2000, i.e. a period ending in the third year and not for twelve months from the first accounting date and within two years of commencement.

Profits (as adjusted for tax purposes)

1.8.98 to 5.4.99	£11,000	
p/e 30.6.2000	£21,000	
y/e 30.6.2001	£25,500	

Taxable

1998/99	1.8.98 to 5.4.99	£11,000	(*a*)
1999/00	1.8.98 to 31.7.99		
	£11,000 + 4/15 × £21,000	£16,600	(*b*)
2000/01	1.7.99 to 30.6.2000		
	(12/15 × £21,000)	£16,800	(*c*)
2001/02	y/e 30.6.2001	£25,500	(*d*)

Notes

(*a*)   *TA 1988, s 61(1); FA 1994, s 201* commencement to 5 April.

(*b*)   *TA 1988, s 61(2)(b); FA 1994, s 201* first twelve months.

(*c*)   *TA 1988, s 62(2)(b); FA 1994, s 202* applies, twelve months to new accounting date.

(*d*)   *TA 1988, s 60(3)(b); FA 1994, s 200.*

The period from 1.8.98 to 5.4.99 is taxed in both 1998/99 and 1999/00 and is therefore an overlap period relievable under *TA 1988, s 63A; FA 1994, s 205* resulting in overlap profits of £11,000. The period from 1.7.99 to 31.7.99 is taxed in both 1999/00 and 2000/01 and is therefore a further overlap period resulting in additional overlap profits of £1,400 (1/15 × £21,000).

Example 8

Change of accounting date in second year

Mr Bakshayev started business on 1 August 1998 and produced accounts to 31 December 1998 and then to 30 April 1999 and annually thereafter.

Profits (as adjusted for tax purposes)

1.8.98 to 31.12.98	£10,000
1.1.99 to 30.4.99	£6,000
y/e 30.4.2000	£30,000
y/e 30.4.2001	£40,000

Taxable (subject to overlap relief under *TA 1988, s 63A; FA 1994, s 205*)

1998/99	1.8.98 to 5.4.99	£14,500	(*a*)
1999/00	1.8.98 to 31.7.99	£23,500	(*b*)
2000/01	y/e 30.4.00	£30,000	(*c*)
2001/02	y/e 30.4.01	£40,000	

Notes

(*a*) *TA 1988, s 61(1); FA 1994, s 201* actual basis for year of commencement £10,000 + (3/4 x £6,000) = £14,500.

(*b*) *TA 1988, s 61(2)(b); FA 1994, s 201* first twelve months. £10,000 + £6,000 + (3/12 × £30,000) = £23,500.

(*c*) *TA 1988, s 60(3)(a); FA 1994, s 200* year ended on accounting date.

The period from 1.8.98 to 5.4.99 is taxed in 1998/99 and 1999/2000. The period from 1.5.99 to 31.7.99 is taxed in 1999/2000 and 2000/01. The overlap period relievable under *TA 1988, s 63A; FA 1994, s 205* is therefore 248 days and 92 days, a total of 340 days and the overlap profits of £14,500 and (3/12 × £30,000) £7,500 a total of £22,000.

Example 9

Change of accounting date in second year more than twelve months from commencement

Mr Gudkov started business on 1 August 1998 and produced accounts to 31 December 1998 and then to 30 September 1999 and annually thereafter.

Profits (as adjusted for tax purposes)

1.8.98 to 31.12.98	£10,000
1.1.99 to 30.9.99	£27,000
y/e 30.9.2000	£35,000
y/e 30.9.2001	£40,000

Taxable (subject to overlap relief under *TA 1988, s 63A; FA 1994, s 205*)

1998/99	1.8.98 to 5.4.99	£19,000	(*a*)
1999/00	y/e 30.9.99	£33,000	(*b*)
2000/01	y/e 30.9.00	£35,000	(*c*)
2001/02	y/e 30.9.01	£40,000	(*d*)

Notes

(*a*)   *TA 1988, s 61(1); FA 1994, s 201* actual basis for year of commencement. £10,000 + (3/9 × £27,000) = £19,000.

(*b*)   *TA 1988, s 60(3)(a); FA 1994, s 200*, twelve months to new accounting date. £27,000 + (3/5 × £10,000) = £33,000.

(*c*)   *TA 1988, s 60(3)(b); FA 1994, s 200*.

(*d*)   *TA 1988, s 60(3)(b); FA 1994, s 200*.

The period from 1.10.98 to 5.4.99 is taxed in 1998/99 and 1999/2000. The overlap period relievable under *TA 1988, s 63A; FA 1994, s 205* is therefore 187 days and the overlap profits are 3/5 × £10,000 and 3/9 × £27,000 − a total of £15,000.

Change of accounting date and basis period

Introduction of statutory code

2.24   Under the preceding year basis of assessment changes of accounting date for unincorporated businesses were dealt with in accordance with the Revenue practice explained in Booklet IR 26 (see Appendix D). Although this procedure had no statutory authority it was approved in *CIR v Helical Bar Ltd 1972 48 TC 221* (see Chapter 16). This is however replaced for the current year basis of assessment by *FA 1994, s 202* introducing substituted *TA 1988, s 62* which is designed to prevent taxpayers obtaining any benefit from deferral of tax on a change of accounting date. Otherwise, for example, an accounting date could be brought forward to defer recognition of profit, or doubly tax a period of abnormally low profit, or defer the accounting date to advance recognition of a loss.

Requirements for valid change

2.25   The statutory revised change of accounting date rules in *section 62* will only apply to changes which meet the requirements of *TA 1988, s 62A; FA 1994, s 203*, except in the case of changes made in the second or third fiscal years. This exception for the second and third years allows a new business complete freedom to change its accounting date where the original date selected has turned out to be inconvenient. As regards partnerships, it is understood that these requirements are to be applied at the level of the partnership, and not the individual partner.

2.26   These requirements are:

(*a*)   that the accounting period to the new accounting date does not exceed a period of 18 months [*TA 1988, s 62A(1)(2); FA 1994, s 203*]; and

(*b*)   notice of the change of accounting date is given to the Revenue by 31 January following the year of assessment in which the accounting change is deemed to take place under substituted *TA 1988, s 62(5)* [*TA 1988, s 62A(3); FA 1994, s 203*] (failure to give notice makes the change ineffective for tax purposes); and either

(*c*)   no accounting date change which has been effective for tax purposes has been made in any of the preceding five years of assessment, other than in the opening years under substituted *TA 1988, ss 60* or *61* [*TA 1988, s 62A(4); FA 1994, s 203*]; or

(*d*)   there has been a change for tax purposes in the preceding five years of assessment but the notice of change of accounting date sets out the reasons for the change, and the Revenue Officer is satisfied that the change is made for *bona fide* commercial reasons, or he does not object to the change within 60 days of receiving the notice. [*TA 1988, s 62A(5); FA 1994, s 203*].

Invalid change of accounting date

2.27   The first two and either the third or fourth of these conditions must be met in order to make the accounting date change effective for tax purposes. If the change is not effective, the new accounting date is ignored in the fiscal year in which it is adopted [*TA 1988, s 62(3); FA 1994, s 202*] and the basis period for tax purposes for the year is twelve months from the end of the previous basis period under *TA 1988, s 60(3)(b); FA 1994, s 200*.

2.28   If a change is thus ineffective in one year, but the new accounting date continues to be used, there is deemed to be a change in the following fiscal year, and each subsequent year, until the change satisfies the requirements in 2.26 and becomes effective, if ever. [*TA 1988, s 62(4); FA 1994, s 202*]. An example would be where the change was not effective because of an earlier change within the five year 'close' season, but became so following the end of that period.

2.29   Moreover, in applying *TA 1988, s 62(1); FA 1994, s 202* the Revenue have confirmed that (for the purposes of the 18-month rule) the 'new date' in the year following the actual date of change is the new accounting date and that the actual accounting period (which is defined by *TA 1988, s 62(1)(a); FA 1994, s 202* as the actual period to which accounts are made up) is the period to the new accounting date which is for 12 months and which does not fail the 18-month maximum period test. This is explained in the following two examples, and also by *Example 5* after 2.35 below.

Example 10

Accounts are made up to 30 June each year until the year 2000. In 2001 the accounting period is extended to 30 April 2002 which is a 22-month accounting period. This therefore fails the 18-month restriction in *TA 1988, s 62A(2); FA 1994, s 203* and the basis period for tax purposes in 2001/02 is the twelve months to 30 June 2001. Similarly there is no valid change in 2002/03 and the basis period is the twelve months to 30 June 2002 (twelve months from the end of the last basis period). In 2003/04 there is a valid change as the actual accounting period is the year ended 30 April 2003 and the basis period is the twelve-month period from 1 May 2002 to 30 April 2003.

Example 11

Accounts are made up to 30 June each year until the year 2000. In 2001 the accounting period is extended to 31 March 2002 which is a 21-month accounting period. This therefore fails the 18-month restriction in *TA 1988, s 62A(2); FA 1994, s 203* and the basis period for tax purposes in 2001/02 is the twelve months to 30 June 2001. If accounts continue to be made up to 31 March in each year, in the year ended 31 March 2003 there is another opportunity to change the accounting date and provided that the remaining conditions are met the basis period for 2002/03 is the period from the end of the basis period in 2001/02, i.e. 1 July 2001 to the new accounting date 31.3.2003.

Appeals

2.30   An appeal may be made against the Revenue rejection of a change of accounting date on *bona fide* commercial grounds within 30 days of the date of the notice that the Revenue is not satisfied with the reasons for the change. [*TA 1988, s 62A(6); FA 1994, s 203*]. The appeal would be to the Commissioners under the normal procedure as if it were an appeal against an assessment to tax [*TA 1988, s 62A(7); FA 1994, s 203*], but the powers of the Commissioners are amended to give them specific power merely to set aside the Inspector's notice of dissatisfaction if they consider that the change was for *bona fide* commercial reasons, otherwise they have to confirm the notice. [*TA 1988, s 62A(8); FA 1994, s 203*].

2.31   Obtaining a tax advantage is not regarded as a *bona fide* commercial reason for a change of accounting date. [*TA 1988, s 62A(9); FA 1994, s 203*]. Tax advantage for this purpose is not defined. It is a term used in *TA 1988, s 709(1)*, but only for the purposes of transactions in securities under *TA 1988, ss 703–709*. Tax advantage therefore is given a wide general meaning and would include a cash flow advantage arising from deferment of tax.

Extended accounting period skipping a fiscal year

2.32   An accounting period for determining changes in accounting date is a period to which accounts are made up. [*TA 1988, s 62A(10); FA 1994, s 203*]. A change of accounting date is deemed to take place either in the fiscal year in which the new date falls, or, if this results in there being no accounting date in the preceding fiscal year, twelve months before the new date. This prevents a fiscal year not being charged to tax on the grounds that there is no accounting date in the fiscal year, which would otherwise have been covered by making the fiscal year itself the basis period under *TA 1988, s 60(1); FA 1994, s 200*. [*TA 1988, s 62(5); FA 1994, s 202*].

Example 12 (continuing)

Mr Bisnovet produced accounts to 5 April each year until 2001 when the accounting date was extended to 30 June 2002 and annually thereafter. There is no accounting period ending in 2001/02 so the change on 30 June 2002 is deemed to take place on 30 June 2001. The 2001/02 basis period is the twelve months to 30 June 2001, the new accounting date.

Shortened accounting period

2.33   If the accounting period from the end of the previous basis period to the new accounting date or deemed accounting date is less than twelve months, or if the year is the year ending in the second fiscal year, the new basis period is the period of twelve months ending with the new accounting date or deemed accounting date. [*TA 1988, s 62(2)(a); FA 1994, s 202*]. If however the new accounting date in the second fiscal year is less than twelve months from commencement, *TA 1988, s 61(2)(b); FA 1994, s 201* applies as explained in 2.16 above. The application of these rules is likely to result in additional overlap profits for an overlap period which would be eligible for overlap relief, dealt with in 2.37 *et seq.* below.

Example 13 (continuing)

Mr Grigorovich produced accounts to 5 April each year until 5 April 2001 after which the accounting date was brought forward to 30 June 2001 and annually thereafter. The basis period for 2001/02 is the twelve months to 30 June 2001, the new accounting date.

Extended accounting period ending in next fiscal year

2.34   If the period from the end of the previous basis period to the new accounting date is in excess of twelve months the whole of the profit for the period to the new accounting date is assessed, unless this period ends in the second fiscal year, in which case the position is as described in 2.16. [*TA 1988, s 62(2)(b); FA 1994, s 202*].

Example 14 (continuing)

Mr Beriev produced accounts to 31 July each year until 31 July 2000 when the accounting date was extended to 31 January 2002 and annually thereafter. No accounts were prepared for the year ended 31 July 2001. The basis period for 2001/02 is from the end of the previous basis period, i.e. 1 August 2000 to the new accounting date 31 January 2002.

Two accounting periods ending in fiscal year

2.35   Where it is intended to change the accounting date in a manner which would result in an accounting period of more than 18 months it would not be an effective change and therefore an account might be prepared for twelve months and a short period of, say, nine months. If both accounting periods ended in the same fiscal year they would be amalgamated under *TA 1988, s 60(5); FA 1994, s 200* (see 2.12 above) and the basis period would be the extended period covering both accounts under *TA 1988, s 62(2)(b); FA 1994, s 202*.

Example 15 (continuing)

Mr Samsonov produced accounts to 31 July each year until 31 July 2001 when the accounting date was changed to 31 March 2002 and annually thereafter. Accounts were prepared for the year ended 31 July 2001 which are amalgamated with those to 31 March 2002. The basis period for 2001/02 is from the end of the previous basis period, i.e. 1 August 2000 to the new accounting date 31 March 2002.

Example 12

Extended accounting period skipping a fiscal year (see 2.32)

Mr Bisnovet started business on 1 August 1998 and produced accounts to 5 April each year until April 2001 when the accounting date was extended to 30 June 2002 and annually thereafter. The requirements of *TA 1988, s 62A; FA 1994, s 203* were met.

Profits (as adjusted for tax purposes)

1.8.98 to 5.4.99	£8,000
y/e 5.4.2000	£18,000
y/e 5.4.2001	£24,000
p/e 30.6.2002	£37,500

Taxable

1998/99	1.8.98 to 5.4.99	£8,000	(a)
1999/00	y/e 5.4.2000	£18,000	(b)
2000/01	y/e 5.4.2001	£24,000	(c)
2001/02	y/e 30.6.2001 (9/12 × £24,000 + 3/15 × £37,500)	£25,500	(d)
2002/03	y/e 30.6.2002 (12/15 × £37,500)	£30,000	(e)

Notes

(a) *TA 1988, s 61(1); FA 1994, s 201.*

(b) *TA 1988, s 60(3)(a); FA 1994, s 200.*

(c) *TA 1988, s 60(3)(b); FA 1994, s 200.*

(d) *TA 1988, s 62(5); FA 1994, s 202* makes this the year in which the accounting date is deemed to change as there is no accounting date in the fiscal year. The period is less than twelve months from the end of the previous accounting date (5.4.2001), therefore *TA 1988, s 62(2)(a); FA 1994, s 202* determines the basis period as twelve months ending with the new accounting date. The period 1.7.2000 to 5.4.2001 is taxed in both 2000/01 and 2001/02 and therefore there is an overlap period relievable under *TA 1988, s 63A; FA 1994, s 205* resulting in overlap profits of £18,000 (9/12 × £24,000).

(e) *TA 1988, s 60(3)(b); FA 1994, s 200.* Although this is the year in which the new accounting date actually falls, the change is deemed to take place in 2001/02 under *TA 1988, s 62(5); FA 1994, s 202* (see above), therefore the basis period is twelve months from the end of the basis period for the previous year.

Example 13

Shortened accounting period (see 2.33)

Mr Grigorovich started business on 1 August 1998 and produced accounts to 5 April each year until 2001 when the accounting date was brought forward to 30 June and annually thereafter. The requirements of *TA 1988, s 62A; FA 1994, s 203* were met.

Profits (as adjusted for tax purposes)

1.8.98 to 5.4.99	£8,000
y/e 5.4.2000	£18,000
y/e 5.4.2001	£24,000
p/e 30.6.2001	£7,500
y/e 30.6.2002	£30,000

Taxable

1998/99	1.8.98 to 5.4.99	£8,000	(a)
1999/00	y/e 5.4.2000	£18,000	(b)
2000/01	y/e 5.4.2001	£24,000	(c)
2001/02	y/e 30.6.2001		
	(9/12 × £24,000 + £7,500)	£25,500	(d)
2002/03	y/e 30.6.2002	£30,000	(e)

Notes

(a)   *TA 1988, s 61(1); FA 1994, s 201.*

(b)   *TA 1988, s 60(3)(a); FA 1994, s 200.*

(c)   *TA 1988, s 60(3)(b); FA 1994, s 200.*

(d)   *TA 1988, s 62(5); FA 1994, s 202* makes this the year in which the accounting date is deemed to change as accounts are made up to a new date in the fiscal year. The period is less than twelve months from the end of the previous accounting date (5.4.2001), therefore *TA 1988, s 62(2)(a); FA 1994, s 202* determines the basis as twelve months ending with the new accounting date. The period 1.7.2000 to 5.4.2001 is taxed in both 2000/01 and 2001/02 and therefore there is an overlap period under *TA 1988, s 63A; FA 1994, s 205* resulting in overlap profits of £18,000 (9/12 × £24,000).

(e)   *TA 1988, s 60(3)(b); FA 1994, s 200.*

Example 14

Extended accounting period ending in next fiscal year (see 2.34)

Mr Beriev started business on 1 August 1998 and produced accounts to 31 July each year until 2001/02 when the accounting date was extended to

31 January 2002 and annually thereafter. The requirements of *TA 1988, s 62A; FA 1994, s 203* were met.

Profits (as adjusted for tax purposes)

y/e 31.7.1999	£14,000
y/e 31.7.2000	£20,000
p/e 31.1.2002	£41,000
y/e 31.1.2003	£30,000

Taxable

1998/99	1.8.98 to 5.4.99	£9,333	(a)
1999/00	y/e 31.7.99	£14,000	(b)
2000/01	y/e 31.7.00	£20,000	(c)
2001/02	1.8.00 to 31.1.02		
	(£41,000 − 6/8		
	£9,333)	£34,000	(d)
2002/03	y/e 31.1.03	£30,000	(e)

Notes

(a)   *TA 1988, s 61(1); FA 1994, s 201.*

(b)   *TA 1988, s 60(3)(a); FA 1994, s 200* overlap 1.8.98 to 5.4.99 = £9,333.

(c)   *TA 1988, s 60(3)(b); FA 1994, s 200.*

(d)   *TA 1988, s 62(5); FA 1994, s 202* makes this the year in which the accounting date is deemed to change as accounts are made up to a new date in the fiscal year. The period is more than twelve months from the end of the previous basis period (31.7.00), therefore *TA 1988, s 62(2)(b); FA 1994, s 202* determines the basis as the period ending on the new accounting date (i.e. 31.1.02 falling in the fiscal year ended 5.4.02). This is an 18-month accounting period, subject to overlap relief under *TA 1988, s 63A; FA 1994, s 205* of the appropriate proportion of the overlap relief brought forward, i.e. (18 − 12) six months which releases approximately 6/8 of the overlap profits available in (b) above, i.e. (say) £7,000 leaving £2,333 to continue to carry forward under *TA 1988, s 63A; FA 1994, s 205*.

(e)   *TA 1988, s 60(3)(b); FA 1994, s 200.*

Example 15

Two accounting periods ending in fiscal year (see 2.35)

Mr Samsonov started business on 1 August 1998 and produced accounts to 31 July each year until 2001/02 when the accounting date was changed to 31 March 2002 and annually thereafter. The requirements of *TA 1988, s 62A; FA 1994, s 203* were met by preparing an account to 31 July 2001 and an eight-month account to 31 March 2002.

Profits (as adjusted for tax purposes)

y/e 31.7.1999	£28,000
y/e 31.7.2000	£40,000
y/e 31.7.2001	£50,000
1.8.2001 to 31.3.2002	£35,000
y/e 31.3.2003	£60,000

Taxable

1998/99	1.8.98 to 5.4.99	£18,667	(a)
1999/00	y/e 31.7.99	£28,000	(b)
2000/01	y/e 31.7.00	£40,000	(c)
2001/02	1.8.00 to 31.3.02	£85,000	(d)
2002/03	y/e 31.3.03	£60,000	(e)

Notes

(a)   *TA 1988, s 61(1); FA 1994, s 201.*

(b)   *TA 1988, s 60(3)(a); FA 1994, s 200*, overlap 1.8.98 to 5.4.99 = £18,667.

(c)   *TA 1988, s 60(3)(b); FA 1994, s 200.*

(d)   *TA 1988, s 62(2)(b); FA 1994, s 202.* The change of accounting date takes effect in 2001/02, the first year of assessment in which accounts are made up to the new date under *TA 1988, s 62(5); FA 1994, s 202. TA 1988, s 60(5); FA 1994, s 200* amalgamates the two accounting periods and *TA 1988, s 62(2)(b); FA 1994, s 202* applies to fix the basis period as the period from the end of the basis period in the previous fiscal year to the new accounting date.

(e)   *TA 1988, s 60(3)(b); FA 1994, s 200.*

Example 16

Requirements for change not met (see 2.27)

Mr Hackel started business on 1 August 1998 and produced accounts to 31 July each year until 2001/02 when the accounting date was changed to 31 March 2002 and annually thereafter. The requirements of *TA 1988, s 62A; FA 1994, s 203* were not met as the accounting period was 20 months to 31 March 2002. The remaining conditions were met so there is a deemed change at 31 March 2003 under substituted *TA 1988, s 62(4); FA 1994, s 202.*

Profits (as adjusted for tax purposes)

y/e 31.7.1999	£28,000
y/e 31.7.2000	£40,000
1.8.2000 to 31.3.2002	£85,000
y/e 31.3.2003	£60,000

Taxable

1998/99	1.8.98 to 5.4.99	£18,667	(a)
1999/00	y/e 31.7.99	£28,000	(b)
2000/01	y/e 31.7.00	£40,000	(c)
2001/02	y/e 31.7.01	£51,000	(d)
2002/03	1.8.01 to 31.3.03	£94,000	(e)

Notes

(a)   *TA 1988, s 61(1); FA 1994, s 201.*

(b)   *TA 1988, s 60(3)(a); FA 1994, s 200*, overlap 1.8.98 to 5.4.99 = £18,667.

(c)   *TA 1988, s 60(3)(b); FA 1994, s 200.*

(d)   *TA 1988, s 60(3)(b); FA 1994, s 200*, 12/20 × £85,000 = £51,000. Twelve months from end of previous basis period as not a valid change of accounting date for tax purposes to 31.3.2002 (see 2.24).

(e)   *TA 1988, s 62(2)(b); FA 1994, s 202*, 8/20 × £85,000 = £34,000 + £60,000 total £94,000.

Discontinuance

2.36   In the fiscal year in which cessation takes place the basis period is from the end of the basis period ending in the preceding fiscal year to the date of discontinuance. [*TA 1988, s 63(b); FA 1994, s 204*]. Where the cessation takes place in the second fiscal year the basis period is from 6 April to the date of cessation. [*TA 1988, s 63(a); FA 1994, s 204*]. Overlap relief may be available as explained below.

Example 17

Mr Lavochkin had been in business many years and made up his accounts to 30 April each year. He ceased to trade on 31 December 2002.

Profits (as adjusted for tax purposes)

y/e 30.4.2001	£30,000
y/e 30.4.2002	£20,000
p/e 31.12.2002	£5,000

Taxable (subject to overlap relief under *TA 1988, s 63A*)

2001/02	y/e 30.4.2001	£30,000	(a)
2002/03	p/e 31.12.2002	£25,000	(b)

Notes

(a)   *TA 1988, s 60(3)(b); FA 1994, s 200.*

(*b*) *TA 1988, s 63(b); FA 1994, s 204* beginning on 1.5.2001 immediately after the basis period for the preceding year of assessment (2001/02, 30.4.2001) and ending at the date of cessation, 31.12.2002.

Overlap relief

General position

2.37 The double charge to tax which results from the inclusion of the profits in more than one basis period is partially relieved if there is a change of accounting date to a date later in the fiscal year, resulting in a basis period in excess of twelve months. Any remaining relief is given on cessation. The relief given on a change of accounting date depends on the overlap period doubly charged and the extent to which the extended accounting period exceeds twelve months. See 2.12 above for the definition of 'overlap profits' and 'overlap period'.

Overlap formula

2.38 The proportion of the overlap profits relieved is found by applying the statutory formula [*TA 1988, s 63A(1); FA 1994, s 205*]:

$$A \times \frac{(B - C)}{D}$$

where
A   is the aggregate amount of the overlap profit which has not previously been allowed as an overlap adjustment;
B   is the number of days in the basis period, which for the formula to apply at all must be more than 365;
C   is the number of days in the year of assessment, either 365 or 366 in the case of a leap year; and
D   is the aggregate of the overlap periods of any overlap profits arising on commencement or on an earlier change of accounting date or on transition to the current year basis less any overlap periods already relieved on previous occasions.

[*TA 1988, s 63A(2); FA 1994, s 205*].

Overlap relief and change of accounting date

2.39 It will be appreciated that an overlap period can arise not only on commencement, but also on a change of accounting date resulting in an accounting period of less than twelve months for which the basis period is extended to twelve months under *TA 1988, s 62(2)(a); FA 1994, s 202* and under the transitional provisions of *FA 1994, 20 Sch 2(4)*.

Example 18 (continuing)

Mr Nieman started business on 1 August 1998 and produced accounts to 31 July each year until 2001/02 when the accounting date was extended to 31 January 2002 and annually thereafter. The requirements of *TA 1988, s 62A; FA 1994, s 203* were met.

Profits (as adjusted for tax purposes)

y/e 31.7.1999	£28,000
y/e 31.7.2000	£40,000
p/e 31.1.2002	£82,000
y/e 31.1.2003	£60,000

Taxable

1998/99	1.8.98 to 5.4.99	£18,667	(*a*)
1999/00	y/e 31.7.99	£28,000	(*b*)
2000/01	y/e 31.7.00	£40,000	(*c*)
2001/02	1.8.00 to 31.1.02		
	(£82,000 − £13,850)	£68,150	(*d*)
2002/03	y/e 31.1.03	£60,000	(*e*)

Notes

(*a*) *TA 1988, s 61(1); FA 1994, s 201*.

(*b*) *TA 1988, s 60(3)(a); FA 1994, s 200*, overlap 1.8.98 to 5.4.99 = £18,667.

(*c*) *TA 1988, s 60(3)(b); FA 1994, s 200*.

(*d*) *TA 1988, s 62(5); FA 1994, s 202* makes this the year in which the accounting date is deemed to change as accounts are made up to a new date in the fiscal year. The period is more than twelve months from the end of the previous basis period (31.7.00), therefore *TA 1988, s 62(2)(b); FA 1994, s 202* determines the basis as the period ending on the new accounting date, i.e. 31.1.02 falling in the fiscal year ended 5.4.02. This is an 18-month accounting period, subject to overlap relief under *TA 1988, s 63A(2); FA 1994, s 205* of the appropriate proportion of the overlap relief brought forward.

$$A \times \frac{(B - C)}{D}$$

$$£18,667 \times \frac{549 - 365}{248} = £13,850$$

A = overlap profit £18,667 as in (*b*) above
B = long accounting period 1.8.2000 to 31.1.2002 = 549 days
C = days in 2001/02 = 365
D = overlap period available, 1.8.98 to 5.4.99 = 248 days

(*e*) *TA 1988, s 60(3)(b); FA 1994, s 200*.

Overlap relief on cessation

2.40   On cessation the overlap relief is the aggregate of any overlap profits, i.e. the amount doubly charged, less any overlap relief previously given on a change of accounting date. [*TA 1988, s 63A(3); FA 1994, s 205*].

Example 18

In the previous example, Mr Nieman ceased to trade on 30 June 2003.

Profit (as adjusted for tax purposes)
    p/e 30.6.03   £45,000

Taxable
    2003/04   p/e 30.6.03
           (£45,000 − £4,817)   £40,183   *(f)*

Note

(f)   *TA 1988, s 63; FA 1994, s 204*, 1.2.03 to 30.6.03 less overlap relief under *TA 1988, s 63A(3); FA 1994, s 205* = £18,667 (*(b)* above) less relief on change in accounting date (*(d)* above) £13,850 leaving £4,817 overlap relief against the profits for the final period. If the relief exceeds the profits a loss will result, relievable in the normal way or as a terminal loss.

Losses and overlap relief

2.41   If a loss making period is included in the basis periods for two successive fiscal years it is only included in the first such period. The loss is treated as nil in the second period to avoid giving excess relief. [*TA 1988, s 63A(4); FA 1994, s 205*]. See Chapter 4.

Transitional provisions

General

2.42   Where a business was in existence prior to 6 April 1994, it continues to be assessed under the old provisions for 1994/95 and 1995/96. There is then a transitional year 1996/97 before the new rules take effect in 1997/98. The transitional provisions are set out in *FA 1994, 20 Sch 1–3*. Businesses ceasing before 6 April 1997 are dealt with entirely under the old rules. [*FA 1994, 20 Sch 3(1)*].

Basis period for 1996/97 and 1997/98

2.43   Where there is an accounting date in 1996/97 the basis period for 1996/97 is that twelve-month period ending with the latest accounting date falling in the year. [*FA 1994, 20 Sch 1(2)(a)*]. This is the 'primary' basis period. But if there is no accounting period ending in 1996/97 the basis period is the fiscal year itself. [*FA 1994, 20 Sch 1(2)(b)*].

2.44   The primary basis period for 1997/98 will be the twelve months from the end of the basis period for 1996/97 [*TA 1988, s 60(3)(b); FA 1994, s 200*]. Where the fiscal year is the appropriate basis period for 1996/97, as a result of a change in accounting date, *TA 1988, s 62; FA 1994, s 202* is applied as if the accounting change were made in the first year of assessment in which accounts are made up to the new date. If the accounting date falls in 1997/98 therefore, the basis period for that year would be the twelve months ending with the new accounting date.

Assessment for 1996/97 where 1995/96 on actual basis

2.45   Where the profits for 1995/96 are assessed on an actual basis under existing *TA 1988, ss 61(4), 62(2)* or *(4)*, the assessment for 1996/97 is also on a fiscal year basis. [*FA 1994, 20 Sch 2(3)*].

Assessment for 1996/97 in all other cases – averaging

2.46   In other cases the assessment for 1996/97 is based on the 'appropriate percentage' of the total of (*a*) the amount of profits or gains of the 'primary' basis period (see 2.43 above) as calculated under substituted *TA 1988, ss 60–63A*, and (*b*) the amount of profits or gains of the 'relevant period'. [*FA 1994, 20 Sch 2(2)*]. The relevant period begins immediately after the end of the basis period for 1995/96 computed under the old rules and ends immediately before the beginning of the primary basis period for the year 1996/97 computed under the new rules. The appropriate percentage is 365 divided by the total number of days in the basis period for 1996/97 (which will be 365 or 366 under *FA 1994, 20 Sch 1(2)*) plus the number of days in the relevant period.

2.47   The transitional profit assessed is therefore the annualised profits for the period from the end of the basis period for 1995/96, on the old rules, to the end of the basis period for 1996/97, on the new rules. [*FA 1994, 20 Sch 2(5)*]. Simply stated, this means that in the case of an established business with annual accounts made up to the same date in 1995/96 and 1996/97, the taxable profit for 1996/97 will be 50 per cent of the aggregate profits for the two years.

Example 19 (continuing)

Mr Mikoyan produces accounts to 5 April each year. The assessment for 1996/97 is on half the combined profits for the years ended 5 April 1996 and 5 April 1997.

Example 20 (continuing)

Mr Gurevich produces accounts to 30 September each year. The assessment for 1996/97 is on half the combined profits for the years ended 30 September 1995 and 30 September 1996.

Example 21 (continuing)

Mr Myasishchyev produces accounts each year to 30 April. The assessment for 1996/97 is on half the combined profits for the years ended 30 April 1995 and 30 April 1996.

Example 22 (continuing)

Mr Yakovlev started business on 1 April 1994 and produced accounts each year to 31 December. The assessment for 1995/96 is on the first twelve months to 31 March 1995. The basis period for 1996/97 is the year ended on the accounting date in the fiscal year, i.e. 31 December 1996. The relevant period is from the end of the basis period for 1995/96, i.e. 1 April 1995 to the beginning of the primary basis period for 1996/97, i.e.

31 December 1995. The assessment for 1996/97 is on $\dfrac{365}{365 + 275}$ (days

in the combined period) of the combined profits of the basis period (y/e 31.12.96) and the relevant period (1.4.95 to 31.12.95).

If Mr Yakovlev elects for the actual basis for 1994/95 and 1995/96, 1996/97 is on the actual profits of the fiscal year with no averaging. The 1997/98 assessment is however based on the year ended in the accounting period, i.e. the year ended 31 December 1997, being twelve months from the end of the primary basis period for 1996/97, the year ended 31 December 1996.

Example 23 (continuing)

Mr Sikorsky produces accounts to 31 December each year until 1996/97 when the accounting date is changed to 31 March. The primary basis period for 1996/97 is the year ended 31 March 1997. The primary period for 1995/96 is the year ended 31 December 1994. The relevant period is from the end of the basis period for 1995/96, i.e. 1 January 1995 to the beginning of the primary basis period for 1996/97, i.e. 31 March 1996. The assessment for 1996/97 is on $\dfrac{365}{365 + 455}$ (days in combined period) of the combined profits of the primary basis period (y/e 31.3.97) and the relevant period (1.1.95 to 31.3.96).

Transitional overlap

2.48   If the basis period for the year 1997/98 begins prior to 6 April 1997, which it would do in most cases other than where accounts are made up for the fiscal year, there is an additional overlap profit relievable on cessation or on a change of accounting date resulting in a basis period in excess of twelve months [*FA 1994, 20 Sch 2(4)*], amounting to the profits of the period which fall before 6 April 1997.

Example 19 (continuing)

Mr Mikoyan produces accounts to 5 April. The 1997/98 basis period is the year ended 5 April 1998, no part of which falls before 6 April 1997 so there is no transitional overlap.

Example 20 (continuing)

Mr Gurevich produces accounts to 30 September. The 1997/98 basis period is the year ended 30 September 1997. The transitional overlap period is from 1.10.96 to 5.4.97.

Example 21 (continuing)

Mr Myasishchyev produces accounts to 30 April. The 1997/98 basis period is the year ended 30 April 1997. The transitional overlap period is from 1.5.96 to 5.4.97.

Example 22 (continuing)

Mr Yakovlev produces accounts to 31 December. The 1997/98 basis period is the year ended 31 December 1997. The transitional overlap relief period is from 1.1.97 to 5.4.97.

Example 23 (continuing)

Mr Sikorsky produces accounts to 31 March. The 1997/98 basis period is the year ended 31 March 1998. The transitional overlap period is from 1.4.97 to 5.4.97.

Example 19

Mr Mikoyan has been in business for many years and produces accounts each year to 5 April.

Profits (as adjusted for tax purposes)
y/e 5.4.94	£20,000
y/e 5.4.95	£22,000
y/e 5.4.96	£26,000
y/e 5.4.97	£24,000
y/e 5.4.98	£30,000
y/e 5.4.99	£28,000

Assessable/taxable
1994/95	preceding year basis	£20,000	(a)
1995/96	preceding year basis	£22,000	(b)
1996/97	transitional year	£25,000	(c)
1997/98	current year basis	£30,000	(d)
1998/99	current year basis	£28,000	(e)

Notes

(a)   *TA 1988, s 60(3)* (original version).

(b)   *TA 1988, s 60(3)* (original version).

(c)   Primary basis period for 1996/97 under
      TA 1988, s 60(3)(b); FA 1994, s 200   £24,000

      Relevant period under *FA 1994*
      20 Sch 2(2)(b), (5)
      i.e. 6.4.95 to 5.4.96   £26,000

      Aggregate, *FA 1994, 20 Sch 2(2)*   £50,000

41

Appropriate percentage under *FA 1994, 20 Sch 2(5)*

$$£50,000 \times \frac{365}{365 + 365} = £25,000$$

There is no transitional overlap period under *FA 1994, 20 Sch 2(4)* as the basis period for 1997/98 begins on 6 April 1997 under *TA 1988, s 60(3)(b); FA 1994, s 200.*

(*d*)   Substituted *TA 1988, s 60(3)(b); FA 1994, s 200.*

(*e*)   Substituted *TA 1988, s 60(3)(b); FA 1994, s 200.*

Example 20

Mr Gurevich has been in business for many years and produces accounts each year to 30 September.

Profits (as adjusted for tax purposes)

y/e 30.9.93	£20,000
y/e 30.9.94	£22,000
y/e 30.9.95	£26,000
y/e 30.9.96	£24,000
y/e 30.9.97	£30,000
y/e 30.9.98	£28,000

Assessable/taxable

1994/95	preceding year basis	£20,000	(*a*)
1995/96	preceding year basis	£22,000	(*b*)
1996/97	transitional year	£25,000	(*c*)
1997/98	current year basis	£30,000	(*d*)
1998/99	current year basis	£28,000	(*e*)

Notes

(*a*)   *TA 1988, s 60(3)* (original version, accounting year ending in preceding fiscal year).

(*b*)   *TA 1988, s 60(3)* (original version).

(*c*)   Basis period for 1996/97 under
TA 1988, s 60(3)(b); FA 1994, s 200
(accounting year to 30.9.96
ending in current fiscal year)   £24,000

Relevant period under *FA 1994, 20 Sch
2(2)(b), (5)*
i.e. 1.10.94 to 30.9.95   £26,000

Aggregate, *FA 1994, 20 Sch 2(2)*   £50,000

Appropriate percentage under *FA 1994, 20 Sch 2(5)*

$$£50,000 \times \frac{365}{365 + 365} = £25,000$$

Overlap period under *FA 1994, 20 Sch 2(4)*: part of basis period for 1997/98, year ending 30 September 1997, which falls before 6 April 1997 i.e. 1.10.96 to 5.4.97, i.e. 187 days,

overlap profits $£30,000 \times \dfrac{187}{365} = £15,370$

(*d*)   Substituted *TA 1988, s 60(3)(b); FA 1994, s 200.*

(*e*)   Substituted *TA 1988, s 60(3)(b); FA 1994, s 200.*

Example 21

Mr Myasishchyev has been in business for many years and produces accounts each year to 30 April.

Profits (as adjusted for tax purposes)

y/e 30.4.93	£20,000
y/e 30.4.94	£22,000
y/e 30.4.95	£26,000
y/e 30.4.96	£24,000
y/e 30.4.97	£30,000
y/e 30.4.98	£28,000

Assessable/taxable

1994/95	preceding year basis	£20,000	(*a*)
1995/96	preceding year basis	£22,000	(*b*)
1996/97	transitional year	£25,000	(*c*)
1997/98	current year basis	£30,000	(*d*)
1998/99	current year basis	£28,000	(*e*)

Notes

(*a*)   *TA 1988, s 60(3)* (original version, accounting year ending in preceding fiscal year).

(*b*)   *TA 1988, s 60(3)* (original version).

(*c*)   Basis period for 1996/97 under
TA 1988, s 60(3)(b); FA 1994, s 200
(accounting year to 30.4.96
ending in current fiscal year)   £24,000

Relevant period under *FA 1994,
20 Sch 2(2)(b), (5)*
i.e. 1.5.94 to 30.4.95   £26,000

Aggregate, *FA 1994, 20 Sch 2(2)*   £50,000

Appropriate percentage under *FA 1994, 20 Sch 2(5)*

$$£50,000 \times \frac{365}{365 + 365} = £25,000$$

Overlap period under *FA 1994, 20 Sch 2(4)*: part of basis period for 1997/98, year ending 30 April 1997, which falls before 6 April 1997 i.e. 1.5.96 to 5.4.97, i.e. 340 days, overlap profits

$$£30,000 \times \frac{340}{365} = £27,945$$

(*d*)   *TA 1988, s 60(3)(b); FA 1994, s 200.*

(*e*)   *TA 1988, s 60(3)(b); FA 1994, s 200.*

Example 22

Mr Yakovlev started business on 1 April 1994 and made up his accounts to 31 December each year.

Profits (as adjusted for tax purposes)
1.4.94 to 31.12.94	£12,000
y/e 31.12.95	£14,000
y/e 31.12.96	£6,000
y/e 31.12.97	£24,000
y/e 31.12.98	£21,000

Assessable/taxable
1993/94	1.4.94 to 5.4.94			
	5/275 × £12,000	=	£218	(*a*)
1994/95	1.4.94 to 31.3.95			
	£12,000 + £3,500			
	(3/12 × £14,000)	=	£15,500	(*b*)
1995/96	1.4.94 to 31.3.95			
	£12,000 + £3,500			
	(3/12 × £14,000)	=	£15,500	
1996/97	Transitional year		£9,410	(*c*)
1997/98	y/e 31.12.97		£24,000	
1998/99	y/e 31.12.98		£21,000	

Notes

(*a*)   *TA 1988, s 61(1)* (original version, profits from commencement to next 5 April).

(*b*)   *TA 1988, s 60(4)* (original version, no accounting years ending in previous fiscal year, usual Revenue choice of twelve-month period).

(c)   Basis period for 1996/97 under
      TA 1988, s 60(3)(b); FA 1994, s 200
      (accounting year to 31.12.96 ending
      in current fiscal year)   £6,000

Relevant period under *FA 1994, 20 Sch
2(2)(b), (5)* i.e.
1.4.95 to 31.12.95 9/12 × £14,000   £10,500

Aggregate *FA 1994, 20 Sch 2(2)*   £16,500

Appropriate percentage under *FA 1994, 20 Sch 2(5)*

$$£16,500 \times \frac{365}{365 + 275} = £9,410$$

Overlap period under *FA 1994, 20 Sch 2(4)*: part of basis period
from 1997/98, year ended 31 December 1997, which falls before 6
April 1997, i.e. 1.1.97 to 5.4.97 i.e. 95 days, overlap profits

$$£24,000 \times \frac{95}{365} = £6,247$$

Mr Yakovlev has the option to elect for the second and third years of
assessment to be charged on an actual basis under *TA 1988, s 62; FA
1994, s 202*. If he so elects the figures become:

Assessable/taxable
1993/94	1.4.94 to 5.4.94			
	5/275 × £12,000	=	£218	(a)
1994/95	6.4.94 to 5.4.95			
	270/275 × £12,000	= £11,782		
	95/365 × £14,000	= £3,644	£15,426	(b)
1995/96	6.4.95 to 5.4.96			
	270/365 × £14,000	= £10,356		
	95/365 × £6,000	= £1,562	£11,918	(c)
1996/97	6.4.96 to 5.4.97			
	270/365 × £6,000	= £4,438		
	95/365 × £24,000	= £6,246	£10,684	(d)
1997/98	y/e 31.12.97		£24,000	(e)
1998/99	y/e 31.12.98		£21,000	(f)

Notes

(a)   *TA 1988, s 61(1)* (original version) profits from commencement to
      next 5 April.

(b)   *TA 1988, s 62(2)* (original version) profits on actual basis for fiscal
      year.

(c)   *TA 1988, s 62(2)* (original version) profits on actual basis for fiscal
      year. The total for 1994/95 and 1995/96 on actual basis is £27,344

(£15,426 + £11,918) compared with £31,000 (£15,500 + £15,500) on the original basis so the election is likely to be made.

(d) *FA 1994, 20 Sch 2(3)*, as 1995/96 is assessed on an actual basis so is 1996/97 instead of the usual transitional provisions.

(e) *TA 1988, s 60(3)(b); FA 1994, s 200.*

(f) *TA 1988, s 60(3)(b); FA 1994, s 200.* The overlap period and overlap profits under *FA 1994, 20 Sch 2(4)* remain unchanged.

Example 23

Mr Sikorsky produces accounts to 31 December each year until 1996/97 when the accounting date is changed to 31 March as a result of a 15-month accounting period.

Profits (as adjusted for tax purposes)

y/e 31.12.94	£25,000
y/e 31.12.95	£30,000
1.1.96 to 31.3.97	£45,000
y/e 31.3.98	£40,000

Assessable/taxable

1995/96	preceding year basis	£25,000	(a)
1996/97	transitional year	£33,384	(b)
1997/98	current year basis	£40,000	(c)

Notes

(a) *TA 1988, s 60(3)* (original version).

(b) Primary basis period for 1996/97 under *FA 1994, 20 Sch 1(2)(a)* (twelve months to 31.3.97)

$$\frac{12}{15} \times £45,000 = \qquad\qquad £36,000$$

Relevant period under *FA 1994, 20 Sch 2(2)(b)*, i.e. 1.1.95 to 31.3.96

1.1.95 to 31.12.95	£30,000
1.1.96 to 31.3.96 3/15 × £45,000	£9,000
Aggregate, *FA 1994, 20 Sch 2(2)*	£75,000

Appropriate percentage under *FA 1994, 20 Sch 2(5)*

$$£75,000 \times \frac{365}{365 + 455} = \qquad\qquad £33,384$$

(c) *TA 1988, s 60(3)(b); FA 1994, s 200.*

Cessation pre-6 April 1998

2.49   In order to prevent exploitation of the preceding year basis of assessment by avoiding Revenue adjustments on cessation by delaying the cessation until after 5 April 1997, anti-avoidance provisions are introduced. If the cessation was prior to 6 April 1997 the old rules continue to apply. [*FA 1994, 20 Sch 3(1)*]. If the cessation took place in 1997/98 the Revenue may direct that the old rules continue to apply. In the first instance the self-assessment provisions will apply to 1996/97 under the normal transitional rules, but the Revenue may make a direction for the old rules to apply if the profits or gains chargeable for 1995/96 and 1996/97 are increased by adjusting the assessments to an actual basis. [*FA 1994, 20 Sch 3(2)*].

2.50   This has the effect of charging the final year 1997/98 on the actual basis, not on the new basis, with overlap relief in spite of the Revenue's Tax Bulletin No 10, February 1994, page 112 which incorrectly states that 1997/98 is not affected by the direction.

Example 24

Mr Antonov had been in business for many years and produced accounts to 30 June each year until 31 January 1998 when he ceased to trade.

Profits (as adjusted for tax purposes)

y/e 30.6.93	£36,000
y/e 30.6.94	£30,000
y/e 30.6.95	£24,000
y/e 30.6.96	£18,000
y/e 30.6.97	£12,000
p/e 31.1.98	£5,000

Assessable/taxable

1994/95	preceding year basis	£36,000	(*a*)
1995/96	preceding year basis	£30,000	(*b*)
1996/97	transitional year	£21,000	(*c*)
1997/98	year of cessation	£8,822	(*d*)

Notes

(*a*)   *TA 1988, s 60(3)* (original version) accounting year ending in preceding year of assessment.

(*b*)   *TA 1988, s 60(3)* as above.

(*c*)   Basis period for 1996/97 under *TA 1988, s 60(3)(b); FA 1994, s 200*, accounting year, ending 30 June 1996 in fiscal year.   £18,000

Relevant period under *FA 1994, 20 Sch 2(2)(b)(5)*
i.e. 1.7.94 to 30.6.95   £24,000

Aggregate, *FA 1994, 20 Sch 2(2)*   £42,000

Appropriate percentage under *FA 1994, 20 Sch 2(5)*

$$£42,000 \times \frac{365}{365 + 365} = £21,000$$

(*d*)   *TA 1988, s 63; FA 1994, s 204*, period from end of basis period for 1996/97, 1 July 1996 to date of cessation 31 January 1998, i.e. £12,000 year ended 30 June 1997 plus £5,000 period ending 31 January 1998, i.e. £17,000 less overlap relief under *TA 1988, s 63A(3); FA 1994, s 205* £8,178 (see below).

Overlap period under *FA 1994, 20 Sch 2(4)*, part of basis period for 1997/98 which falls before 6 April 1997, 1.7.96 to 5.4.97 i.e. 279 days

overlap profits $£17,000 \times \dfrac{279}{580^*} = £8,178$

* period 1.7.1996 to 31.1.1998 365 + 215 days.

Revenue direction
The Revenue may direct that the new rules do not to apply under *FA 1994, 20 Sch 3(2)*.

1994/95	preceding year basis	£36,000	(*a*)
1995/96	preceding year basis	£30,000	(*b*)
1996/97	preceding year basis	£24,000	(*c*)
1997/98	6 April to date of cessation	£8,000	(*d*)

Notes

(*a*)   *TA 1988, s 60(3)* (original version).

(*b*)   *TA 1988, s 60(3)* (original version).

(*c*)   *TA 1988, s 60(3)* (original version).

(*d*)   *TA 1988, s 63(1)(a)* (original version), i.e. £3,000 (3/12 × £12,000) + £5,000. The total of 1996/97 and 1997/98 on this basis is £32,000 (£24,000 + £8,000) compared with £29,822 (£21,000 + £8,822) on the new basis so the Revenue are likely to make this direction.

The Revenue have a further option to compute 1995/96 and 1996/97 on an actual fiscal year basis under *TA 1988, s 63(1)(b)* (original version).

1995/96 actual basis
   3/12 × £24,000 =   £6,000
   9/12 × £18,000 = £13,500

                                £19,500

1996/97 actual basis
    3/12 × £18,000 =   £4,500
    9/12 × £12,000 =   £9,000
                                                            £13,500
                                                            £33,000

However, this is less than as originally computed under the old rules which amounted to £54,000 (£30,000 + £24,000) and this further option would not be exercised in this instance.

Cessation in 1998/99

2.51   Where the cessation takes place in 1998/99 and the profits which would have been charged to tax for 1996/97, had they been calculated on an actual basis, exceed those charged under the transitional provisions, or would have done had it not been for the losses brought forward under *TA 1988, s 385*, the Revenue may make a direction for 1996/97 to be assessed on an actual basis instead of following the transitional year rules. Losses can be brought forward against the recalculated profits. [*FA 1994, 20 Sch 3(3), (4)*]. Note that the direction does not disapply the new rules for 1996/97, as stated incorrectly in the Revenue's Tax Bulletin No 10, page 112. 1996/97 is charged on the fiscal year basis under *FA 1994, 20 Sch 3(4)*.

2.52   Any adjustments arising from the direction should be made by an additional assessment or a reduction or discharge, as necessary. [*FA 1994, 20 Sch 3(5)*].

Example 25

Mr Adler had carried on trading for many years, making up his accounts to 30 June each year until he ceased to trade on 31 December 1998.

Profits (as adjusted for tax purposes)
y/e 30.6.94	£30,000
y/e 30.6.95	£28,000
y/e 30.6.96	£24,000
y/e 30.6.97	£22,000
y/e 30.6.98	£16,000
1.7.98 to 31.12.98	£3,000

Assessable/taxable
1995/96	preceding year basis	£30,000	(*a*)
1996/97	transitional year	£26,000	(*b*)
1997/98	current year basis	£22,000	(*c*)
1998/99	year of discontinuance	£2,500	(*d*)

Notes

(*a*)   *TA 1988, s 60(3)* (original version).

(*b*)   Basis period for 1996/97

y/e 30.6.96 [*FA 1994, 20 Sch 1(2)(a)*]	£24,000
Relevant period under *FA 1994, 20 Sch 2(2)(b)*	
y/e 30.6.95	£28,000
Aggregate *FA 1994, 20 Sch 2(2)*	£52,000

Appropriate percentage under *FA 1994, 20 Sch 2(5)*

$$£52,000 \times \frac{365}{365 + 365} = \qquad £26,000$$

(*c*)   *TA 1988, s 60(3)(b); FA 1994, s 200*, y/e 30.6.97

(*d*)   *TA 1988, s 63(b); FA 1994, s 204* y/e 30.6.98 = £16,000

+ p/e 31.12.98 £3,000, total	£19,000
less overlap relief, overlap period	
1.7.96 to 5.4.97, overlap profits	
9/12 × £22,000 =	£16,500
final assessment £19,000 − £16,500 =	£2,500

Possible Revenue direction under *FA 1994,*	
20 Sch 3(3), (4). 1996/97 on transitional rules (as above)	£26,000
1996/97 on actual basis	
3/12 × y/e 30.6.96 (£24,000)	£6,000
9/12 × y/e 30.6.97 (£22,000)	£16,500
	£22,500

As this is less than the amount assessed for 1996/97 under the transitional rules there would be no Revenue direction.

Example 26

Mr Bartini had been in business for many years and produced accounts to 30 September each year until 30 September 1998 when he ceased to trade.

Profits (as adjusted for tax purposes)

y/e 30.9.94	£20,000
y/e 30.9.95	£25,000
y/e 30.9.96	£30,000
y/e 30.9.97	£60,000
y/e 30.9.98	£20,000

Assessable/taxable

1995/96	y/e 30.9.94	£20,000	(*a*)
1996/97	transitional year or	£27,500	(*b*)
	on Revenue direction	£45,000	
1997/98	y/e 30.9.97	£49,260	(*c*)
1998/99	y/e 30.9.98	£Nil	(*d*)

Notes

(*a*)   *TA 1988, s 60(3)* (original version).

(*b*)   Basis period for 1996/97 under
TA 1988, s 60(3)(b); FA 1994, s 200
accounting year ending 30 September 1996
in fiscal year under *FA 1994, 20 Sch 2(2)(a)*   £30,000

Relevant period under *FA 1994, 20 Sch 2(2)(b), (5)*
i.e. 1.10.94 to 30.9.95   £25,000

Aggregate, *FA 1994, 20 Sch 2(2)*   £55,000

Appropriate percentage under *FA 1994, 20 Sch 2(5)*

$$£55,000 \times \frac{365}{365 + 365} = £27,500$$

but see Revenue option below.

Overlap period under *FA 1994, 20 Sch 1(4)* part of basis period for
1997/98 which falls before 6 April 1997, i.e. 1.10.96 to 5.4.97, 187
days, overlap profits

$$£60,000 \times \frac{187}{365} = £30,740.$$

(*c*)   *TA 1988, s 60(3)(b); FA 1994, s 200*, accounting year ending in fiscal year, £60,000 y/e 30.9.97, less overlap relief under *TA 1988,
s 63A(4); FA 1994, s 205* carried back as a loss under substituted *TA
1988, s 380 (1)(b)* £10,740 (£30,740 less relieved in 1998/99
£20,000).

(*d*)   Substituted *TA 1988, s 63; FA 1994, s 204* period from end of previous basis period, i.e. 1.10.97 to date of cessation 30.9.98, i.e.
£20,000 less overlap relief as above £30,740, excess overlap relief
available for loss relief £10,740, as above.

Revenue direction
Under *FA 1994, 20 Sch 3(3)(4)* the Revenue may direct the substitution of
the actual profits in the fiscal year 1996/97 for those assessed where there
is a cessation prior to 6 April 1999. The actual profits for 1996/97 would
be:

6/12 × £30,000 (y/e 30.9.96)	£15,000
6/12 × £60,000 (y/e 30.9.97)	£30,000
	£45,000

As £45,000 is greater than the amount charged under the transitional year provisions of £27,500, the Revenue should make the direction and assess £45,000 for 1996/97.

Transitional anti-avoidance measures

2.53   The measures to prevent tax avoidance via exploitation of the transitional rules will necessarily be complex because of the numerous ways in which these rules could be so exploited. These include a change of accounting policies, deferment of expenses, an acceleration of income or a change of accounting date in the transitional period, all with a view to maximising the profits falling in the transitional period which are averaged down to the annual equivalent under the transitional rules (see Chapter 16).

Lloyd's underwriters

2.54   Lloyd's underwriters are assessed on a calendar year basis and the calendar year is coterminous with the fiscal year in which it ends. Therefore an underwriter commencing on 1 January 1994 is deemed to have commenced on 6 April 1994, which under the old rules would have been assessed for 1994/95. This does not however work for Simplified Assessing and it is in future provided that the year in which the under-writing results are declared will be the fiscal year in respect of which they are taxed.

2.55   Because Lloyd's runs a three-year rolling account, the 1994 calendar year is not closed until 31 December 1996 and the results for that year would be declared in May 1997. These figures therefore form the basis of assessment for 1997/98 under *FA 1994, s 218(3)*. The detailed amendments for Lloyd's underwriters are contained in *FA 1994, ss 219–230* and *21 Sch*, and are outside the scope of this work.

Chapter 3

New Rules of Assessment under Schedule D, Cases III to VI

Schedule D, Case III

3.1   Shortly stated Schedule D, Case III charges tax in respect of:

(*a*)   any interest of money whether yearly or otherwise, or any annuity or other annual payment, whether such payment is payable within or out of the United Kingdom, but not including any payment chargeable under Schedule A; and

(*b*)   all discounts; and

(*c*)   income, except income charged under Schedule C, from securities bearing interest payable out of the public revenue.

[*TA 1988, s 18(3)*].

The location of the source will usually determine whether it falls within Case III or within Cases IV or V.

Fiscal year basis

3.2   Under *TA 1988, s 64; FA 1994, s 206* income tax under Schedule D, Case III will be chargeable on the full amount of the income arising in the year of assessment without any deduction. The only exceptions will be income received by a partnership, dealt with in 7.9 below, and income falling within the transitional provisions.

Commencement date for new rules

3.3   The fiscal year basis applies to new sources arising on or after 6 April 1994 and for existing sources from 6 April 1997 (1997/98) provided that they continue beyond 5 April 1998 [*FA 1994, 20 Sch 4(1)*], with the transitional year being 1996/97.

Example 1

Mr Lebed opened a bank deposit account on 5 October 1994 with £100,000, on which interest was payable gross at 10 per cent p.a.

Interest was received as follows:

1994/95	£100,000 × 10% × $\dfrac{6}{12}$ =	£5,000
1995/96	£100,000 × 10%	£10,000
1996/97	£100,000 × 10%	£10,000
1997/98	£100,000 × 10%	£10,000

Assessable/taxable
1994/95	fiscal year basis	£5,000
1995/96	fiscal year basis	£10,000
1996/97	fiscal year basis	£10,000
1997/98	fiscal year basis	£10,000

New sources

3.4   Each lodgement is strictly a new source (*Hart v Sangster 1957 37 TC 231*) although this point is not normally taken by the Revenue. The Revenue will not continue their practice of assessing new accounts on a preceding year basis until 1996/97 merely because there is in existence an account dealt with on the preceding year basis, particularly if they consider that the taxpayer is trying to maximise transitional relief. New accounts from 6 April 1994 will be dealt with on a strict fiscal year basis under the new rules in all cases (see 16.27 *et seq*. below).

Cessation before 6 April 1998

3.5   If the source ceases prior to 6 April 1998 the transitional provisions do not apply and the old rules apply throughout. [*FA 1994, 20 Sch 5*].

Example 2

Mr Lebed closed the deposit account referred to in the previous example on 31 December 1997. The interest received in 1997/98 was

$$£100,000 \times 10\% \times \frac{9}{12} = £7,500$$

Assessable/taxable
1994/95	actual basis	£5,000
1995/96	actual basis	£10,000
1996/97	preceding year basis	£10,000
1997/98	actual basis	£7,500

The taxpayer has the option to put 1996/97 on an actual basis under *TA 1988, s 66(1)(c)* (original enactment). The Revenue has the option to put 1996/97 on an actual basis under *TA 1988, s 67* (original enactment) under *FA 1994, 20 Sch 5*.

Transitional provisions – averaging

3.6   Other than as mentioned in 3.5 and 3.7 the transitional year 1996/97
is assessed on one-half of the aggregate of the full amount of the income
arising in 1996/97 and the full amount of the income arising in the year 1995/
96 (which under the old rules would have been assessed for 1996/97 on the
preceding year basis of assessment). [*FA 1994, 20 Sch 4(1)(2)*].

Example 3

Mr Gribovsky had the following interest received, taxable under
Schedule D, Case III.

1993/94	£1,000
1994/95	£2,000
1995/96	£4,000
1996/97	£8,000
1997/98	£9,000

Assessable/taxable

1994/95	preceding year basis	£1,000	
1995/96	preceding year basis	£2,000	
1996/97	transitional year	£6,000	*(a)*
1997/98	fiscal year basis	£9,000	

Note

(*a*)   *FA 1994, 20 Sch 4(2)(a)*

income arising in 1996/97	£8,000
FA 1994, 20 Sch 4(2)(b) income	
arising in 1995/96	£4,000
aggregate	£12,000
50% thereof	£6,000

Transitional provisions where 1995/96 on actual basis

3.7   If the 1995/96 assessment is on the fiscal year basis, as a result of a
taxpayer's election for the actual basis, under *TA 1988, s 66(1)(c)* the
assessment for 1996/97 will also be made on an actual basis, not on the
averaging basis. [*FA 1994, 20 Sch 4(3)*].

Example 4

Mr Petlyakov opened an account in 1993/94 and received the following
deposit interest.

1993/94	£3,000
1994/95	£12,000
1995/96	£8,000
1996/97	£10,000
1997/98	£9,000
Total received	£42,000

Assessable/taxable

1993/94	actual basis	£3,000	
1994/95	actual basis	£12,000	
1995/96	preceding year	£12,000	
1996/97	transitional year	£9,000	*(a)*
1997/98	fiscal year basis	£9,000	
Total assessed		£45,000	

Notes

(*a*) Transitional period

1995/96 *FA 1994, 20 Sch 4(2)(a)*	£8,000
1996/97 *FA 1994, 20 Sch 4(2)(b)*	£10,000
	£18,000
50% thereof *FA 1994, 20 Sch 4(1)(2)*	£9,000

Mr Petlyakov elected to apply the actual basis for 1995/96 under *TA 1988, s 66(1)(c)* (original enactment).

Assessable/taxable

1993/94	actual basis	£3,000	
1994/95	actual basis	£12,000	
1995/96	actual basis	£8,000	
1996/97	fiscal year basis	£10,000	*(b)*
1997/98	fiscal year basis	£9,000	
Total assessed		£42,000	

Note

(*b*) *FA 1994, 20 Sch 4(3)*, 1996/97 assessed on a fiscal year basis as 1995/96 assessed on an actual basis.

Partnerships

3.8   Partnership investment income is not chargeable on a fiscal year basis but by reference to the basis period for Schedule D, Cases I or II under *TA 1988, s 111(4)(b); FA 1994, s 215*. The transitional provisions for such income will be included in the *Finance Act 1995*.

Schedule D, Cases IV and V

3.9   Schedule D, Case IV charges tax in respect of income arising from securities out of the United Kingdom, except income charged under Schedule C. Schedule D, Case V charges tax in respect of income arising from possessions out of the United Kingdom, not being income consisting of emoluments of any office or employment. [*TA 1988, s 18*]. The assessing provisions of *TA 1988, s 65* are modified to assess such income on a current fiscal year basis from 6 April 1994 for new sources, and from 6 April 1997 for sources in existence on or before 5 April 1994, and continuing beyond 5 April 1998. [*FA 1994, s 207(6) and 20 Sch 6(1)*].

Fiscal year basis

3.10   The alteration in the legislation is accomplished by deleting reference to 'the year preceding' in the existing legislation. [*FA 1994, s 207(1)(3)*]. The special rules for new sources of income and ceased sources in *TA 1988, ss 66, 67* no longer have effect [*FA 1994, s 207(4)*] and the provisions which preserve the arising basis for property etc. situated in the Republic of Ireland under *TA 1988, s 68* are amended to refer to the provisions of the main charging section in *TA 1988, s 65* only. [*FA 1994, s 207(5)*].

Example 5

Mr Belyayev, resident and domiciled in England, let out his holiday villa in Spain for the first time in the summer of 1994. He received the following net income as adjusted for tax purposes:

1994/95	£5,000
1995/96	£7,000
1996/97	£8,000
1997/98	£10,000

The profit chargeable to tax for each fiscal year is the net income as computed above.

Foreign trades and professions

3.11   A material change is made by *FA 1994, s 207(2)* which provides that income arising from a trade, profession or vocation, managed and controlled from outside the United Kingdom will remain chargeable under Schedule D, Case V, but the current year basis of assessment applicable to Schedule D, Cases I and II will apply. This means that the provisions relating to opening years, overlaps, change of accounting date, cessation and overlap relief will apply to such income, which will therefore be assessed by reference to basis periods and not the fiscal year. The rules as explained in Chapter 2 will therefore apply without amendment for a person assessed on an arising basis.

3.12 Income from a trade, profession or vocation carried on either solely or in partnership outside the UK by a UK ordinarily resident and domiciled individual is taxed on such an arising basis, regardless of remittances to the UK. The fact that the income is computed under Schedule D, Case I or II rules can cause considerable practical difficulties where overseas accounts are prepared locally and in accordance with the accounting and fiscal requirements of the source country. Losses and capital allowances may only be used against foreign income falling within *TA 1988, s 65*.

3.13 The remittance basis continues for non-UK domiciled individuals or not ordinarily resident British subjects or citizens of the Republic of Ireland. In order to qualify for the remittance basis the trade has to be carried on entirely outside the UK, because if the activities are from a single trade or profession carried out partly in the UK and partly abroad it will be taxable under Schedule D, Cases I or II (and not Case V) under *Davies v Braithwaite 1933 18 TC 198*. It is therefore often desirable to carry out overseas activities through an overseas partnership controlled and managed outside the UK under *TA 1988, s 112* or through an overseas employment.

Example 6

Mr Bolkhovitinov, resident and domiciled in England, was a partner in Borovkov-Florov a business managed and controlled outside the UK. The business made up its accounts to 31 December each year.

Profits (as adjusted for UK tax purposes) applicable to Mr Bolkhovitinov

y/e 31.12.94	£24,000
y/e 31.12.95	£30,000
y/e 31.12.96	£36,000
y/e 31.12.97	£42,000
y/e 31.12.98	£48,000

Assessable/taxable
1995/96 income arising in preceding year

9/12	y/e 31.12.94	£18,000
3/12	y/e 31.12.95	£7,500
		£25,500 *(a)*
1996/97	transitional year	£33,448 *(b)*
1997/98	current year basis	£42,000 *(c)*
1998/99	current year basis	£48,000 *(d)*

Notes

(a)   *TA 1988, s 66(1)(a)* (original enactment).

(b)   Primary basis period 1996/97, y/e 31.12.96
      [*FA 1994, 20 Sch 1(2)(a)*]   £36,000

      Relevant period under *FA 1994, 20 Sch
      2(2)(b), 2(5)*

      6.4.95 to 31.12.95

$$\frac{270}{365} \times £30,000 =$$ £22,191

      Aggregate *FA 1994, 20 Sch 2(2)*   £58,191

$$£58,191 \times \frac{365}{270 + 365} =$$ £33,448

(c)   *TA 1988, s 60(3)(b); FA 1994, s 200*. Overlap period under *FA
      1994, 20 Sch 2(4)*: part of basis period 1997/98, year ended
      31.12.1997 which falls before 6 April 1997, i.e. 1.1.97 to 5.4.97, i.e.
      95 days, overlap profits

$$£42,000 \times \frac{95}{365} = £10,931$$

(d)   *TA 1988, s 60(3)(b); FA 1994, s 200*.

Determination of chargeable income

3.14   Income from abroad is assessed under Schedule D, Cases IV or
V on the amount computed as if it were income arising in the UK, but
subject to a deduction for any annual payments to a non-resident out of
income which is not excluded by *TA 1988, s 347A(5)*. Interest is not
deductible from rents from a foreign investment property, *Ockenden v
Mackley* [1982] *STC 513*.

3.15   There is no express provision enabling expenses to be deducted
in computing Schedule D, Case V income. The Revenue practice in the
case of let property is to allow certain expenses such as rates, insurance
premiums and agent's commissions. However, the Revenue maintain
that in strictness only expenses incurred abroad are deductible. They
argue that the Parliamentary debate on the *Finance Bill 1914*, which provided for income from overseas properties to be assessed on the arising
rather than the remittance basis for the first time, shows that the intention
of the original legislation was to liken the arising and remittance bases
and it would therefore be unfair to give greater relief for income arising
than income remitted. This view is disputed.

Remittance basis

3.16   Schedule D, Case IV or V income is taxed on an arising basis, except where the taxpayer is not domiciled in the UK or is a Commonwealth citizen or citizen of the Republic of Ireland and not ordinarily resident in the UK, in which case the income assessed is that remitted to the UK (if any). Income from foreign licences of UK patents is treated as foreign income for double taxation relief purposes (Extra-statutory concession B8 (1992)).

Example 7

Mr Bratukhin, resident in the UK but domiciled abroad, let out his holiday villa in Spain for the first time in the summer of 1994. He received the following net income from the letting:

1994/95	£4,000
1995/96	£7,000
1996/97	£8,000
1997/98	£10,000

However the rents were paid into his bank account in Jersey from which he remitted sums to the UK as follows:

1994/95	£1,000
1995/96	£3,000
1996/97	£10,000
1997/98	£2,000

The profits chargeable to tax for each fiscal year was the amount remitted to the UK in the fiscal year.

Partnerships

3.17   Partnership investment income is not chargeable on a fiscal year basis but by reference to the basis period for Schedule D, Cases I or II under *TA 1988, s 111(4)(b); FA 1994, s 215*. The transitional provisions for such income will be included in the *Finance Act 1995*. A trade controlled from the UK is charged under Schedule D, Case I, *Ogilvie v Kitton 1908 5 TC 338*, but if controlled abroad under Schedule D, Case V, *Colquhoun v Brooks 1889 2 TC 490*.

Planning remittances

3.18   If a non-UK domiciled individual is assessable on a remittance basis it is important to ensure that so far as possible remittances to the UK are out of capital, which means that foreign income should be paid into a separate account with a different bank. However, chargeable gains are also assessed on a non-domiciled UK resident on a remittance basis under *TCGA 1992, s 12(1)* and therefore the proceeds arising on the sale at a profit of overseas investments should be paid into yet another account and not remitted unless necessary. Remittances proved not to be of income are not taxed under Schedule D (*Timbrell v Lord Aldenham's Executor 1947 28 TC 293*).

3.19   Remittances within the same tax year but after the source has ceased are caught (*Joffe v Thain 1955 36 TC 199*). Remittances of income in a fiscal year following the cessation of the source are not taxable, unless the remittances are of remuneration assessable under Schedule E, Case III, which are caught by *TA 1988, s 19(1)4A*.

Pensions

3.20   Foreign pensions or annuities are charged to tax (whether remitted to the UK or not) subject to a deduction of 10 per cent. Pensions granted in respect of Nazi persecution as a civil service or social security pension are brought within the total exemption enjoyed by annuities under *TA 1988, s 330*. The provisions apply to pensions charged under Schedule E under *TA 1988, s 19(1)(4)*. The remittance basis is maintained for non-UK domiciled pensioners.

Transitional provisions – averaging

3.21   Where income assessed under Schedule D, Case IV or V arose prior to 6 April 1994, and continues beyond 5 April 1998, the 1996/97 assessment will normally be on one-half of the aggregate of the income arising in 1996/97 and 1995/96. [*FA 1994, 20 Sch 6(1)(2)(a)*]. Under the old rules income arising in 1995/96 would on a preceding year basis have been assessed for 1996/97. Normal allowances and deductions are made from the appropriate source of income.

Example 8

Mr Dudakov, resident and domiciled in England, let out his holiday villa in Spain for many years. He received the following net income, as adjusted for tax purposes:

1993/94	£1,000
1994/95	£2,000
1995/96	£4,000
1996/97	£8,000
1997/98	£9,000

Assessable/taxable

1994/95	preceding year basis	£1,000	
1995/96	preceding year basis	£2,000	
1996/97	transitional year	£6,000	(a)
1997/98	fiscal year basis	£9,000	

Notes

(a) *FA 1994, 20 Sch 6(2)(a)(i)*
income arising in 1996/97 £8,000

FA 1994, 20 Sch 6(2)(a)(ii)
income arising in 1995/96 £4,000

aggregate £12,000

50% thereof £6,000

This is precisely the same rule as applies for Schedule D, Case III (see 3.6 above).

3.22   Where the remittance basis applies, because, for example, the taxpayer is not domiciled in the United Kingdom, the charge for 1996/97 will under Schedule D, Case IV be one-half of the total of the remittances in 1995/96 and 1996/97 (so far as can be computed) without any other deduction. [*FA 1994, 20 Sch 6(2)(b)*]. Where the remittance basis applies to Schedule D, Case V income, the assessment for 1996/97 will be on one-half of the actual remittances in 1995/96 and 1996/97 with no other deduction. [*FA 1994, 20 Sch 6(2)(c)*]. The reason for the slight difference in the wording between Schedule D, Cases IV and V in respect of remittances in the transitional period is not clear.

Example 9

Mr Chetverikov is a non-UK domiciled UK resident who had remitted to the UK income from his international trading partnership which is managed and controlled in the Bahamas.

Remittances received in the UK are:

1993/94	£1,000
1994/95	£2,000
1995/96	£4,000
1996/97	£8,000
1997/98	£9,000

Assessable/taxable

1994/95	preceding year basis	£1,000	
1995/96	preceding year basis	£2,000	
1996/97	transitional year	£6,000	(a)
1997/98	fiscal year basis	£9,000	

Notes

(*a*) *FA 1994, 20 Sch 6(2)(c)*

(i)	income remitted in 1996/97	£8,000
(ii)	income remitted in 1995/96	£4,000
	Aggregate	£12,000
	50% thereof	£6,000

Transitional provisions where 1995/96 on actual basis

3.23 If 1995/96 was assessed on the fiscal year basis as a result of the taxpayer's election under existing *TA 1988, s 66(1)(c)* the averaging provisions do not apply for 1996/97 which will also be assessed on a fiscal year basis. [*FA 1994, 20 Sch 6(3)*].

Example 10

Mr Ekonomov, resident and domiciled in England, first let his villa in Spain in the summer of 1993. He received the following income, as adjusted for tax purposes:

1993/94	£5,000
1994/95	£8,000
1995/96	£6,000
1996/97	£7,500
1997/98	£10,000

Assessable/taxable

1993/94	actual basis	£5,000	(*a*)
1994/95	actual basis	£8,000	(*b*)
1995/96	preceding year basis	£8,000	(*c*)
1996/97	transitional year	£6,750	(*d*)
1997/98	fiscal year basis	£10,000	(*e*)

Notes

(*a*) *TA 1988, s 66(1)(a)* (original enactment).

(*b*) *TA 1988, s 66(1)(b)* (original enactment).

(*c*) *TA 1988, s 65(1)* (original enactment).

(*d*) *FA 1994, 20 Sch 6(2)(a)*

Income arising in 1996/97	£7,500
FA 1994, 20 Sch 6(2)(a)(i)	

Income arising in 1995/96	£6,000
FA 1984, 20 Sch 6(2)(a)(ii)	
Aggregate	£13,500
50% thereof	£6,750

(e)   *TA 1988, s 65(1); FA 1994, s 207(1).*

Mr Ekonomov elects for 1995/96 to be on an actual basis under *TA 1988, s 66(1)(c)* (original enactment) and the income for that year therefore becomes £6,000.

This election causes the transitional year to be adjusted to the actual basis too, *FA 1994, 20 Sch 6(3)*, i.e. to £7,500. The total for 1995/96 and 1996/97 therefore becomes:

1995/96	£6,000
1996/97	£7,500
	£13,500

compared with:	
1995/96	£8,000
1996/97	£6,750
	£14,750

so the election saves tax on the difference of £1,250.

Transitional overlap relief

3.24   Where income from an overseas trade, profession or vocation is assessed under Schedule D, Case V on a current year basis, as under Schedule D, Cases I and II, the tax is charged on the accounting period ending in the fiscal year and not on the fiscal year basis. The overlap provisions in *TA 1988, s 63A; FA 1994, s 205* apply to any transitional overlap arising on any part of the profits or gains for the basis period for 1997/98 which falls prior to 6 April 1997 as under Schedule D, Cases I and II under *FA 1994, 20 Sch 2(4)*. [*FA 1994, 20 Sch 6(4)*]. (See Chapter 2, 2.37–2.41 and 2.48.)

Cessation prior to 6 April 1998

3.25   If a source chargeable under Schedule D, Cases IV or V which commenced prior to 6 April 1994 ceases prior to 6 April 1998 the old rules continue to apply. [*FA 1994, 20 Sch 7*].

Example 11

Mr Kanstantinov, resident and domiciled in England, had let his villa in Spain for many years until it was sold on 30 September 1997. He received the following income as adjusted for tax purposes:

1993/94		£6,˄00
1994/95		£7,000
1995/96		£8,000
1996/97		£9,000
1997/98		£5,000

Assessable/taxable

1994/95	preceding year	£6,000	(a)
1995/96	preceding year	£7,000	(b)
1996/97	preceding year	£8,000	(c)
1997/98	actual basis	£5,000	(d)

Notes

(a)   *TA 1988, s 65(1)* (original enactment).

(b)   *TA 1988, s 65(1)* (original enactment).

(c)   *TA 1988, s 65(1)* (original enactment).

(d)   *TA 1988, s 67(1)(b)* (original enactment).

The assessment for 1996/97 is adjusted to the income for that year on an actual basis of £9,000 under *TA 1988, s 67(1)(b)* (original enactment) because the new rules are disapplied by *FA 1994, 20 Sch 7*.

Schedule D, Case VI

Fiscal year basis

3.26   Case VI is the sweep up charge which relates to tax in respect of any annual profits or gains not falling under any other case of Schedule D and not charged by virtue of Schedules A, C or E. *TA 1988, s 69; FA 1994, s 208* provides that income under Schedule D, Case VI shall be computed on the full amount of the profits or gains arising in the fiscal year. Previously there was an option for an averaging method that was little used in practice. There are no transitional provisions as Schedule D, Case VI income has always been assessed on a current year basis in theory.

3.27   In practice, certain income assessable under Schedule D, Case VI, in particular from furnished lettings, has been computed on a non-statutory preceding year basis on the income arising in the preceding fiscal year. In such cases the Revenue have confirmed that they will apply non-statutory transitional relief and assess 1996/97 on the appropriate proportion of the income arising in 1996/97 and 1995/96 which would have been assessed in 1996/97, had the *de facto* preceding year basis continued, generally following the Schedule D, Cases I and II provisions.

Example 12

Mr Fedorov produced accounts for his income from furnished lettings on a calendar year basis and by agreement with the Revenue was assessed on a preceding year basis.

Profits (as adjusted for tax purposes)

y/e 31.12.94	£40,000
y/e 31.12.95	£45,000
y/e 31.12.96	£50,000
period 1.1.97 to 5.4.97	£13,000
y/e 5.4.98	£53,000

Assessable/taxable

1995/96	preceding year basis	£40,000	(*a*)
1996/97	transitional year	£47,782	(*b*)
1997/98	fiscal year	£53,000	

Notes

(*a*) *TA 1988, s 69* (original enactment) non-statutory agreed basis.

(*b*) Extra statutory transitional relief.

1996/97 primary basis period	
y/e 5.4.97	
1.1.97 to 5.4.97	£13,000
y/e 31.12.96	
50,000 × 9/12	£37,500
	£50,500
Relevant period 1.1.95 to 5.4.96	
y/e 31.12.95	£45,000
y/e 31.12.96	
£50,000 × 3/12	£12,500
	£57,500
aggregate	£108,000

$$\text{appropriate percentage } \frac{365}{365 + 460} = \qquad £47,782$$

Partnerships

3.28 Partnership investment income is not chargeable on a fiscal year basis but by reference to the basis period for Schedule D, Cases I or II under *TA 1988, s 111(4)(b); FA 1994, s 215*. The transitional provisions for such income will be included in the *Finance Act 1995*.

Transitional anti-avoidance

3.29   The Revenue have recognised that by assessing the income for 1996/97 on one-half of the total income for 1995/96 and 1996/97 a considerable incentive is given to taxpayers to accelerate income into the transitional period, only half of which will be taxed. The *Finance Act 1995* will contain provisions to counter such avoidance, details of which are contained in Chapter 16.

Chapter 4

Loss Relief

Introduction

4.1   Under the existing provisions of *TA 1988, s 380* losses arising in a fiscal year, or by Revenue practice, losses in respect of an accounting year ending in a fiscal year, can be set against the total income of that year. This will include the profits of the preceding year assessed in that year under the normal preceding year basis. Alternatively, losses can be carried forward against the total income of the following year. The provisions are recast to reflect the current year basis while preserving the intention behind the existing legislation.

Set-off

4.2   As profits are assessed on the basis of the accounting year ending in the fiscal year, a loss may be set against the total income of the preceding fiscal year, thus preserving the one-year carry back, or set against total income for the year in which the losses arise.[*TA 1988, s 380(1); FA 1994, s 209(1)*]. The loss is computed in the same way as a profit by reference to the accounting year ending in the fiscal year, not by apportioning the loss over the fiscal year, as under the previous statutory provisions. [*TA 1988, s 382(3); FA 1994, s 209(3)*]. Relief cannot be given for the same loss twice and it is not possible to claim part of the loss except to the extent that it exceeds available income.

4.3   A claim must be made within one year of the filing date of 31 January following the end of the year of assessment in which the loss arises. The taxpayer may determine whether he prefers to set the loss against the income of the year of the loss before carrying back any balance to the preceding year, or claim relief so far as possible against the income of the preceding year and any balance in the year of the loss. Relief given for a loss arising in the current year takes precedence over a loss arising in a succeeding period carried back. [*TA 1988, s 380(2); FA 1994, s 209(1)*]. The loss is claimed against the current year income under *TA 1988, s 380(1)(a); FA 1994, s 209(1)* and against the preceding year under *TA 1988, s 380(1)(b); FA 1994, s 209(1)*.

Example 1 (continuing)

Mr Kamov started business on 1 August 1998 and produced accounts to 31 December 1998 and annually thereafter. He made a loss in the year ended 31 December 2000 which could be claimed against any other income in 2000/01 and/or carried back and set against total income for 1999/2000.

Loss in early years of trade

4.4 *TA 1988, s 381* allows relief for losses in the first four fiscal years of a trade to be carried back against total income of the three preceding years, using the earliest available income first. There is a minor amendment to these provisions to make it clear that the loss relief is available against the whole of the claimant's income up to the amount of the loss. Apparently, it was considered that the existing wording might not cover the situation where the loss exceeded the claimant's income, although this was not a point which the Revenue have taken or would take in practice. [*FA 1994, s 209(2)*].

Example 2 (continuing)

Mr Yuriev started business on 1 August 1998 and made up accounts to 31 July 1999 and annually thereafter. The first year's accounts showed a loss. The loss for 1998/99 (proportion to 5 April 1999 as first year) can be set against total income for 1998/99 and/or 1997/98 under *TA 1988, s 380; FA 1994, s 209(1)* and the balance of the loss which falls in 1999/2000 (6 April 1999 to 31 July 1999) can be set against total income for 1999/2000 and/or 1998/99.

However as the loss arises in the first four years of trading it may, under *TA 1988, s 381; FA 1994, s 209(2)*, be carried back. The loss for 1998/99 can be set against total income for 1995/96 (carried back three years) with any excess against total income for 1996/97, and any further excess against total income for 1997/98. Any remaining balance can be set against 1998/99 under *TA 1988, s 380(1)(a); FA 1994, s 209(1)*.

The loss for 1999/2000 can similarly be set against any remaining total income for 1996/97, then 1997/98, then 1998/99 under amended *TA 1988, s 381; FA 1994, s 209(2)* with any balance claimed in 1999/2000 under *TA 1988, s 380(1)(a); FA 1994, s 209(1)*.

No double counting of losses

4.5   Where a loss would be included in the computation of two successive years of assessment, for example, under the opening provisions or on a change of accounting date, the loss is only given in the first year in which it is available and is treated as zero in the second year. [*TA 1988, s 382(4); FA 1994, s 209(3)*].

Example 3 (continuing)

Mr Zhukovsky had produced accounts for the year to 5 April up to and including the year 2000/01 which produced a loss. He then produced accounts for a short period to 30 June 2001 and annually thereafter. The assessment for 2001/02 would be the twelve months ending on the new accounting date 30 June 2001, which includes nine months of the loss for the year ended 5 April 2001. As the loss has been included in 2000/01 however it is treated as nil in 2001/02 to prevent double counting.

Loss carry forward

4.6   The loss carry forward provisions of *TA 1988, s 385* are largely recast to take account of the fact that losses are calculated on the same basis as profits and therefore under the current year basis include capital allowances as a trading expense. *TA 1988, s 385(1); FA 1994, s 209(4)* provides that where a loss has been sustained in a trade, profession or vocation carried on alone or in partnership and relief has not otherwise been given, a claim may be made for the unrelieved loss to be carried forward and set off against the income of the trade, profession or vocation for subsequent years of assessment. Losses must be set against the first available profit and reduce the taxable income by the amount of the loss brought forward. It is no longer necessary to claim for the unrelieved loss for each profitable year, as under the old rules. A single claim will suffice if made within six years of the end of the year of assessment in which the loss arises, or five years from the filing date under *FA 1994, 19 Sch 14* from 1996/97. [*FA 1994, s 209(4)(5)*].

Example 1 (continuing)

Mr Kamov, making up his accounts to 31 December each year, suffered a loss in the calendar year 2000. A loss remained unrelieved after setting the loss against total income in 2000/01 and carrying back so far as possible. The balance of the loss unrelieved can be carried forward under *TA 1988, s 385; FA 1994, s 209(4)(5)* and set-off against future profits of the same trade, profession or vocation.

4.7 *Loss Relief*

Terminal losses

4.7   A minor alteration is made to the terminal loss provisions to enable terminal loss relief to be available for the final year of assessment as well as for the three preceding fiscal years. [*FA 1994, s 209(6)*].

Example 4

Mr Gurshin made up his accounts to 30 November each year until 31 August 2003 when the business ceased. He had no other income until 1 January 2004 when he took a job which produced earnings of £10,000 in 2003/04. The results (as adjusted for tax purposes) were as follows:

y/e 30.11.1999	£85,000
y/e 30.11.2000	£65,000
y/e 30.11.2001	£50,000
y/e 30.11.2002 loss	(£20,000)
1.12.2002 to 31.8.2003 loss	(£110,000)

Assessable/taxable before loss relief

1999/2000	current year	£85,000
2000/01	current year	£65,000
2001/02	current year	£50,000
2002/03	current year	£Nil
2003/04	current year	£Nil

Loss relief available

2001/02 current year	£50,000
Less loss carried back under	
TA 1988, s 380(1)(b); FA 1994, s 209(1)	£20,000
Amended assessment	£30,000

Terminal loss

2003/04 loss in last twelve months of trading	
1.12.2002 to 31.8.2003	£110,000
1.9.2002 to 30.11.2002	
	£Nil

(already relieved under *TA 1988, s 380(1)(b);* *FA 1994, s 209(1)*)	
Total terminal loss	£110,000
Set-off against income in 2003/04	£10,000
Loss carried back	£100,000
Set-off against income in 2002/03	£Nil
Loss carried back	£100,000

Set-off against income in 2001/02	£30,000
Loss carried back	£70,000
Set-off against income in 2000/01	£65,000
Loss unrelieved	£5,000

Commencement date for new rules

4.8   The new rules for loss relief apply from 1997/98 and subsequent years of assessment for businesses which commenced prior to 6 April 1994 so that the averaging provisions of the transitional year 1996/97 do not restrict the relief available. [*FA 1994, s 209(7)*].

Example 5 (continuing)

Mr Groppius made up his accounts to 30 September each year. He had no other income. He incurred a loss in the year ended 30 September 1996, the 'primary' basis period for the transitional year 1996/97. The transitional year assessment is calculated by treating the profits and gains for the year ended 30 September 1996 as nil, as there are no such profits or gains. The transitional year is therefore half the income for the year ended 30 September 1995. The loss relief is then given under the existing loss relief provisions of *TA 1988, s 380* for the loss falling in 1995/96 and 1996/97, the loss for the year ended 30 September 1996 being apportioned over those two years on the strict old rule basis.

Example 1

Set-off and carry forward

Mr Kamov started business on 1 August 1998 and produced accounts to 31 December 1998, i.e. for a period of less than twelve months ending in the fiscal year of commencement, and annually thereafter. He also had investment income of £2,000 a year.

Profits and losses (as adjusted for tax purposes)

1.8.98 to 31.12.98	£5,000
y/e 31.12.99	£16,500
y/e 31.12.2000 (loss)	£(22,500)
y/e 31.12.2001	£28,500

Taxable – subject to loss relief
1998/99 1.8.98 to 5.4.99
   £5,000 + (3/12 × £16,500)   £9,125   (*a*)

73

1999/00 y/e 31.12.99	£16,500	(*b*)
2000/01 y/e 31.12.00	Nil	(*c*)
2001/02 y/e 31.12.01	£28,500	(*d*)

Notes

(*a*)   *TA 1988, s 61(1); FA 1994, s 201* commencement to 5 April.

(*b*)   *TA 1988, s 61(2); FA 1994, s 201* does not apply, although the second year of assessment, as the period from commencement 1.8.98 to the accounting date given by *TA 1988, s 60(5); FA 1994, s 200*, 31.12.99, is not less than twelve months. Therefore, this is the first year of assessment in which there is an accounting date which falls not less than twelve months after the commencement date and the basis period is fixed by *TA 1988, s 60(3)(a); FA 1994, s 200*.

(*c*)   *TA 1988, s 60(3)(b); FA 1994, s 200*.

(*d*)   *TA 1988, s 60(3)(b); FA 1994, s 200*.

The period from 1.1.99 to 5.4.99 is taxed both for 1998/99 and 1999/00 and is therefore an overlap period relieved under *TA 1988, s 63A; FA 1994, s 205* resulting in overlap profits of £4,125 (3/12 × £16,500).

Loss relief available
The loss for the year ended 31 December 2000 is £22,500. This may be relieved as follows (ignoring relief under *TA 1988, s 381; FA 1994, s 209(2)*):

Against investment income in 2000/01 [*TA 1988, s 380(1)(a); FA 1994, s 209(1)*]	£2,000
Against trading profits and investment income in 1999/00	£2,000
[*TA 1988, s 380(1)(b); FA 1994, s 209(1)*]	£16,500
Against trading profits for the year ended 31 December 2001 (balance) [*TA 1988, s 385; FA 1994, s 209(4)(5)*]	£2,000
	£22,500

However, as the investment income in 2000/01 is covered by personal allowances, it is probably better not to claim relief against total income in that year (i.e. not to claim under *TA 1988, s 380(1)(a); FA 1994, s 209(1)*) which would increase the loss carried forward against the profits for the year ended 31 December 2001 to £4,000.

Example 2

Set-off, carry forward and early year losses

Mr Yuriev started business on 1 August 1998 and produced accounts to 31 July 1999, i.e. for a period of twelve months, and annually thereafter. He also had investment income of £3,000 a year and a salary of £6,000 p.a. up to 31.3.1998.

Profits and losses (as adjusted for tax purposes)

y/e 31.7.1999 (loss)	£(14,000)
y/e 31.7.2000	£20,000
y/e 31.7.2001	£26,000

Taxable – subject to loss relief

1998/99 (1.8.98 to 5.4.99 8/12 × (£14,000))	Nil	(*a*)
1999/00 y/e 31.7.1999	Nil	(*b*)
2000/01 y/e 31.7.2000	£20,000	(*c*)
2001/02 y/e 31.7.2001	£26,000	(*d*)

Notes

(*a*)   *TA 1988, s 61(1); FA 1994, s 201*, commencement to 5 April.

(*b*)   *TA 1988, s 61(2); FA 1994, s 201* inapplicable as period from commencement 1.8.98 to accounting date 31.7.99 is not less than twelve months *TA 1988, s 61(2)(a); FA 1994, s 201*. Therefore, the basis period for the first year of assessment in which there is an accounting period under *TA 1988, s 60(3)(a); FA 1994, s 200* is the year ended 31.7.99.

(*c*)   *TA 1988, s 60(3)(b); FA 1994, s 200*.

(*d*)   *TA 1988, s 60(3)(b); FA 1994, s 200*.

The period from commencement on 1.8.98 to 5.4.99 is taxed both for 1998/99 and 1999/00 and is therefore an overlap period relieved under *TA 1988, s 63A; FA 1994, s 205* but no overlap profits.

Loss relief available
The loss of £14,000 for the year ended 31 July 1999 may be relieved as follows (ignoring relief under *TA 1988, s 381; FA 1994, s 209(2)*):

Against investment income in 1997/98 on the basis of the loss in 1998/99 of £9,333 (8/12 × £14,000 for 1.8.98 to 5.4.99) limited to total income [*TA 1988, s 380(1)(b); FA 1994, s 209(1)*]	£9,000
Against investment income in 1998/99 on loss as above unrelieved (£9,333 − £9,000) limited to total income of £3,000 [*TA 1988, s 380(1)(a); FA 1994, s 209(1)*]	£333

Against the same income in respect
of the loss for the year ended
31 July 1999 [*TA 1988, s 380(1); FA 1994,
s 209(1)*] £4,667
limited to total income (£3,000–£333)   £2,667

Against future profits from the same
trade under *TA 1988, s 385; FA 1994,
s 209(4)(5)* £14,000 less
relieved £12,000 leaving   £2,000
to be claimed against profits for
the year ended 31 July 2000

                                                         £14,000

Example 2 as above, but giving loss relief under *TA 1988, s 381; FA 1994, s 209(2).*

Loss for 1998/99	£9,333	
Loss for 1999/00	4,667	
Total losses available for relief	£14,000	

Loss relief		£
1995/96	Earned income	6,000
	Investment income	3,000
		9,000
	Loss arising 1998/99 £9,333 (limited to total income)	(9,000)
	(balance £333 c/f to 1996/97)	
	Chargeable to tax	Nil
1996/97	Earned income	6,000
	Investment income	3,000
		9,000
	Balance of loss arising 1998/99 (£9,333 − £9,000)	(333)
	Loss arising 1999/00	(4,667)
	Chargeable to tax	£4,000

Example 3

Losses on change of accounting date

Mr Zhukovsky started business on 1 August 1998 and produced accounts to 5 April each year until 2001 when the accounting date was brought forward to 30 June and annually thereafter. The requirements of *TA 1988, s 62A; FA 1994, s 203* were met. He had no other income.

Profits and losses (as adjusted for tax purposes)

1.8.98 to 5.4.99	£8,000
y/e 5.4.2000	£20,000
y/e 5.4.2001 (loss)	£(24,000)
p/e 30.6.2001	£7,500
y/e 30.6.2002	£30,000

Taxable – subject to loss relief

1998/99	1.8.98 to 5.4.99	£8,000	(a)
1999/00	y/e 5.4.2000	£20,000	(b)
2000/01	y/e 5.4.2001	£Nil	(c)
2001/02	y/e 30.6.2001		
	9/12 × (£24,000) + £7,500	£7,500	(d)
2002/03	y/e 30.6.2002	£30,000	

Notes

(a)   *TA 1988, s 61(1); FA 1994, s 201.*

(b)   *TA 1988, s 60(3)(a); FA 1994, s 200.*

(c)   *TA 1988, s 60(3)(b); FA 1994, s 200.*

(d)   *TA 1988, s 62(5); FA 1994, s 202* makes this the year in which the accounting date is deemed to change as accounts are made up to a new date in the fiscal year. The period is less than twelve months from the end of the previous accounting date (5.4.2001), therefore *TA 1988, s 62(2)(a); FA 1994, s 202* determines the basis as twelve months ending with the new accounting date. The loss is counted as nil in the apportionment as it has already been taken into 2000/01, and *TA 1988, s 382(4); FA 1994, s 209(3)* excludes it from being included twice. The period 1.7.2000 to 5.4.2001 is taxed in both 2000/01 and 2001/02 and therefore there is an overlap period under *TA 1988, s 63A; FA 1994, s 205*, but no overlap profits in view of the overall loss for the period.

Loss relief available
The loss for the year ended 5 April 2001 is £24,000. This may be relieved as follows (ignoring relief under *TA 1988, s 381; FA 1994, s 209(2)*):

Against profits for the year ended 5 April 2000 [*TA 1988, s 380(1)(b); FA 1994, s 209(1)*]	£20,000
There is no other income in 2000/01 so no relief under *TA 1988, s 380(1)(a); FA 1994, s 209(1)*.	

The relief to carry forward of
(£24,000 − £20,000) £4,000 is used
against the profits for the year
ending 30 June 2001 of £7,500   £4,000
reducing them to £3,500 under
TA 1988, s 385; FA 1994, s 209(4)(5)

                                                    £24,000

Example 4

Loss in 1996/97

Mr Groppius made up his accounts to 30 September each year. He had no other income. The results, as adjusted for tax purposes, were as follows:

y/e 30.9.94	£6,000
y/e 30.9.95	£25,000
y/e 30.9.96 (loss)	(£35,000)
y/e 30.9.97	£8,000
y/e 30.9.98	£28,000

Assessable/taxable – before loss relief

1995/96	preceding year basis	£6,000	
1996/97	transitional year	£12,500	*(a)*
1997/98	current year basis	£8,000	
1998/99	current year basis	£28,000	

Notes

(a) Primary basis period 1996/97
     y/e 30.9.96 [*FA 1994, 20 Sch
     1(2)(a) and 2(2)(a)*]   Nil

Relevant period [*FA 1994, 20 Sch 2(5)*]
     y/e 30.9.95   £25,000

Aggregate   £25,000

Appropriate percentage *FA 1994, 20
Sch 2(2)*

$£25,000 \times \dfrac{365}{365 + 365} =$ £12,500

Loss relief available
  Loss in year ended 30.9.96 £35,000, apportioned to 1996/97
  6/12 = £17,500, 1995/96 6/12 = £17,500

1995/96 assessable income	£6,000
loss relief under *TA 1988, s 380(1)*	
(original enactment)	£6,000
Assessment	Nil
Loss relief carried forward	
1995/96 loss £17,500 − £6,000 =	£11,500
1996/97 assessable income	£12,500
Loss relief under *TA 1988, s 380(2)*	
(original enactment)	£11,500
	£1,000
Loss relief under *TA 1988, s 380(1)*	
(original enactment)	£1,000
Assessment	Nil
Loss relief carried forward	
1996/97 loss £17,500 − £1,000	£16,500
1997/98 assessable income	£8,000
Less loss relief brought forward under	
TA 1988, s 385; FA 1994, s 209(4)(5)	£8,000
Assessment	Nil
Loss relief carried forward	
£16,500 − £8,000	£8,500
1998/99 assessable income	£28,000
Less loss relief brought forward under	
TA 1988, s 385; FA 1994, s 209(4)(5)	£8,500
Assessment	£19,500

Example 5

Loss 1997/98

Mr Isacco made up his accounts to 30 April each year. He had no other income.

The results, as adjusted for tax purposes, were as follows:

y/e 30.4.94	£18,000
y/e 30.4.95	£20,000
y/e 30.4.96	£15,000
y/e 30.4.97 loss	(£30,000)
y/e 30.4.98	£22,000

4.9   *Loss Relief*

Assessable/taxable – before loss relief

1995/96 preceding year basis	£18,000	
1996/97 transitional year	£17,500	(a)
1997/98 current year basis	Nil	
1998/99 current year basis	£22,000	

Notes

(a) primary basis period 1996/97

y/e 30.4.96 [*FA 1994, 20 Sch 1(2)(a) and 2(2)(a)*]	£15,000
Relevant period [*FA 1994, 20 Sch 2(5)*]	£20,000
Aggregate	£35,000

Appropriate percentage *FA 1994, 20 Sch 2(2)*

$$£35,000 \times \frac{365}{365 + 365} = \qquad £17,500$$

Loss relief available

1996/97 assessable income	£17,500
loss carried back under *TA 1988, s 380(1)(b); FA 1994, s 209(1)*	£17,500
Assessment	Nil

Loss carried forward £30,000 less relieved £17,500 = £12,500.

1997/98 assessable income therefore no loss relief available	Nil
1998/99 assessable income	£22,000
Less loss relief brought forward under *TA 1988, s 385; FA 1994, s 209(4)(5)*	£12,500
Assessment	£9,500

Transitional rules

4.9   There are no particular transitional provisions relating to losses except that *FA 1994, 20 Sch 8* confirms that the time limit for lodging claims for loss relief for losses sustained in 1994/95 and 1995/96 remains two years from the end of the year of assessment and not one year from the filing date of 31 January following the end of the year of assessment, which applies from 1996/97 onwards.

Relief for losses on unquoted shares

4.10   *TA 1988, s 574* is re-enacted by *FA 1994, s 210* to mirror the changes introduced in *TA 1988, s 380* by *FA 1994, s 209(1)*. The loss as computed for capital gains tax purposes on the shares in an unquoted trading company subscribed for may be set against the total income for the year in which the loss arises under *TA 1988, s 574(1)(a); FA 1994, s 210*, or against the total income of the preceding year under *TA 1988, s 574(1)(b); FA 1994, s 210*. The claim must be made within twelve months from 31 January following the fiscal year in which the loss arises. It is not possible to claim relief twice for the same loss, or to claim a capital gains tax loss relief in respect of the loss claimed for income tax purposes.

4.11   A loss claimed against income for the current year is given in priority to relief brought back from the following year under the carry back provisions. [*TA 1988, s 574(2); FA 1994, s 210*]. Relief is given in priority to relief for trading losses under *TA 1988, s 380* or *381*. This would normally be in the taxpayer's favour as such trading losses could be carried forward under *TA 1988, s 385* if the income was insufficient to absorb all the losses available for relief.

Example 6

Mr Kolpakov sustained a capital loss on the disposal of shares subscribed for in Komta Ltd of £23,000 on 1 May 1999. His total income for 1999/2000 was £18,000 and for 1998/99, £20,000. He claimed relief as follows:

Against 1998/99 under *TA 1988, s 574(1)(b); FA 1994, s 210*, £20,000 reducing his taxable income for that year to nil.

Against 1999/2000 the balance of the loss under *TA 1988, s 574(1)(a); FA 1994, s 210* (£23,000 − £20,000) £3,000 reducing his taxable income from £18,000 to £15,000.

Chapter 5

Capital Allowances

Introduction

5.1 The Simplified Assessing rules do not change the assets eligible for capital allowances, nor do they make any fundamental change in the way the allowances are calculated. They do however make a fundamental change to the way in which the allowances are actually given and the chargeable period for which they are given.

Commencement date for new rules

5.2 The new arrangements apply to new businesses commencing on or after 6 April 1994, but not until 1997/98 for businesses already in existence at that date, i.e. after the transitional year 1996/97 to ensure that there is no loss of relief. [*FA 1994, s 211(2)*].

Trading expense

5.3 Under the new arrangements capital allowances are treated as a trading expense instead of an allowance for which a separate claim is necessary. This applies to capital allowances on industrial buildings and structures, machinery and plant, dwelling houses let on assured tenancies, mineral extraction assets, agricultural buildings and works, and dredging. [*CAA 1990, s 140(1); FA 1994, s 211*]. Allowances given by way of discharge or repayment of tax which are available primarily against a specified class of income are deductible by reference to a period of account and not for the fiscal year.

5.4 Writing-down allowances, initial allowances and balancing charges are given by treating the allowances as a trading expense in the period of account, or in the case of a balancing charge as a trading receipt in that period, under *CAA 1990, s 140(2); FA 1994, s 211*. This brings the basis for unincorporated businesses onto a similar treatment to that of companies under *CAA 1990, s 144*. The claim for capital allowances is made in the tax return and not as a separate claim under *TMA 1970, s 42* which is repealed for such claims which relate to a trade under *CAA 1990, s 140(3); FA 1994, s 211*.

5.5 Scientific research allowances have always been allowed as a deduction in computing the profits of a trade, and continue to be treated as trading expenses in the same way as other capital allowances, under *CAA 1990, s 140(5); FA 1994, s 211*.

5.6 The revised arrangements for capital allowances apply to professions, vocations, employments and offices as they apply to trades [*CAA 1990, s 140(4); FA 1994, s 211*] and a toll road undertaking is deemed to be a trade for industrial buildings allowance purposes. [*CAA 1990, s 140(6); FA 1994, s 211*].

Example 1

Mr Kazlov made up accounts to 30 June annually. In the year ended 30 June 1999 he incurred expenditure on plant and machinery of £40,000. His capital allowances pool brought forward was £100,000 and he had disposals of £4,000. His profits before capital allowances, but otherwise as adjusted for tax purposes were £52,000.

Capital allowances for y/e 30.6.99

Written down value brought forward	£100,000
Less disposals	£4,000
	£96,000
Additions	£40,000
	£136,000
Writing-down allowance at 25% p.a.	£34,000
Written down value carried forward	£102,000
Profits for accounting period	£52,000
Less capital allowances	£34,000
Taxable profit	£18,000

The adjusted profit of £18,000 for the y/e 30 June 1999 is assessed for 1999/2000 on the current year basis.

Chargeable period

5.7 The basis period rules for capital allowances are abolished under the Simplified Assessing rules and replaced by a revised definition of chargeable period in *CAA 1990, s 161(2); FA 1994, s 212(2)*. The chargeable period is, in the case of an unincorporated business, the period of account which is the period for which accounts are made up [*CAA 1990, s 60(1)(2); FA 1994, s 212(1)*], subject to gaps and overlaps dealt with in 5.8 to 5.10 below. The chargeable period for capital allowances purposes may fall into one or more basis periods for income tax purposes but it is the profit after capital allowances which is doubly charged, giving rise to overlap relief in due course.

Example 2

In the previous example, had Mr Kazlov started business on 1 July 1998 and incurred expenditure on plant of £140,000, less disposals of £4,000 the computation would have been:

Plant additions	£140,000
Less disposals	£4,000
	£136,000
Writing-down allowance at 25% p.a.	£34,000
Written down value carried forward	£102,000
Profit for accounting period	£52,000
Less capital allowances	£34,000
Adjusted profit	£18,000

Assessable/taxable
1998/99 1.7.98 to 5.4.99
9/12 × £18,000 = £13,500

Commencement to next 5 April
TA 1988, s 61(1); FA 1994, s 201

1999/2000 y/e 30.6.99 = £18,000

Twelve months to accounting date,
TA 1988, s 60(3)(a); FA 1994, s 200

Overlap

5.8 Where there is an overlap of two periods of account the period common to both is deemed to fall in the first period of account only, which means that assets qualifying for capital allowances would be treated as being acquired in the first period of account and not the second. An overlapping of two periods includes the coincidence of the two periods and the inclusion of one period in another. [*CAA 1990, s 160(6); FA 1994, s 212(1)*].

5.9 It would be most unusual for two periods of account to overlap but it could happen; for example, where a partner retired or died, and accounts were made up to the date of his leaving in order to arrive at the amount due to him on dissolution. The remaining partners might continue to prepare an annual set of accounts to the normal accounting date, which would mean that the period to the date the partner left would appear in two sets of accounts. [*CAA 1990, s 160(3)(a); FA 1994, s 212(1)*].

5.10   It should be noted that these rules only apply where the same period appears in two sets of accounts, not where there is an overlap in basis periods, i.e. where the same profits after capital allowances are charged to tax more than once on the transition to Simplified Assessing on a commencement, or on a change of accounting date under the new rules, and which would be relieved by way of overlap relief on a cessation or change of accounting date under the provisions of substituted *TA 1988, ss 60–63A.*

Example 3

Pashinin and Porokhovshchikov were in partnership, making up accounts to 31 December annually until 1999 when Porokhovshchikov died on 30 June. Accounts were prepared to the date of death and for the year ended 31 December 1999.

The capital allowances pool at 1.1.1999 was £120,000 and there were acquisitions of plant and machinery of £9,000 and £12,000 in each half year and disposals of £1,000 and £2,000 respectively.

The capital allowances are:
1.1.99 to 30.6.99

Written down value brought forward at 1.1.99	£120,000
Additions 1.1.99 to 30.6.99	£9,000
	£129,000
Disposals 1.1.99 to 30.6.99	£1,000
	£128,000
Writing-down allowance £128,000 × 25% × 6/12 =	£16,000
Written down value at 30.6.99	£112,000
Additions 1.7.99 to 31.12.99	£12,000
	£124,000
Disposals 1.7.99 to 31.12.99	£2,000
	£122,000
Writing-down allowance £122,000 × 25% × 6/12 =	£15,250
Written down value at 31.12.99	£106,750

Gap

5.11   The converse of the same period falling in two sets of accounts is a gap between two sets of accounts, which would again be a most unusual situation. It is however catered for in substituted *CAA 1990, s 160(3)(b)* by providing that any interval between sets of accounts is deemed to be part of the first period of account. Therefore any acquisitions or disposals in the interval are related to the earlier period. This rule would appear to apply where there was a suspension of trading, for example, on a farmer selling one farm and after a short period acquiring a new farm. It is likely that the Revenue would agree that the farming trade continued throughout [*TA 1988, s 53*], but accounts would probably be prepared to the date of sale of the first farm and from the acquisition of the second farm.

Capital allowances – basis periods

5.12   Under the previously applying basis period rules in the original *CAA 1990, s 160* the basis period for capital allowances was the same as the basis period for income tax, except in the opening and closing years of assessment where special rules applied. Where two basis periods overlapped the period common to both fell in the first basis period only. If there was a gap between basis periods for example, on a change of accounting date, the interval fell into the second basis period except where that period was one in which the trade was permanently discontinued, in which case the interval was added to the first basis period. A full year's writing-down allowance was given in each basis period except for the opening period and period of cessation, in which case a proportionate part of the writing-down allowances was given.

Example 4

Mr Laville commenced business on 29 December 1988 and ceased 17 August 1996. Accounts were made up to 30 April each year.

	Income tax basis period		Capital allowances basis period	
1988–89	29.12.88	– 5.4.89	29.12.88	– 5.4.89
1989–90	29.12.88	– 28.12.89	6.4.89	– 28.12.89
1990–91	29.12.88	– 28.12.89*	no basis period	
1991–92	1.5.89	– 30.4.90	29.12.89	– 30.4.90
1992–93	1.5.90	– 30.4.91	1.5.90	– 30.4.91
1993–94	1.5.91	– 30.4.92	1.5.91	– 30.4.92
1994–95	1.5.92	– 30.4.93	1.5.92	– 30.4.93
1995–96	1.5.93	– 30.4.94	1.5.93	– 5.4.96
1996–97	6.4.96	– 17.8.96	6.4.96	– 17.8.96

* Probable Revenue selection, although the Revenue have power under *TA 1988, s 60* to choose any twelve-month period ending in 1990/91.

Had an election been made for the actual basis of assessment for the two years following commencement under *TA 1988, s 62* and also the Revenue applied the actual basis on discontinuance under *TA 1988, s 63*, the capital allowances basis period would have been as follows:

Income tax basis period			Capital allowance basis period		
1988–89	29.12.88	– 5.4.89	29.12.88	– 5.4.89	
1989–90	6.4.89	– 5.4.90	6.4.89	– 5.4.90	
1990–91	6.4.90	– 5.4.91	6.4.90	– 5.4.91	
1991–92	1.5.89	– 30.4.90	no basis period		
1992–93	1.5.90	– 30.4.91	6.4.91	– 30.4.91	
1993–94	1.5.91	– 30.4.92	1.5.91	– 30.4.92	
1994–95	6.4.94	– 5.4.95	1.5.92	– 5.4.95	
1995–96	6.4.95	– 5.4.96	6.4.95	– 5.4.96	
1996–97	6.4.96	– 17.8.96	6.4.96	– 17.8.96	

In both cases a full year's writing-down allowance would be made for all years other than 1988–89 and 1996–97 which would be time apportioned. Balancing allowances and charges would fall into the appropriate basis periods in which disposals took place.

If Mr Laville commenced a new and separate trade on 29 December 1996 making up accounts to 30 April each year, the capital allowances by reference to each accounting period would be given in the computation adjusting the profits for that period as if they were trading expenses, and then the resultant net profit, as adjusted for tax purposes, would be allocated to the income tax basis period. These would be:

1996/97   29.12.1996 to 5.4.1997 [*TA 1988, s 61(1); FA 1994, s 201*]
1997/98   29.12.1996 to 28.12.1997 [*TA 1988, s 61(2)(a); FA 1994, s 201*]
1998/99   1.5.1997 to 30.4.1998 [*TA 1988, s 60(3)(a); FA 1994, s 200*]
1999/2000 1.5.1998 to 30.4.1999 [*TA 1988, s 60(3)(b); FA 1994, s 200*]

Amount of allowances

5.13   Under the old rules a full year's writing-down allowances were given for each fiscal year, irrespective of the length of the capital allowance basis period, other than in the years of commencement or cessation. However, under the Simplified Assessing rules if the period of account in which the expenditure is incurred is for less than or more than twelve months, as it could be, not only on commencement or cessation, but also on a change of accounting date to a period earlier or later in the fiscal year, the writing-down allowance is adjusted pro rata in accordance with the length of the accounting period. [*FA 1994, s 213(3)–(10)*]. For example, if the rate of writing-down allowance is 25 per cent per annum and the accounting period is for 15 months, the effective rate of writing-down allowances becomes 31.25 per cent (25 × 15/12). Conversely if the accounting period is nine months the writing-down allowance becomes 18.75 per cent (25 × 9/12). However, no period of account may exceed

18 months and an accounting period of greater length is divided into twelve-month (or less) periods of account. [*CAA 1990, s 160(4); FA 1994, s 212(1)*].

Example 5

Mr Bedunkovich made up accounts each year to 31 December until 1999 when he produced a short set of accounts to 30 June which was a valid change of accounting date for tax purposes and annually thereafter. In the six months to 30 June 1999 he incurred expenditure on plant and machinery of £25,000. His capital allowances pool brought forward was £80,000 and disposals in the period realised £5,000.

Capital allowances for six-month period ending 30.6.99:

Pool value brought forward	£80,000
Less disposals	£5,000
	£75,000
Additions in period 1.1.99 to 30.6.99	£25,000
	£100,000
Writing-down allowances at 25% p.a. for six months $(25 \times \dfrac{6}{12})$	£12,500
Written down value carried forward at 30 June 1999	£87,500
Adjusted pre-capital allowances profits were:	
y/e 31.12.98	£60,000
1.1.99 to 30.6.99	£27,500
Capital allowances for y/e 31.12.98 were £20,000	

Assessable/taxable	
1998/99 y/e 31.12.98	£40,000
(£60,000 less capital allowances £20,000)	
1999/2000 year to new accounting date	
1.1.99 to 30.6.99	£15,000
(£27,500 less capital allowances £12,500)	
1.7.98 to 31.12.98	
(£40,000 × 6/12)	£20,000
Assessment	£35,000

Example 6

Mr Lisichkin made up accounts each year to 30 June until 1999 when he produced a long set of accounts to 31 December, which was a valid change of accounting date for tax purposes, and annually thereafter. In the 18 months to 31 December 1999 he incurred expenditure on plant and machinery of £50,000. His capital allowances pool was £110,000 and disposals in the period realised £8,000.

Capital allowances for 18-month period ending 31.12.99:

Pool value brought forward	£110,000
Less disposals	£8,000
	£102,000
Additions in period 1.7.98 to 31.12.99	£50,000
	£152,000

Writing-down allowances at 25% p.a. for

$$18 \text{ months } (25 \times \frac{18}{12}) \qquad\qquad £57,000$$

Written down value carried forward at 31 December 1999	£95,000
Adjusted pre-capital allowances profits were:	
y/e 30.6.98	£80,000
1.7.98 to 31.12.99	£95,000

Capital allowances for y/e 30.6.98 were £30,000

Assessable/taxable	
1998/99 y/e 30.6.98	£50,000
(£80,000 less capital allowances £30,000)	
1999/2000 period 1.7.98 to 31.12.99	
(£95,000 less capital allowances £57,000)	£38,000

Subject to overlap relief under *TA 1988, s 63A; FA 1994, s 205*, ignored in this example.

Non-traders

5.14   Where a person is not carrying on a trade, profession or vocation but is still entitled to capital allowances, for example, a landed estate where the allowances are given by way of discharge or repayment, the period of account means the year of assessment. [*CAA 1990, s 160(5); FA 1994, s 212(1)*].

Chargeable period – amendments

5.15   Legislative changes to the *Capital Allowances Act 1990* are made by *FA 1994, s 213*. This makes a number of amendments, including deleting references to basis period throughout the *Capital Allowances Act*, which leaves such references as referring to the chargeable period, i.e. the period of account as redefined by *CAA 1990, s 161(2); FA 1994, s 212(2)*.

5.16   *FA 1994, s 213(3)(a)* deletes the references to years of assessment and basis periods for industrial buildings allowance purposes in *CAA 1990, s 8* which results in such allowances being due at the end of the chargeable period as redefined. The provisions relating to long as well as short periods of account for industrial buildings allowances are brought into effect by *FA 1994, s 213(2)*, amending *CAA 1990, s 3(2)*; those for plant by *FA 1994, s 213(4)*, amending *CAA 1990, s 24(2)(a)(ii)*; those for motor cars used for the purpose of a trade costing more than £12,000, where it is necessary to provide for the maximum annual allowance of £3,000 per annum, to be adjusted pro rata for long and short periods, by *FA 1994, s 213(5)*, amending *CAA 1990, s 34(a)(b)*. The corresponding rules relating to contributions for such cars are covered in *FA 1994, s 213(6)*, amending *CAA 1990, s 35(1)(b)*.

5.17   Similar provisions relating to dwelling houses let on assured tenancies are covered in *FA 1994, s 213(7)*, amending *CAA 1990, s 85(2)*; for mineral extraction allowances by *s 213(8)*, amending *CAA 1990, s 98(6)*; for dredging by *s 213(9)* amending *CAA 1990, s 134(1)* and for scientific research allowances by *FA 1994, s 213(10)*, amending *CAA 1990, s 137(5)–(7)*. The scientific research allowance provisions are considerably simplified by this amendment, which also provides that the relevant chargeable period is to be the chargeable period in which the expenditure was incurred, or in the case of pre-trading expenditure, in the chargeable period beginning with the commencement of the trade. Finally, *FA 1994, s 213(11)* amends *CAA 1990, s 161(5)* by providing that any reference to capital allowances being made in taxing a trade is a reference to them being made in computing the trading income for corporation tax or income tax purposes.

Crown property

5.18   If an industrial building is owned by the Crown, or a person not within the charge to UK tax, the residue of expenditure is calculated as if the owner were entitled to all the normal allowances. The owner is assumed for this purpose to have a fiscal year accounting period which ended immediately before the beginning of the next following year of assessment. [*Substituted CAA 1990, s 8(13)(d)*]. This enables the residue of expenditure to be calculated as the starting point for the purchaser's industrial buildings allowances.

Losses

5.19   The extension of loss relief to include capital allowances becomes unnecessary where the allowances are treated as trading expenses and for the purpose of the loss relief restriction under *TA 1988, s 384* and the inclusion of capital allowances in terminal loss relief. The necessary alterations are made by *FA 1994, s 214(1)(b)–(e)*. The anti-avoidance provisions to prevent the exploitation of capital allowances through the leasing of assets such as narrow boats and containers are retained subject to the necessary amendments in *TA 1988, s 384(6)* introduced by *FA 1994, s 214(2)*.

Farming

5.20   Farm profit averaging in *TA 1988, s 96* used to be on the basis of the profits before capital allowances. However, by treating capital allowances as a trading expense averaging will be by reference to the profits after capital allowances. [*FA 1994, s 214(1)(a)*]. This will affect new businesses from 6 April 1994, but for existing trades the new rules do not come into effect until 1997/98, which means that farm profit averaging for the years up to and including 1995/96, with 1996/97, will be done under the old rules before capital allowances are deducted. The averaging for 1996/97 with 1997/98 and any later pair of years will be done under the new rules after deducting capital allowances. [*FA 1994, s 214(7)*].

Example 7

Mr Putilov farmed in East Anglia and produced the following results:

Year ended 30 September	Adjusted profit before capital allowances	Capital allowances		Adjusted profit after capital allowances
	£	£		£
1994	100,000	95/96	10,000	
1995	80,000 ⎤			
1996	40,000 ⎬	96/97	8,000	
1997	112,000 ⎦		12,000	100,000

Assessable/taxable
1995/96
  y/e 30.9.94 — 100,000
1996/97
primary basis period
  y/e 30.9.96 — £40,000
Relevant period
  y/e 30.9.95 — £80,000

Aggregate — £120,000

Appropriate proportion

$$\frac{365}{365 + 365}$$ £60,000

Total for two years	£160,000

1996/97 is less than 70% of 1995/96
Therefore, applying farm profit averaging
under *TA 1988, s 96*

1995/96 becomes	£80,000
Less capital allowances	£10,000
	£70,000
1996/97 becomes	£80,000
Less capital allowances	£8,000
	£72,000

1996/97, as before	£72,000
1997/98 y/e 30.9.97 (after	
capital allowances)	£100,000

1996/97 is between 70% and 75% of
1997/98, therefore applying farm
profit averaging under *TA 1988, s 96*
(marginal relief)

Difference (£100,000 − £72,000) =	£28,000
multiplied by three	£84,000
Less 3/4 of £100,000	£75,000
	£9,000

Final assessment 1996/97	
£72,000 + £9,000 =	£81,000

Assessment 1997/98	
£100,000 − £9,000 =	£91,000

which might change if averaged with 1998/99 in due course.

Patents and know-how

5.21   Patent rights qualify for capital allowances with a writing-down allowance of 25 per cent per annum. This requires amendment to cater for long periods of account of more than twelve months as well as short periods of account, and this is achieved by amending *TA 1988, s 520(4)(a)(ii)* by *FA 1994, s 214(4)*. The supplementary provisions relating to capital expenditure on patent rights in *TA 1988, s 521* will be by reference to the chargeable period, not the basis period, as a result of *FA 1994, s 214(5)*, amending *TA 1988, ss 521, 528* and *530*.

5.22   The provisions relating to capital allowances on know-how, extending the allowance pro rata for an accounting period in excess of twelve months, is achieved by an amendment to *TA 1988, s 530(2)(a)(ii)* by *FA 1994, s 214(6)*.

Transitional provisions

5.23   Any unused capital allowances carried forward under *CAA 1990, s 140(4)* which have not been relieved in 1996/97 or earlier periods are treated as due in the first period of account ending after 5 April 1997. [*FA 1994, 20 Sch 9*]. The effect of this is that if the allowances are not relieved in 1997/98 they would be included in the figure for losses carried forward under *TA 1988, s 385; FA 1994, s 209(4)(5)*.

Example 8

Mr Shchyerbakov had agreed tax losses at 5.4.97 of £27,000 and unused capital allowances of £19,000 at the same date. In the year ended 30 September 1997, to which date he made up his annual accounts, the profit as adjusted for tax purposes after capital allowances, amounted to £40,000.

Assessable/taxable 1997/98

y/e 30.9.97		£40,000
Less brought forward		
losses	£27,000	
capital allowances	£19,000	
		£46,000
Assessment		Nil
Losses carried forward		
£46,000 − £40,000		£6,000

5.24   Because the new rules do not apply for existing businesses until 1997/98 the transitional period 1996/97 is dealt with under the old rules which means that the capital allowances basis period for 1996/97 is from the end of the basis period for 1995/96 to the beginning of the basis period for 1997/98.

Example 9

If in the earlier example Mr Laville had not ceased business on 17 August 1996 but had continued to trade, the position would have been as follows:

Income tax basis period		*Capital allowances basis period*
1995–96	1.5.93 – 30.4.94	1.5.93 – 30.4.94
1996–97 ½	(1.5.94 – 30.4.96)	1.5.94 – 30.4.96
1997–98	1.5.96 – 30.4.97	no separate basis period, deducted as expense in period 1.5.96 – 30.4.97

Note that all purchases in the lengthened period 1.5.1994 to 30.4.1996 would qualify for a writing-down allowance in 1996/97. However this is one years writing-down allowance under the old rules, irrespective of the length of the capital allowance basis period.

Farming losses

5.25   The restriction for farming losses where there have been losses in the five preceding years under *TA 1988, s 397* has been based on losses before capital allowances. In order to preserve the status quo in determining whether such losses can be set against other income, it is provided by *FA 1994, s 214(3)* that the results are to be computed without reference to capital allowances in order to determine whether there has been a loss in each of the previous five years. Otherwise by treating losses as trading expenses the comparison of results would automatically have been after capital allowances which would have had a material effect on the calculation in many cases.

Chapter 6

Double Taxation Relief

Commencement – existing rules

6.1 Simplified Assessing does not require any change to the basic provisions for the relief of double taxation by crediting the foreign tax charged against the UK tax liability on the same income. The complication that arises under the existing system is that under the commencement provisions, profits are doubly assessed until the preceding year basis of assessment is running, and *TA 1988, s 804* gives relief for the foreign tax on those profits, or the proportion of them, every time they are brought into assessment. This in turn results in the foreign tax for the opening period being credited more than once.

Cessation – existing rules

6.2 The converse of this is that on a cessation part of the profits, and therefore the double tax credit applicable thereto, falls out of assessment. On a cessation it is necessary to make an adjustment if as a result of the opening and closing provisions more double tax credit has been given than the foreign tax which was suffered. This is done by clawing back any excess relief by means of a charge under Schedule D, Case VI at the basic rate of an amount such that at the basic rate it equates with the excess foreign tax credit.

Commencement – new rules

6.3 The double relief is one of the complications not simplified under the Simplified Assessing rules because there is still a double assessment on commencement in all cases other than where the accounting period ends with the end of the fiscal year. There can also be a double assessment on a change of accounting date resulting in a period of account of less than twelve months, in view of the requirement to tax at least twelve months profits in each fiscal year. Because the profits, to an extent, are doubly taxed it is necessary to give an additional double tax credit and *TA 1988, s 804(1)* is amended accordingly by *FA 1994, s 217*. Double taxation relief is therefore given against overlap profits notwithstanding the fact that relief has already been given in respect of the same overseas tax against the same profits in the first period common to the overlap period.

Excess relief

6.4   The withdrawal of excess credit applies where credit has been allowed in respect of an overlap profit, and overlap relief becomes available under *TA 1988, s 63A(1)* or *(3)* on a change of accounting date resulting in a period of in excess of twelve months, or on a cessation. [*TA 1988, s 804(5); FA 1994, s 217(2)*].

To ascertain the excess credit, it is first necessary to determine the difference between:

(*a*)   the amount of double tax credit actually allowed as a result of giving credit twice on overlap profits [*substituted TA 1988, s 804(5A)(a)(i)*], and

(*b*)   the amount of tax credit which would have been available had relief only been given once [*substituted TA 1988, s 804(5A)(a)(ii)*].

This difference must then be compared with;

(*c*)   the credit which would have been allowed in the subsequent year of clawback had the profits not been restricted by overlap relief [*substituted TA 1988, s 804(5A)(b)*].

6.5   Where (*a*) minus (*b*) exceeds (*c*), there is an excess credit which is recovered by way of a Schedule D, Case VI charge at the basic rate, such that the tax due equals the excess credit. Where there has been an insufficient credit, i.e. where (*c*) exceeds (*a*) minus (*b*) it is given as a credit in the year of overlap relief in place of that otherwise available. [*TA 1988, s 804(5B); FA 1994, s 217(2)*].

Change of accounting date

6.6   Where the overlap profits are only partially relieved as a result of a change of accounting date, the proportion of the double tax credit in relation to each element of the overlap is treated as contributing proportionately to the adjustment required. The overlap profit references are introduced by *FA 1994, s 217(3)*.

Example 1

Mr Kalinin, domiciled and resident in the UK, started business in Canada on 1 August 1998 and produced accounts to 30 June 1999, i.e. for a period of less than twelve months ending in the fiscal year following that of commencement, and annually thereafter until 30 June 2001 when the business was sold. His other income absorbed his personal allowances and lower and basic rate bands except in 1998/99 when he was liable at the basic rate of (say) 25 per cent. The UK higher rate is assumed to be 40 per cent.

Profits (as adjusted for UK tax purposes)

1.8.98 to 30.6.99	£12,500	Canadian tax	£4,375
y/e 30.6.2000	£19,500	Canadian tax	£6,825
y/e 30.6.2001	£25,500	Canadian tax	£8,925
			£20,125

Taxable

1998/99   1.8.98 to 5.4.99

$8/11 \times £12,500$ £9,090 (*a*)

UK tax payable £9,090 @ 25%	£2,272

Less credit for Canadian tax

$£9,090 \times \dfrac{4,375}{12,500}$ limited to £2,272

UK tax payable	£Nil

1999/00 1.8.98 to 31.7.99

$(£12,500 + 1/12 \times £19,500)$ £14,125 (*b*)

UK tax £14,125 @ 40%	£5,650

Less credit for Canadian tax

$£14,125 \times \left(\dfrac{4,375}{12,500} + \dfrac{6,825}{19,500} \right)$ £4,944

UK tax payable	£706
2000/01 y/e 30.6.2000	£19,500 (*c*)
UK tax £19,500 @ 40%	£7,800

Less credit for Canadian tax

$£19,500 \times \dfrac{6,825}{19,500}$ £6,825

UK tax payable	£975
2001/02 y/e 30.6.2001	£25,500 (*d*)

Less overlap relief

1.8.98 to 5.4.99		£9,090
1.7.99 to 31.7.99	$\dfrac{£19,500}{12} =$	£1,625
		£10,715 (*e*)
		£14,785

UK tax £14,785 @ 40%	£5,914

Less credit for Canadian tax

£8,925 limited to	£5,914
UK tax payable	£Nil

Notes

(*a*)   *TA 1988, s 61(1); FA 1994, s 201* commencement to 5 April.

(*b*)   *TA 1988, s 61(2); FA 1994, s 201* first twelve months.

(c) *TA 1988, s 60(3)(a); FA 1994, s 200.*

(d) *TA 1988, s 60(3)(b); FA 1994, s 200.*

(e) *TA 1988, s 63A(3); FA 1994, s 205.*

Applying FA 1994, s 217(5A)
Credit available in opening years but for *TA 1988, s 804; FA 1994, s 217*

1998/99		£2,272

1999/00 $3/11 \times £12,500 \times \dfrac{4,375}{12,500}$ £1,194

$1/12 \times £19,500 \times \dfrac{6,825}{19,500} = $ £569 £1,763

2000/01 $11/12 \times £19,500 \times \dfrac{6,825}{19,500}$ £6,256

£10,291

FA 1994, s 217(5A)(a)(ii)
Credit allowed
1998/99

	£2,272
1999/00	£4,944
2000/01	£6,825
	£14,041

FA 1994, s 217(5A)(a)(i)
difference £ 3,750

Credit available y/e 30.6.2001 on assumption no overlap relief given.

Profits	£25,500
UK tax £25,500 @ 40%	£10,200
Less credit for Canadian tax	£8,925
Less difference as above	£3,750
Credit available *FA 1994, s 217(5B)(b)*	£5,175
UK tax payable – as before	£5,914
Less credit as restricted	£5,175
Final UK tax payable	£739

The credit finally allowed of £14,041 as above plus £5,175 for 2001/02 i.e.
£19,216 compares with the foreign tax suffered of £20,125, i.e. a shortfall
of credit of £909, which is the loss of credit in 1998/99 of £9,090 at the
difference between the UK tax rate of 25% and the Canadian rate of 35%

$\left(\dfrac{14,375}{£12,500}\right)$ i.e. £9,090 @ 10%, £909.

Transitional provisions

Relief for Schedule D, Cases I and II

6.7   The transitional rules relating to double taxation relief apply where income first arose prior to 6 April 1994 and continues after 5 April 1998, unless there is a cessation in 1998/99. [*FA 1994, 20 Sch 10(1)*]. The credit for foreign tax in 1996/97 is one-half of the aggregate of the foreign tax paid on income arising in 1995/96 and 1996/97. [*FA 1994, 20 Sch 10(2)*]. This does not apply where Schedule D, Case I or II income for 1995/96 has been assessed on an actual basis, as this would have attracted its own foreign tax credit and there would be no double allowance. In 1996/97 the foreign tax paid in respect of the actual income for that year will be allowed as a credit in 1996/97, which will be assessed on an actual basis under *FA 1994, 20 Sch 2(3)*. [*FA 1994, 20 Sch 10(3)*].

6.8   The straightforward 50 per cent rule cannot apply where the aggregate period used in the transitional year 1996/97 is a shorter or longer period than two years because, for example, of a change of accounting date. In such circumstances the foreign tax credit for the two years 1995/96 and 1996/97 is reduced or increased proportionately by reference to the transitional period basis period under *FA 1994, 20 Sch 2(2)*. [*FA 1994, 20 Sch 10(4)*].

Example 2

Mr Sheremetyev, resident and domiciled in England, was a partner in a foreign partnership which made up its accounts to 30 September each year until 1997 when it made up accounts to 31 March. His UK income absorbed his personal allowances and lower and basic rate tax bands.

The profits as adjusted for UK tax purposes, applicable to Mr Sheremetyev, and the related foreign tax credit, were as follows:

	Profits	FTC
	£	£
y/e 30.9.94	40,000	11,000
y/e 30.9.95	38,000	12,000
y/e 30.9.96	45,000	15,000
1.10.96 to 31.3.97	25,000	7,000
y/e 31.3.98	50,000	14,000

Assessable/taxable
1995/96 y/e 30.9.94   £40,000

Tax payable at 40%   £16,000
Less foreign tax credit   £11,000

Tax due   £5,000

1996/97 primary basis period y/e 31.3.97

1.10.96 to 31.3.97	£25,000
(FTC £7,000)	
½ y/e 30.9.96	£22,500
(FTC £7,500)	
relevant period 1.10.94 to 31.3.96	
y/e 30.9.95	£38,000
(FTC £12,000)	
½ y/e 30.9.96	£22,500
(FTC £7,500)	
Aggregate	£108,000

Appropriate fraction

$$£108,000 \times \frac{365}{365 + 365 + 183} = \qquad £43,176$$

Tax payable at 40%	£17,270
Less foreign tax credit (£7,000 +	
£7,500 + £12,000 + £7,500) =	

$$£34,000 \times \frac{365}{365 + 365 + 183} = \qquad £13,593$$

Tax due	£3,677
1997/98 y/e 31.3.98	£50,000
Tax payable at 40%	£20,000
Less foreign tax credit	£14,000
Tax due	£6,000

Relief for Schedule D, Cases IV and V

6.9   Where the income is assessed under Schedule D, Case IV or V, by reference to the income arising in the fiscal year, the foreign tax credit is one-half of the foreign tax paid in the two years 1995/96 and 1996/97, i.e. the same basis on which the income is assessed. Where the income is assessed by reference to remittances, the foreign tax applicable to those remittances is credited and in the transitional year one-half of the foreign tax applicable to remittances in 1995/96 and 1996/97 is credited. [*FA 1994, 20 Sch 10(5)*].

Cessation before 6 April 1998

6.10   If the source of income eligible for double tax credits commenced prior to 6 April 1994 and ceases prior to 6 April 1998 the Revenue may direct that the old rules should apply for 1996/97 under *FA 1994, 20 Sch*

3(2), 7. If the Revenue makes such a direction the tax credit would follow and any withdrawal of excess credit would be made under the old rules. [*FA 1994, 20 Sch 12(1)*].

Cessation in 1998/99

6.11   If the cessation takes place in 1998/99, the Revenue have the power to make a direction for 1996/97 to be assessed on an actual fiscal year basis under *FA 1994, 20 Sch 3(4)*. If they make such a direction the old rules continue to apply for calculating the withdrawal of excess relief, if any. [*FA 1994, 20 Sch 12(2)*].

Cessation after 5 April 1998

6.12   Where the business commenced prior to 6 April 1994 and continues after 5 April 1998, the double foreign tax credit will have been given under the old commencement provisions and the clawback will be charged under the new Simplified Assessing rules. There are provisions in *FA 1994, 20 Sch 11* for calculating the excess relief to be recovered in such cases where a source of income ceases in 1998 or later; save when the Revenue make a direction to assess 1996/97 on an actual basis as set out in 6.11. The recovery provisions for excess relief are broadly similar to the new rules under substituted *TA 1988, s 804(5)(2)(5C)*. [*FA 1994, 20 Sch 11(2)(3)*]. It is necessary to compare:

(*a*)   the tax credit actually allowed; with

(*b*)   the aggregate of the credit which would have been allowed had there been no double allowance on commencement and as if the transitional credit had not been reduced.

[*FA 1994, 20 Sch 11(4)*].

6.13   The object of the calculation is to make sure that the credit that is actually allowed, taking into account the double allowance under the old commencement provisions, does not exceed the credit which falls out of assessment on the transitional provisions when only part of the credit is allowed. The transitional provisions do not appear to take account of the overlap relief on cessation, however, which could cause a loss of foreign tax credit in the final period.

6.14   The excess foreign tax credit as calculated is recovered by means of a Schedule D, Case VI charge of such an amount as at the basic rate equals the excess relief.

6.15   It is not clear that these provisions take the necessary account of any restriction in foreign tax credits arising as a result of overlap relief.

6.16   Where income for 1996/97 has been charged on the basis of the actual income in the fiscal year there is no loss of credit except by reference to overlap relief causing the foreign tax credit to be restricted, which is ignored, so the excess credit is merely the amount doubly allowed on commencement. [*FA 1994, 20 Sch 11(5)*]. The clawback arises whether the excess credit was given under the old or new provisions. [*FA 1994, 20 Sch 11(6)*].

6.17 Where foreign tax is given as an expense under *TA 1988, s 811*, instead of as a credit, the transitional rules are applied to the profits as reduced. [*FA 1994, 20 Sch 13*].

Chapter 7

Partnerships

Introduction

7.1   There are fundamental changes to partnership taxation under Simplified Assessing. Under the existing rules partnerships are assessed to tax as a single unit and the partnership profits are allocated among the partners in accordance with their profit sharing ratio in the year of assessment, not in accordance with the ratio in which they actually share the accounting profits forming the basis period for that assessment. Moreover the tax payable by the partnership is calculated as a joint and several liability of the partners. Under the new provisions each partner will be responsible for his own taxation in connection with his share of the partnership profit and there will be no joint liability. The suggestion that UK resident partners might be jointly liable for the payment of tax of nonresident partners in the Consultative Document has not been reflected in the legislation, but may be included in the *Finance Act 1995*.

Partners as notional sole traders

7.2   Once the new rules come into force a partner who joins a firm will be treated as commencing a new trade or profession and his share of profits will be taxed on him personally under the commencement provisions, including an overlap. Conversely a partner who leaves the firm will be treated as ceasing to carry on the trade or profession and he will be entitled to overlap relief.

No separate taxable entity

7.3   New *TA 1988, s 111(1)* as introduced by *FA 1994, s 215(1)* provides that a partnership is not treated for tax purposes as an entity separate and distinct from the partners who carry it on. This radical change means partnerships will not be assessed in the partnership name under the new provisions.

Partnership as deemed individual

7.4   Substituted *TA 1988, s 111(2)* provides that a partnership is to be treated as an individual for the purpose of computing the profits chargeable to tax where all the partners are subject to income tax as individuals or trustees. So even though a partnership is not a separate entity for tax purposes under the new provisions, it is effectively treated as such for determining the amount of chargeable profits.

Allocation of profits

7.5   Substituted *TA 1988, s 111(3)* provides that each partner is taxed as if he were carrying on a separate business, but the measure of profit is his share of the adjusted results of the partnership for the period. This means that usually the only difference between the accounting profit on which the partner's drawings are based and the taxable profit is that arising from the normal adjustments for tax purposes; i.e. disallowing depreciation, entertaining etc., and allowing capital allowances and other statutory deductions. The provisions of *TA 1988, s 277(2)* which allocated a partner's share by reference to his share in the fiscal year, and not in the accounting period which formed the basis for that assessment, are repealed by *FA 1994, s 215(3)(c)*.

Commencement date for new provisions

7.6   The new provisions come into force from 1997/98 in respect of partnerships carrying on a trade, profession or business on 5 April 1994. Partnerships commencing on or after 6 April 1994 are subject to the new rules from the start. If there is a change in partners after 5 April 1994 and the partners do not elect for continuation under *TA 1988, s 113(2)* there will be a deemed cessation and commencement and the new rules will therefore apply on the commencement. [*FA 1994, s 215(4)(5)*].

Example 1

Messrs Shishmaryev, Silvansky and Sukhoi were in partnership as solicitors sharing profits equally and preparing accounts, on a bills delivered basis, to 30 April each year. On 30 April 1994, Mr Sukhoi retired and Mr Kuznetsov joined. The goodwill passed under the partnership agreement to the new firm without payment and work in progress passed at a nominal £1, under *TA 1988, s 101*. There was no election for continuation under *TA 1988, s 113(2)*.

Profits (as adjusted for tax purposes, ignoring work in progress were):

y/e 30 April 1991	£150,000
y/e 30 April 1992	£140,000
y/e 30 April 1993	£120,000
y/e 30 April 1994	£100,000
y/e 30 April 1995	£140,000
y/e 30 April 1996	£180,000
y/e 30 April 1997	£200,000

Work in progress, on the basis of cost of professional staff time plus attributable overheads, was £120,000 at 30 April 1995, £145,000 at 30 April 1996, and £130,000 at 30 April 1997.

SP A27 requires work in progress to be taken into account in computing the profits of the new partnership commencing on 30 April 1994. The profit for the year ended 30 April 1995 of £140,000 has to be adjusted to £260,000 to reflect the closing work in progress of £120,000. The profit for the year ended 30 April 1996 has likewise to be adjusted to £205,000 to reflect the increase in work in progress (£145,000 – £120,000); and that for the year ended 30 April 1997 has to be adjusted to £185,000 to reflect the reduction in work in progress (£145,000 – £130,000).

Assessable/taxable

		Total £	*Sh* £	*Si* £	*Su* £	*K* £
(a)	1992/93					
	y/e 30.4.91	150,000	50,000	50,000	50,000	
(b)	1993/94					
	y/e 30.4.92	140,000	46,667	46,667	46,666	
(c)	1994/95					
	cessation					
	6.4.94 to 30.4.94					
	$\frac{25 \times £100,000}{365}$	6,849	2,283	2,283	2,283	
(d)	1994/95					
	recommencement					
	1.5.94 to 5.4.95					
	$\frac{340 \times £260,000}{365}$	242,191	80,730	80,730	–	80,731
(e)	1995/96					
	y/e 30.4.95	260,000	86,667	86,667		86,666
(f)	1996/97					
	y/e 30.4.96	205,000	68,333	68,333		68,334
(g)	1997/98					
	y/e 30.4.97	185,000	61,667	61,667		61,666
Total 1992/93						
to 1997/98		1,189,040	396,347	396,347	98,949	297,397

Notes

(a)   Preceding year basis, *TA 1988, s 60(3)* (original enactment).

(b)   Preceding year basis, *TA 1988, s 60(3)* (original enactment).

Total for 1992/93 and 1993/94 £290,000.

7.6 Partnerships

Revenue option for actual basis under *TA 1988, s 63(1)(b)* (original enactment):

1992/93	$\dfrac{25}{365} \times £140,000$	£9,589
	$\dfrac{340}{365} \times £120,000$	£111,780
		£121,369
1993/94	$\dfrac{25}{365} \times £120,000$	£8,219
	$\dfrac{340}{365} \times £100,000$	£93,151
		£101,370
		£222,739

which is less than £290,000 originally assessed so there is no Revenue adjustment on cessation.

(*d*) Commencement to 5 April, substituted *TA 1988, s 61(1)*.

(*e*) Twelve months to first accounting date, substituted *TA 1988, s 60(3)(a)*. Overlap credit for £242,191 already assessed in 1994/95.

(*f*) Current year basis, substituted *TA 1988, s 60(3)(b)*.

(*g*) Current year basis, substituted *TA 1988, s 60(3)(b)*.

Had there been a continuation election on Mr Sukhoi's retirement and Mr Kuznetsov's arrival the position would have been markedly different. The absence of a cessation would have enabled the bills delivered basis to have been retained throughout.

Assessable/taxable

		Total £	Sh £	Si £	Su £	K £
(*a*)	1992/93 y/e 30.4.91	150,000	50,000	50,000	50,000	
(*b*)	1993/94 y/e 30.4.92	140,000	46,667	46,667	46,666	
(*c*)	1994/95 y/e 30.4.93	120,000	40,000	40,000	2,740	37,260
(*d*)	1995/96 y/e 30.4.94	100,000	33,333	33,333		33,334
(*e*)	1996/97 transitional year	160,000	53,333	53,333		53,334
(*f*)	1997/98 y/e 30.4.97	200,000	66,667	66,667		66,666
		870,000	290,000	290,000	99,406	190,594

	Total £	Sh £	Si £	Su £	K £
As originally computed	1,189,040	396,347	396,347	98,949	297,397
Difference caused by failure to elect for continuation	319,040	106,347	106,347	(457)	106,803

Notes

(*a*) Preceding year basis, *TA 1988, s 60(3)* (original enactment).

(*b*) Preceding year basis, *TA 1988, s 60(3)* (original enactment).

(*c*) Preceding year basis, *TA 1988, s 60(3)* (original enactment).

Mr Sukhoi $\dfrac{25}{365} \times £40,000 =$ £2,740

Mr Kuznetsov $\dfrac{340}{365} \times £40,000 =$ £37,260

(*d*) Preceding year basis, *TA 1988, s 60(3)* (original enactment).

(*e*) Basis period 1996/97, *FA 1994, 20 Sch 1(2)*.

y/e 30.4.96   £180,000

Relevant period, *FA 1994, 20 Sch 2(5)*

y/e 30.4.95   £140,000

Aggregate *FA 1994, 20 Sch 2(2)*   £320,000

Appropriate percentage, *FA 1994, 20 Sch 2(5)*

£320,000 $\times \dfrac{365}{365 + 365} =$ £160,000

(*f*) Current year basis, substituted *TA 1988, s 60(3)(b)*. Transitional overlap, *FA 1994, 20 Sch 2(4)*.

$\dfrac{340}{365} \times £200,000 =$ £186,301

The substantially increased taxable income arises from the combination of the work in progress adjustment increasing the profits of the commencement year, taxed nearly twice and the acceleration of increasing profits on moving to the current year basis in 1994/95 instead of 1997/98.

Equitable adjustments

7.7 The effect of the new rule is that the desirability of having an equitable adjustment in the partnership agreement to cater for the imbalance that can apply under the existing rules between the profits in which the partner actually shares in a year and the assessment for that year (the latter being based on the profits of the basis period, but allocated in accordance with the profit sharing arrangements in the fiscal year) should no longer arise. However, an equitable adjustment might still be desirable if there are prior charges such as salaries to certain partners, and the total salaries exceed the adjusted profits.

Example 2

Messrs Semyenov, Sutugin and Gorylev were in partnership trading as 'Tri Druga'. Mr Semyenov and Mr Sutugin were entitled to 'salaries' of £30,000 each as a prior share of profits which were thereafter shared in the proportion 20, 20 and 60.

The profits, as adjusted for tax purposes, were:

y/e 30.6.98	£140,000
y/e 30.6.99	£ 40,000
y/e 30.6.2000	£180,000

Assessable/taxable

	Total £	Se £	Su £	G £
1998/99				
y/e 30.6.98				
Prior share	60,000	30,000	30,000	–
Profit/loss	80,000	16,000	16,000	48,000
	140,000	46,000	46,000	48,000
1999/2000				
y/e 30.6.99				
Prior share	60,000	30,000	30,000	–
Profit/loss	(20,000)	–	–	(20,000)
	40,000	30,000	30,000	(20,000)
G's notional loss				
shared equally		(10,000)	(10,000)	20,000
		£20,000	£20,000	–
2000/01				
y/e 30.6.2000				
Prior share	60,000	30,000	30,000	–
Profit/loss	120,000	24,000	24,000	72,000
	180,000	54,000	54,000	72,000

The loss shown in the accounts after the salaries of Mr Semyenov and Mr Sutugin in the year ended 30 June 1999, which is borne by Mr Goryelov, is not an allowable loss for tax purposes as the partnership shows an overall profit, which is allocated to those partners which share in it in their profit sharing ratio, i.e. Mr Semyenov and Mr Sutugin equally. They each receive £30,000 but pay tax on £20,000 while Mr Goryelov who suffers a loss of £20,000 obtains no relief for it. Equity would suggest that in these circumstances Messrs Semyenov and Sutugin should surrender their tax saved on £10,000 each to Mr Goryelov as an equitable adjustment under an appropriate clause in the partnership agreement.

Cessation provisions

7.8   Not only will each partner calculate his chargeable profits under the opening provisions of substituted *TA 1988, ss 60* and *61*, but on leaving the partnership he will fall within the cessation provisions of *TA 1988, s 63* and be eligible for overlap relief in respect of his partnership share under *TA 1988, s 63A; FA 1994, s 205*. Individual partners will of course also be affected by additional overlap or overlap relief arising on a change of accounting date under *TA 1988, s 62* and *62A*. [*FA 1994, ss 202, 203*].

Example 3

Mr Polikarpov and Mr Shavrov started business in partnership on 1 August 1998 sharing profits equally and produced accounts to 31 December 1999 and annually thereafter. On 1 July 2000 they were joined by Mr Michaelson and shared profits equally until 30 September 2001 when Mr Shavrov was tragically killed in an aircraft crash. The surviving partners continued to share profits equally.

Profits (as adjusted for tax purposes)

1.8.98 to 31.12.99	£43,000
y/e 31.12.2000	£45,000
y/e 31.12.2001	£57,000
y/e 31.12.2002	£48,000

Taxable	*Total* £	*P* £	*S* £	*M* £	
1998/99 1.8.98 to 5.4.99					
8/17 × £43,000	20,235	10,117	10,118	–	(*a*)
1999/00 1.1.99 to 31.12.99					
12/17 × £43,000	30,352	15,176	15,176	–	(*b*)

111

Taxable	Total £	P £	S £	M £	
2000/01 y/e 31.12.2000					
1.1.00 to 30.6.00	22,500	11,250	11,250	–	(c)
1.7.00 to 31.12.00	22,500	7,500	7,500	7,500	(d)
1.1.01 to 5.4.01	4,750	–	–	4,750	(e)
	49,750	18,750	18,750	12,250	
2001/02 y/e 31.12.2001					
1.1.01 to 30.9.01	42,750	14,250	14,250	14,250	(f)
Less Overlap relief	(3,794)		(3,794)		(g)
1.10.01 to 31.12.01	14,250	7,125	–	7,125	(h)
	53,206	21,375	10,456	21,375	
2002/03 y/e 31.12.2002	48,000	24,000	–	24,000	(i)

Notes

(a) Substituted *TA 1988, s 61(1)* commencement to 5 April.

(b) Substituted *TA 1988, s 60(3)(a)* twelve months to first accounting date. Overlap period 1.1.99 to 5.4.99, overlap profits for P and S

$$3/17 \times \frac{£43,000}{2} = £3,794 \text{ each.}$$

(c) Substituted *TA 1988, ss 60(3)(b), 111(3)(a)*.

(d) Substituted *TA 1988, ss 60(3)(b), 111(3)(a)*.

(e) Substituted *TA 1988, s 111(3)(b)* overlap period 1.1.01 to 5.4.01,

overlap profits $3/12 \times \frac{£57,000}{3} = £4,750.$

(f) Substituted *TA 1988, ss 60(3)(b), 63, 111(3)(a)* period to date of cessation on death.

(g) Substituted *TA 1988, ss 63A(3), 111(3)(c)* overlap relief fully relieved on cessation (see (b) above).

(h) Substituted *TA 1988, ss 60(3)(b), 111(3)(a)* period to end of accounting period.

(i) Substituted *TA 1988, ss 60(3)(b), 111(3)(a)* accounting year ending in fiscal year apportioned to partners in profit sharing ratio.

Investment income

7.9 All income accruing to a partner from the partnership is computed by reference to the partnership basis period applicable to the trade or profession under *TA 1988, s 111(4); FA 1994, s 215(1)*. This applies to property income assessable under Schedule A, interest and other income assessable under Schedule D, Case III, income from overseas securities under Schedule D, Cases IV and V and even sundry income such as furnished lettings under Schedule D, Case VI as well as dividends under Schedule F and taxed income. The fact that all income is assessed by reference to the accounting period should simplify each partner's self-assessment in respect of his partnership share and may be the precursor to the eventual abolition of the schedular system which has long ago outlived its usefulness.

Example 4

Zlokazov & Co was a partnership consisting of Mr Zlok and Mr Kazov sharing profits equally, which has the following income, as adjusted for tax purposes, which is assumed to accrue evenly throughout the period.

	£	*Sch D* *Case I* £	*Sch A* £	*Sch D* *Case III* £	*Sch D* *Case V* £
y/e 30.4.94	113,000	80,000	20,000	5,000	8,000
y/e 30.4.95	130,000	90,000	24,000	6,000	10,000
y/e 30.4.96	141,000	100,000	25,000	4,000	12,000
y/e 30.4.97	129,000	85,000	22,000	2,000	20,000

Assessable/taxable

	Total £	*Z* £	*K* £
1995/96			
Schedule D, Case I – y/e 30.4.94	80,000	40,000	40,000

Schedule A – y/e 5.4.96

$$\frac{25}{365} \times £24,000 \qquad 1,644$$

$$\frac{340}{365} \times £25,000 \qquad 23,288$$

	24,932	12,466	12,466

Schedule D, Case III – y/e 5.4.95 (PYB)

$$\frac{25}{365} \times £5,000 \qquad 343$$

$$\frac{340}{365} \times £6,000 \qquad 5,589$$

	5,932	2,966	2,966

Schedule D, Case V – y/e 5.4.95 (PYB)

$$\frac{25}{365} \times £8,000 \qquad 548$$

	Total £	Z £	K £
$\dfrac{340}{365} \times £10,000$	9,315		
	9,863	4,932	4,932

1996/97 transitional year
Schedule D, Case I
   primary basis period
   y/e 30.4.96   £100,000

relevant period
   y/e 30.4.95   £90,000
   Aggregate   £190,000

Appropriate percentage

$$£190,000 \times \dfrac{365}{365 + 365} = \qquad 95,000 \quad 47,500 \quad 47,500$$

Schedule A – y/e 5.4.97

$\dfrac{25}{365} \times £25,000$	1,712		
$\dfrac{340}{365} \times £22,000$	20,493		
	22,205	11,103	11,102

Schedule D, Case III – y/e 5.4.96

$\dfrac{25}{365} \times £6,000 =$	411	
$\dfrac{340}{365} \times £4,000 =$	£3,726	

y/e 5.4.97

$\dfrac{25}{365} \times £4,000 =$	£274	
$\dfrac{340}{365} \times £2,000 =$	£1,863	
Aggregate	£6,274	

50% thereof	3,137	1,569	1,569

	Total £	Z £	K £

Schedule D, Case V – y/e 5.4.96

$$\frac{25}{365} \times £10,000 = \qquad £\ 685$$

$$\frac{340}{365} \times £12,000 = \qquad £11,178$$

y/e 5.4.97

$$\frac{25}{365} \times £12,000 = \qquad £\ 822$$

$$\frac{340}{365} \times £20,000 = \qquad £18,630$$

Aggregate   £31,315

	Total £	Z £	K £
50% thereof	15,658	7,829	7,829
1997/98 Schedule D, Case I – y/e 30.4.97	85,000	42,500	42,500

transitional overlap relief
FA 1994, 20 Sch 2(4)

$$£85,000 \times \frac{340}{365} =$$

	Total £	Z £	K £
	79,178	39,589	39,589
Schedule A – y/e 30.4.97	22,000	11,000	11,000
Schedule D, Case III – y/e 30.4.97	2,000	1,000	1,000
Schedule D, Case V – y/e 30.4.97	20,000	10,000	10,000

There is a need for transitional overlap relief for:

Schedule A

$$\frac{340}{365} \times £22,000$$

Schedule D, Case III

$$\frac{340}{365} \times £2,000$$

Schedule D, Case V

$$\frac{340}{365} \times £20,000$$

	£	£	£
Schedule A	20,493	10,246	10,247
Schedule D, Case III	1,863	932	931
Schedule D, Case V	18,630	9,315	9,315

There is no statutory provision for this but it is understood that it will be included in the *Finance Act 1995*. (See 7.22 below.)

Non-trading businesses

7.10   If the partnership carries on a business but not a trade, the same rules apply as if it were carrying on a trade. This is presumably intended to cover income such as that from furnished holiday accommodation which is assessable under Schedule D, Case VI but under the rules of Schedule D, Case I or other quasi-trading income. It is understood that this does not presage any move by the Revenue to extend the meaning of trade, but to permit joint investment activities which are carried on as a business to be treated as a partnership for tax purposes (as indeed it may need to be for VAT purposes in order to obtain VAT registration where appropriate so that input tax can be recovered). (See also 10.25 below.) It is unclear whether such a business has to use fiscal year accounting on the basis that the income is chargeable under Schedule D, Case VI, or whether as a partnership it can have any accounting date ending in the year and pre-pare accounts and computations accordingly. [*Substituted TA 1988, s 111(5)*]. The latter would be consistent with assimilating partnership businesses to trades.

Joint investments

7.11   The partnership provisions would not extend to mere invest-ments which were jointly owned and where there was no 'business' (*McKee v Luck 1925 9 TC 511*). There is no statutory definition of a partnership for tax purposes and therefore the definition in the *Partnership Act 1890, s 1* of the 'relation which subsists between persons carrying on a business in common with a view of profit', applies. The meaning of business has been considered in the context of VAT and the relevant principles were summarised in the case of *C & E Commissioners v Lord Fisher [1981] STC 238*. The following criteria were considered rel-evant in determining whether an activity constituted a business; whether:

  (i)   the activity was a serious undertaking earnestly pursued;

  (ii) the activity was an occupation or function pursued with reasonable or recognisable continuity;

 (iii) the activity had a measure of substance;

 (iv) the activity was conducted in a regular manner and on sound and recognised business principles;

  (v) the activity was predominantly concerned with making supplies for a consideration; and

 (vi) the supplies were of a kind commonly made by those who sought to profit by them.

Existence or otherwise of partnership

7.12   The basic definition of partnership in the *Partnership Act* has been set out in 7.11. Whether or not a partnership exists has been considered in many cases, the issue being one of fact, (*CIR v Williamson 1928 14 TC 335; Calder v Allanson 1935 19 TC 293*). The presence or absence of a partnership agreement is not conclusive (*Hawker v Compton 1922 8 TC 306; Dickenson v Gross 1927 11 TC 614; Fenston v Johnston 1940 23 TC 29*). A partnership agreement can confirm that a partnership exists and can provide for a partnership to be set up, but it cannot create retrospectively a partnership relationship which did not exist (*Ayshire Pullman Motor Services and Ritchie v CIR 1929 14 TC 754; Waddington v O'Callaghan 1931 16 TC 187; Taylor v Chalklin 1940 26 TC 463*). Even where there is a partnership the question of whether any individual is in reality a true equity partner is a question which also has to be addressed. Minor children were not regarded as effective partners in *Alexander Bulloch & Co v CIR [1976] STC 514*, but in *Stekel v Ellice [1973] 1 All ER 465* a salaried partner was held under the arrangements in existence to be a true equity partner.

Relevance of sharing profits and losses

7.13   The sharing of profits implies partnership (*Morden Rigg & Co and RB Eskrigge & Co v Monks 1923 8 TC 450; George Hall & Son v Platt 1954 35 TC 440; John Gardner & Bowring Hardy & Co Ltd v CIR 1930 15 TC 602*), but it is however not necessarily conclusive. (*Pratt v Strick (1932) 17 TC 459*). The sharing of losses, again although not necessarily conclusive, is highly indicative of a partnership (*Brown v Tapscott 1840 6 M & W 119; Bond v Pittard 1838 3 M & W 357*).

Corporate partners

7.14   Where a corporate partner is involved the provisions relating to partnerships involving companies in *TA 1988, ss 114* and 115 are amended by *FA 1994, s 215(2)* to apply to cases where the partnership is carrying on a profession or business as well as a trade, and to provide that in calculating the corporate partner's taxable profit it is necessary to compute the partnership results as if it were a corporation. However, to arrive at the individual partner's share of profits *TA 1988, s 114(3)*, as amended, provides that the individual's share of losses, profits and gains is arrived at on the basis that the partnership is an individual and ignoring the fact that any of the partners are companies. This enables the new provisions for individuals in substituted *TA 1988, s 111(2)* to apply, even where the partnership contains a company (see 7.4 above).

Deemed company

7.15   Where there is a mixture of partners therefore it is necessary to compute the profits under corporation tax rules to arrive at the corporate partner's share and to recompute the same profits under income tax rules in order to arrive at the individual partner's shares.

Foreign partnerships

7.16   In the case of a partnership managed and controlled abroad, an individual partner is taxed under Schedule D, Case V in view of *TA 1988, s 112*, which remains unaltered, but a corporate partner remains taxable on its share of the profit as if the partnership were UK resident under *TA 1988, s 115(4)*. Where a partnership is controlled abroad the new provisions do not apply until 1997/98. [*FA 1994, s 215(5)(b)*].

Partnership changes

7.17   Under the new rules, as each individual partner is taxed separately on his share of the partnership profits, and by reference to his joining and leaving the partnership, there is no requirement for the partnership itself to be deemed to cease on a change in partners, subject to any election for continuation. The partnership only remains relevant in the sense that there is a single partnership set of accounts and computations and a single partnership return and statement allocating the profits for the partners. The provisions of *TA 1988, s 113(2)* which allowed the partners' to elect for continuation on a change of partners' ceases to have effect. Instead, continuation treatment is automatic where there is at least one continuing partner. Accordingly the opening year and cessation provisions only apply to those individuals who are joining or leaving the firm. The consequences of such an election are no longer relevant and the relevant provisions are repealed.

7.18   Until the new rules come into effect however, in most cases on the 6 April 1997 for existing businesses, it will be necessary to continue to make an election for continuation after a partnership change under *TA 1988, s 113(2)* within two years of the change. Failure to do so would not only give rise to a cessation, but would immediately put the continuing business on the new Simplified Assessing rules because it would be deemed to commence on or after 6 April 1994 if the partnership change took place on or after that date. It is important to appreciate this in deciding whether or not to make the continuation election. (See 7.6 above.)

Farm profit averaging

7.19   Averaging claims under *TA 1988, s 96* will be made by individual partners and not by the firm. [*FA 1994, s 216(3)(a)*]. This will apply for the averaging of 1996/97 with 1997/98 and subsequent pairs of years. Farm profit averaging claims up to and including 1995/96 with 1996/97 will be done under the old rules at the partnership level. [*FA 1994, s 216(5)*]. If, however, the trade was set up and commenced on or after 6 April 1994, the averaging at the individual level applies from 1994/95 with 1995/96 or any subsequent pairs of years. For the treatment of capital allowances see 5.16 above.

Losses

7.20   Prior to Simplified Assessing, it was necessary to provide in loss relief claims for continuing partners to be treated as continuing and not eligible for terminal loss relief or relief for losses in the early years of a trade, but able to carry forward losses as if there had been no cessation, and to claim losses against total income on the same basis. These provisions are not required under the new rules and are deleted by *FA 1994, s 216(3)(b)–(g)*.

Terminal losses

7.21   There are consequential amendments to the terminal loss relief provisions in *FA 1994, s 216(4)*. A trade, profession or vocation shall be treated as discontinued, and a new one set up and commenced, only if:

(*a*)   there is a cessation of the firm as a result of all the existing partners ceasing to be engaged in carrying on the trade, profession or vocation; or

(*b*)   in the case of an individual partner, if he ceases to be a partner.

Transitional provisions

7.22   There are no specific transitional provisions relating to partnerships as there was initially thought to be no need for them. For an existing partnership the provisions in substituted *TA 1988, s 111* provide that the transitional rules applicable to an individual apply to the partnership, and the partnership itself continues to be assessed for years up to and including 1996/97. From 1997/98 each partner is dealt with on an individual basis by reference to his share of the partnership profits or losses shown by the partnership statement.

7.23   However transitional relief is needed for investment income of a partnership assessed on a fiscal year basis in 1996/97, but by reference to the Schedule D, Case I or II basis period for 1997/98 under substituted *TA 1988, s 111(4)(b)*. It is understood that these provisions will be included in the *Finance Act 1995*. (See 7.9 above.)

Chapter 8

Companies: Employees and Directors

Companies

Pay and File

8.1   The corporation tax system has already been streamlined under 'Pay and File', introduced by *F(No 2)A 1987*, as amended and extended by later Acts. A new set of rules governs the payment and assessment procedures for corporation tax, which apply for accounting periods beginning on or after 1 October 1993.

8.2   Briefly stated, a company is obliged to pay its estimate of the corporation tax liability nine months after the end of its accounting period. It is then generally obliged to complete and send its tax return for the period to the Revenue three months later. The form of the return (CT200) is such that the company or its agent can work through the computation and so determine its tax liability. However, the Revenue are to issue the actual assessment, usually once the profits have been agreed.

8.3   Pay and File has a detailed code of its own dealing with reporting requirements, payments, assessing procedures, interest and penalties. It has many of the hallmarks of self-assessment, but it is still partly a hybrid system given that the making of the assessment is by the Revenue. The reader is referred to the textbooks on Pay and File for more detailed information.

Changes under Simplified Assessing

8.4   The general structure of Pay and File is not altered by Simplified Assessing. There are also no changes to the basis of computing a company's tax liability. However, a number of changes are made in *FA 1994* to bring the position for companies in line with that for individuals and trustees essentially relating to management and administration, which take effect in respect of accounting periods ending after 31 March 1996. The changes may be summarised as follows.

(*a*) Notification of chargeability to corporation tax must be made within six months of the end of the accounting period, rather than twelve months as at present.

(*b*) The company tax return is to become a self-assessment, so that responsibility for assessment will be with companies. This is really a change of form rather than substance.

(*c*) The Revenue will be entitled to make enquiries into a company's return for twelve months after the filing date for a timeous return. Thereafter the figures in the return and the self-assessment become final and cannot be reopened other than under a 'discovery'.

(*d*) During this twelve-month period a company will be entitled to amend its return and self-assessment. The Revenue will be entitled to correct any obvious errors or mistakes within nine months.

(*e*) The discovery rules themselves have been revised and are codified in the new legislation. Essentially a discovery assessment can only be raised if there has been fraud, neglect or incomplete disclosure.

(*f*) If the return was not filed on time, the Revenue can determine the tax due. There is no appeal against such a determination, but it is automatically superseded by a completed return and self-assessment.

8.5   These issues are considered in further detail in the Chapters that follow dealing with management and administration.

Employees and directors

Background

8.6   Since the publication in November 1992 of the Inland Revenue's second Consultative Document 'A Simpler System for Assessing Personal Tax' it has been integral to Simplified Assessing that all who receive a tax return – including employees – are to be included within its ambit. Employees who are fully taxed under PAYE and have no other income are not obliged to notify the Revenue of their chargeability (see 10.7 below). But employees who receive a return will be obliged to complete and send it back to the Revenue by 30 September following the end of the tax year if the Revenue are to calculate their liability, or by 31 January if they are to self-assess (see 10.12 and 10.3 below).

8.7   *FA 1994* itself is predominantly concerned with the self-employed, both in respect of the move to the CY basis from 1997/98 and the management provisions for self-assessment which take effect from 1996/97. The provisions relating specifically to employees and company directors have been deferred and will be included in *FA 1995*. This is enabling the Revenue to examine the issues involved with representative bodies, and to devise a system to enable employees to make complete tax returns on a timely basis.

8.8   Whilst the fundamentals of PAYE are not to be altered, employees will have to complete and file their tax returns by the due dates, and be in a position to work out their own tax liability. This will necessitate significant changes to the present legislation relating to the provision of information by employers to employees, particularly regarding expense payments and benefits in kind.

8.9   At present employers have no obligation to give their employees such information. Instead they are required to deliver to the Inspector Form P11D for directors and what used to be called higher paid employees, i.e. those earning over £8,500 per annum, and Form P9D for other employees. Whilst many employers in fact give copies to employees the practice is far from universal. Moreover, even those employees who are aware of the taxable benefits they receive by being given copies of the Form P11D do not necessarily know the cash equivalent on which their liability to tax is based.

8.10   It follows that under Simplified Assessing employers will be required to provide their employees with considerably greater information than they are required to do at present in relation to expenses and benefits in kind. This in turn raises questions as to the nature of that information, the determination of the taxable amount notified to the employee, and the deductions available to the employee. This Chapter reviews the present tax position and reporting obligations in respect of emoluments, expenses and benefits in kind and considers the likely changes to the system which will be necessitated by Simplified Assessing.

Wages, salaries, bonuses etc.

8.11   Under *TA 1988, s 19*, tax is chargeable under Schedule E on 'emoluments', which under *TA 1988, s 131* are defined to include 'all salaries, fees, wages, perquisites and profits whatsoever'. Emoluments paid to an employee fall within the PAYE procedure and no fundamental changes are needed under Simplified Assessing. Information relating to salaries, fees and wages etc. is presently provided by the employer to the employee in the form of monthly payslips and at the end of the year on form P60. No particular changes will be required other than to ensure that the employee receives the P60 well in time to complete his tax return.

Expenses and expenses payments

General position

8.12   The present position regarding the taxability of expenses may be summarised as follows.

(*a*)   Payments by an employer to an employee to reimburse an expense incurred in the performance of the duties of the employment are not emoluments taxable under the general rule for Schedule E (although any profit element is so taxed).

(*b*)   Expenses payments are chargeable as deemed emoluments where they are made to directors or employees earning over £8,500 per annum, except where a dispensation exists.

(*c*)   Where an employer pays a personal bill of the employee, such as a home telephone bill (known as a 'pecuniary liability') the payment is taxable as part of the employee's income, although the employee may obtain a deduction of any amount which would have been deductible if the payment had been made out of his or income from the employment as outlined in (*d*) below.

(*d*)   Under *TA 1988, s 198* an employee is entitled to a deduction for travelling expenses necessarily incurred in the performance of his duties; or for other expenditure incurred wholly, exclusively and necessarily in the performance of those duties. It is well established that this *section* lays down a very strict test. In particular no relief is available for home to work travel.

(*e*)   PAYE is generally applied to round sum allowances, but not to other expense payments, and not to payments to meet employees' pecuniary liabilities.

8.13   Under Simplified Assessing the basic structure of the system relating to chargeability, deductibility and the operation of PAYE will not be changed. But some aspects of the system may need amending, as explored in this Chapter. Moreover, given that employees will be responsible for reporting on their tax return sums received from their employers and from third parties, and for claiming appropriate deductions, and that they will have the ability to self-assess, they will need to be rather more fully informed than at present as to how the rules work, and what records they will need to keep. They will also have to know whether PAYE has been applied to expense payments made to them.

Travelling and subsistence

8.14   Generally a deduction is available for the expense of business journeys, travelling from one work place to another, but not from home to work. Costs of subsistence follow the same rules. The Schedule E deduction rules were devised in a more leisurely and simpler era, and have been subject to growing criticism in recent years. Whilst they are relatively straightforward where there is a stable place of work, problems can arise in the increasingly frequent cases of employees working more at home, or who have different work locations.

8.15   Under Simplified Assessing, to enable an employee to make a claim for expenses reimbursed, where appropriate, he will need to know:

(*a*)   if he has a 'normal place of work', and if so its location, since home to work is not deductible;

(*b*) if he has no normal place of work, whether he has a 'travelling appointment' (i.e. where travelling is an integral part of the job, for example a sales representative) so that expenses are deductible; and

(*c*) if he has no normal place of employment, and does not have a travelling appointment but works at different sites, the extent to which deductions can be claimed.

8.16 The position particularly of such site based employees is a controversial one, although certain practices are adopted by agreement with the Revenue in some cases, such as construction site workers. Many representations have been made to the Revenue seeking a review of the system. The area is likely to pose problems for employees when it comes to their reporting obligations under Simplified Assessing. Considerable guidance will be required from the Revenue as to the precise extent of an employee's obligations, regardless of whether any legislative changes of principle are made.

8.17 A related area is the extent to which the incidental element in overnight subsistence payments is taxable. This applies to such items as newspapers, telephone calls home and laundry etc. These are regarded by the Revenue as personal expenses, so the reimbursement for allowances made to employees are fully taxable. The tax treatment of such minor items is again an issue which will need to be clarified.

Entertaining

8.18 There is a broad prohibition for entertaining costs, either in calculating the employer's tax liability, or in calculating that of the employee. Generally, in trading concerns where an employee receives an allowance specifically earmarked for entertaining, the payment is disallowed in calculating the employer's tax liability. In such circumstances the employee can get tax relief on business entertaining under the Schedule E rules for expenditure incurred wholly, necessarily and exclusively in the performance of the duties of his employment. The position is similar for a reimbursement of expenditure incurred, or where the employer directly pays the particular entertaining bill. Hence the cost of the disallowance falls upon the employer rather than the employee.

8.19 However, where the employee meets the expenditure from an inclusive salary or round sum allowance, the disallowance is made in calculating the employee's tax liability. He is not entitled to a deduction in such circumstances. It seems that these principles will not change under Simplified Assessing, but the employee will clearly need to know in what form the expenditure has been received and whether or not the employer has had a disallowance.

Motor mileage allowance

8.20   The gross amount of motor mileage allowances paid to directors and higher paid employees is chargeable to tax. Relief is given on the business proportion by reference to business miles. For other employees only the 'profit element' is taxable. There is no statutory definition of profit element, but in practice this is taken as the difference between the gross amount received, and the allowable expenditure and capital allowances. Relief is also given for qualifying interest on a loan to buy a car for the same business proportion.

8.21   An administrative arrangement calculating the profit on motor allowances paid known as the fixed profit car scheme ('FPCS') is operated in certain cases. The tax is calculated on any profit element through the employee's PAYE coding, based upon an estimate of business miles in the previous year. If necessary an adjustment is made after the end of the year when the actual figures are returned. Any tax due is then collected or repaid as the case may be through an adjustment to the code or directly by tax assessment.

8.22   Under Simplified Assessing such schemes will still be able to be operated, but full information will need to be provided to employees. Where FPCS is operated an employee will not know until the end of the tax year whether the statutory basis is more beneficial. But if he is to claim relief on the statutory basis he will need full details of mileage and expenses.

Benefits in kind

General position

8.23   The present position regarding the taxability of benefits in kind may be summarised as follows.

(*a*)   There is a general Schedule E charge for goods, property and other assets transferred to employees which can be converted into cash by sale or exchange, tax being imposed by reference to the second-hand value.

(*b*)   This general Schedule E charge has been considerably extended by legislation brought in to deal with items which are incapable of being converted into money, or where the measure of the taxable benefit is less than the commercial benefit, notably in the areas of vouchers/credit tokens, living accommodation, and other benefits applicable to directors and higher paid employees.

(*c*)   Benefits are generally taxable if provided by reason of the employment, whether by the employer or third parties. Also benefits provided for members of the employee's family or household are included.

(*d*) There are a number of exceptions under statute, for example canteens for staff, work place nurseries and some living accommodation.

(*e*) The determination of the taxable amount depends upon the nature of the benefit, being variously linked to cost, the price which the employee would pay and statutory figures. The value of a benefit before any business use deduction is described as the 'cash equivalent'.

(*f*) As regards deductibility for business use, in most cases the employee may deduct from the amount treated as income any amount which would have been deductible if he had incurred the cost out of income from the employment. Exceptions here include company cars instead of mileage allowances, car fuel for private use, vans where the benefit is private use and mobile phones where the benefit is for the use thereof.

8.24 As with expenses and expense payments, the basic structure of the system regarding benefits in kind will not require changing under Simplified Assessing. However, a number of issues do arise in the context of reporting and self-assessing which will need to be resolved. For example, under the present system the cash equivalent of a benefit is sometimes linked to the personal circumstances of the individual employee, and an employer will accordingly not be able to calculate the correct amount without some information from the employee. Moreover, in relation to the cash equivalent of some benefits, for commercial reasons an employer might be reluctant to reveal to an employee his cost of the particular item.

Car, van and fuel benefits

8.25 Relevant information will have to be provided to the employee. The area is quite complicated, since there are various factors which go into the calculation of the benefit in kind for cars, for example list price, extras, the age of the car, the business mileage, the extent to which a car is available for the employee, whether it is a second car, and whether payments have been made by the employee for its use. Moreover, the employer will not necessarily know the business mileage, whether or not the car is a second car and whether there are periods of unavailability for the employee.

8.26 A possible approach is for an obligation on employers to calculate the cash equivalent on the basis that the business mileage was less than 2,500 (or as the case may be 18,000) miles a year and that the car was available to the employee throughout the year, unless the employer specifically knew to the contrary. The system might then permit the employee to adjust the information on his return if he considered it appropriate, for example if he considered that business mileage was in excess of 18,000 miles.

8.27   Similar issues arise in relation to vans and fuel, notably the engine size of the car, whether diesel or petrol is used, whether the car is available for the whole year and whether payments are made by the employee. Again the employer possibly could make certain assumptions as to the availability of the car and other matters unless he knew otherwise to the contrary.

Beneficial loans

8.28   In a case where beneficial loans are provided to an employee by an employer, say at reduced interest rates, the calculation of the cash equivalent is made complicated by the possibility of the interaction with the £30,000 mortgage interest relief and the restriction to the lower rate or less. Changes proposed in *FA 1994* make the calculation of the cash equivalent of a loan separate from any interest relief, but they do not make it possible for employers always to calculate the cash equivalent. This is quite a complicated area and one where detailed information will have to be provided to employees.

Living accommodation

8.29   Where living accommodation is provided by an employer to an employee there is a basic charge by reference to the greater of the rent paid by the employer for the premises or its annual value, the latter being taken from the rating list. Where the cost is over £75,000, the excess is regarded as giving rise to a loan by the employer to the employee who is then charged by reference to the official interest rate on the notional loan. A deduction is permitted for business use or where rent is paid by the employee.

8.30   It seems that under Simplified Assessing there are unlikely to be any particular difficulties in determining the appropriate cash equivalent other than in cases where the property was not valued for rating purposes. In any event, this is an area of the law which is presently under review and there may be changes to the basis of the Schedule E charge prior to the introduction of Simplified Assessing.

Dispensations

8.31   Dispensations are bilateral arrangements between the Inspector and the employer to the effect that certain expense payments (and benefits in kind) need not be included on Form P11D. Dispensations do not reduce any tax liability, as they relate to expenses, and sometimes benefits, for which employees would be able to obtain a matching deduction. Employees are not involved, and there is no requirement on the part of the employer to inform them of arrangements made. Moreover, the Revenue cannot volunteer information to employees because of the confidentiality of the agreement between the employer and the Revenue.

8.32   PAYE does not apply where there is a dispensation. The items need not be shown on Form P11D, and the employee need not show the items on his tax return. Examples are expenses paid in respect of specific claims for allowable items such as business travel, scale rate payments calculated only to reimbursed entertaining expenditure at business occasions where the employer would not claim a deduction, allowable subscriptions, and mileage allowances at or below set levels.

8.33   In principle no change will be required to the system of dispensations under Simplified Assessing. Indeed, in a move towards simplification of the system the trend towards dispensations is likely to be encouraged. But there are issues regarding notification which need to be clarified. For the confidentiality reasons referred to above the Revenue would not be permitted to give the employee details of dispensations agreed with the employer. So an employee might have no knowledge of a dispensation, and might see a mismatch between his own recollection of benefits and the Form P11D. Possibly under Simplified Assessing there will have to be an obligation to let employees know what expenditure and benefits are covered by a dispensation. Alternatively, there could be an arrangement whereby P11Ds were given to employees on the basis that anything which was not shown was covered by a dispensation.

Annual voluntary settlement

8.34   An annual voluntary settlement ('AVS') involves an employer voluntarily settling an employee's tax liability by a single, usually annual, payment. These are typically to cover one-off benefits, such as Christmas parties and/or to save employees facing an unexpected tax charge. An AVS is not based upon statute, but derives from a contract between the employer and the Revenue. There is a dispensation from P11D reporting. Employers do not have to inform employees of their existence, and it seems possible for such a system to be retained under Simplified Assessing with no P11D reporting.

8.35   Normally the Inspector ascertains what proportion of employees are likely to be higher rate taxpayers and calculates a composite rate which is applied to the total of expenditure/benefits. The calculation of the tax is done so the benefits or expenditure are 'grossed up' at the composite rate, to take account of the fact that the employer is paying the employee's tax. There is no individual attribution of income and related tax, and no tax is repaid, even where it might be due. Possibly some formal recognition to AVS is required under Simplified Assessing.

Employer reporting obligation under Simplified Assessing

8.36   Given the various issues raised above, it is inevitable that certain obligations will be imposed upon employers with regard to the provision of information to employees. A balance will have to be struck between a system which ensures that the employee is provided with full information, including information as to the cash equivalent or taxable amount where possible on a timely basis, and one which makes too many compliance demands upon the employer.

8.37 These are issues which are presently being considered by the Revenue, and the outcome of their deliberations will govern the precise reporting requirements. One approach would be to provide employers with an option, either to give full information to the employee in a form prescribed by the Revenue such as a Form P11D, or to have rather greater leeway as to the manner in which data is given to the employee. But whatever approach is adopted, it seems that the following areas will have to be covered.

(*a*) Employers will have to provide employees with a Form P11D or P9D – or an equivalent – by a specified date in addition to the P60.

(*b*) Employers will probably still be required to provide the Revenue with a form P11D, both as a cross check for the Revenue and also to enable the Revenue to determine the employee's tax liability in cases where the employee fails to file his tax return.

(*c*) In the case of expense payments, it seems that the amounts paid and any PAYE applied to the payment would have to be reported to the employee. Except where dispensations have been given, gross payments are likely to have to be shown, and any amounts which the employee has made good.

(*d*) In the case of benefits in kind, employers may have to work out the cash equivalent, possibly with an obligation to ascertain more facts than are at present available to them (for example having to satisfy themselves that business mileage exceeds/is less than 2,500/18,000 miles), indicating also whether and how PAYE has been applied and any amounts made good by the employee.

(*e*) In cases where the taxable amount of a benefit in kind depends on information not available to the employer, there may be a requirement to provide whatever information the employer has to the employee in order to enable the employee to calculate the cash equivalent and to calculate any deduction claimed.

(*f*) In the event that there have been no taxable expenses or payments, the employer may be required to notify employees specifically to this effect.

(*g*) It seems that employees will probably need to be informed by their employers about any dispensations that exist.

(*h*) Employers may be obliged to use their best endeavours to obtain from third parties information about benefits provided to employees, and return the cash equivalent.

Employee responsibilities under Simplified Assessing

8.38   Taking the matters earlier mentioned into account, and in particular the obligation to make a full return of income, the requirements which are likely to fall upon employees under Simplified Assessing will encompass the following.

(*a*)   An obligation to report expense payments received from employers which are taxable.

(*b*)   An obligation to report all benefits, notably the cash equivalent of benefits from employer and third parties, substantially based upon the P11D or equivalent. In the event that this information is available from sources other than the employer, i.e. third parties, this would also need to be reported.

(*c*)   The employee would need to make a claim for available deductions under *ICTA 1988, s 198*, or other applicable *sections*.

(*d*)   Allied to the above will be obligations to keep detailed records, in particular Forms P11D, 9D and P60; to keep originals or photocopies of receipts and other documents, and to keep data where these differ from Form P11D.

8.39   Provision would also have to be made in the event that the P11D was delivered late to the employee, or not at all. Some form of liaison system between the employee and the employer might be introduced statutorily to accelerate the process. But if this failed to elicit the information from the employer, it seems that the system would have to be based upon the employee giving best estimates of the figures, followed by an amended return when he was in full possession of the data.

Underpayments under PAYE

8.40   Provision will be required for tax underpaid by an employee taxed under PAYE. At present the Inspector decides whether to collect the underpayment by coding out under PAYE in the following year, or by direct assessment. Under Simplified Assessing this will be possible where the taxpayer chooses Revenue assessment, as the Inspector can inform the taxpayer before 31 January whether the balance needs to be paid then, or whether it will be coded out.

In the case of self-assessment such an option for coding out would not be easy to provide. Possibly in any event the balance should be paid with the return in January.

Chapter 9

Settlements and Estates in the Course of Administration

Introduction

9.1   Simplified Assessing has no special provisions for the taxation of income and gains of settlements and estates of deceased persons. The position of trustees and personal representatives under the existing law is thus unaffected. Likewise beneficiaries under settlements, and those entitled to income from the estates of deceased persons, will be taxable in the same way as before.

9.2   As regards the management provisions under Simplified Assessing, the basic obligations of trustees to file returns are little changed, these being in line with those of individuals. Likewise trustees may self-assess their income tax and CGT liability. Personal representatives are similarly obliged to make returns, and also have the ability to self-assess.

9.3   As to taxability, trustees and personal representatives are generally liable to income tax and CGT in respect of income and gains accruing to them, albeit tax is charged on them at the basic rate and lower rate on dividend income (and in certain cases applicable to trustees at an additional rate, for example where they are trustees of discretionary trusts) but not at the higher rate. The beneficiaries of settlements may be liable to higher rate tax in addition to the lower and basic rates. Persons entitled to the income of estates of deceased persons are also subject to income tax, as described in this Chapter.

9.4   It is not proposed to consider the position of trustees and personal representatives in any depth in this book, given that there have been no changes under Simplified Assessing addressed specifically at trustees and personal representatives. But an outline of their tax position, as well as that of the beneficiaries of trusts and persons entitled to estate income, is appropriate, particularly as regards the amendments made under Simplified Assessing with regard to reporting requirements, the raising of assessments and the collection of tax.

Settlements

General tax position of trustees

9.5   There are no express charging provisions applicable to trustees, other than in the case of trustees for minors and incapacitated persons discussed below. However, it is well established that trustees are generally assessable in respect of trust income; see for example *Reid's Trustees v IRC 1929 14 TC 512*. Under *FA 1989, s 151*, income arising to trustees of a settlement may be assessed and charged on and in the name of any one or more of the trustees. But their personal circumstances are not relevant to any question of personal reliefs or higher rate tax, the latter issues being linked to the total income of individuals.

9.6   Accordingly trustees are subject to income tax at the basic rate on trust income, or in the case of shares in UK companies, with a tax credit equal to the lower rate. However, income of 'accumulation and maintenance' or discretionary trusts is subject to the 'special' trust rate, being the sum of the basic rate and the additional rate, presently 35 per cent. Trustees are likewise chargeable to CGT on chargeable gains accruing from the disposal of trust assets. The rate of CGT depends upon the particular circumstances of each trust, in particular whether a beneficiary has an interest in possession therein, or whether it is a discretionary or accumulation and maintenance trust.

Reporting and self-assessing by trustees

9.7   Under Simplified Assessing trustees will continue to have an obligation to file returns as set out in *TMA 1970, s 8A* as amended by *FA 1994, s 178(2)* (see 10.10 below). Trustees will also have the ability to self-assess (see 11.5). The general provisions regarding Revenue audit and collection of tax outlined in later Chapters also apply.

Trustees for minors and incapacitated persons

9.8   A person who is legally incapacitated may be assessed and charged to tax through his trustee or guardian. [*TMA 1970, s 72(1)*]. 'Incapacitated person' means an infant, person of unsound mind, lunatic, idiot and insane person. [*TMA 1970, s 118(1)*]. The powers contained in *TMA 1970, ss 7* and *8* (see 10.5 and 10.10 below) relating to the notification of chargeability and the submission of personal tax returns are sufficiently wide to cover the case of persons who are in receipt of income which is not their own but in respect of which they are assessable.

Taxability of beneficiaries

9.9   While income of a trust in the first instance bears tax in the trustees hands as outlined above, whether by deduction at source or direct assessment, it will in certain cases form part of the total income of the beneficiaries. Such cases include those where:

(i) a beneficiary has a vested interest in income, regardless of whether he has actually received it;

(ii) amounts in the nature of income are paid or applied to a beneficiary who is not entitled as of right to that income; and

(iii) other payments made to a beneficiary which have the character of income in his hands, albeit that they are derived from capital (*Brodie's Trustees v IRC 1933 17 TC 432*).

Reporting and self-assessing by beneficiaries

9.10   In all cases where a beneficiary is in receipt of taxable income that beneficiary, as well as the trustees, will have a reporting obligation under Simplified Assessing. This should pose no problem where trust income is actually paid to the beneficiary on a timely basis, and he is aware that the payment is indeed income. But the position is rather more difficult in cases where income has arisen to which the beneficiary is entitled, but which he has not actually received, and indeed which he may not know about.

9.11   Indeed, there may even be cases where the beneficiary's precise entitlement is unclear as a matter of law, for example in the case of a demerger where there is doubt whether the shares in the company demerged constitute income or capital in the trustees' hands. Likewise there may be cases of the kind described in 9.9(iii) where the source of the payment is capital, but where case law may suggest that it nevertheless constitutes income in the beneficiary's hands.

9.12   There are no provisions in the Simplified Assessing legislation requiring the trustees actually to notify beneficiaries of such matters. In this regard the issue is akin to that of information reporting of benefits in kind etc. by employers to employees as discussed in Chapter 8, where legislation may be expected in *FA 1995*. It is not clear whether there will be corresponding legislation for trustees and beneficiaries or whether, for example, this is a matter which will be dealt with by some form of code of Revenue practice, or at all.

9.13   It may be that a beneficiary will have to use estimates in those cases where he is unsure of the position, adopting the procedure outlined in 11.28 *et seq*. Moreover, in cases where he has received payments which are from a capital source, but which may have the quality of recurrence in his hands, or where it is uncertain whether a receipt in the trustees hands is capital or income in, for example, the case of a demerger, the beneficiary may perhaps avail himself of any post-transaction rulings provisions (see 11.40). But beneficiaries must be mindful of their possible exposure to surcharges, interest and penalties if they are in default, as outlined in the following Chapters.

Personal representatives

General position

9.14 On a person's death, his property vests in his personal representatives, whose responsibility is to administer the estate by getting in the property, discharging the deceased's debts, and distributing the residue to the persons entitled under the Will or intestacy. They are liable for any tax chargeable on the deceased, albeit to the extent of assets of the deceased, out of which they may recover any payments made. [*TMA 1970, s 74*].

9.15 Moreover, during the administration period, the income of the estate is at common law that of the personal representatives, in their representative capacity, rather than that of the beneficiaries. Accordingly, income other than that received under deduction of tax is, under the present system, in the first place assessable on them in accordance with the various schedules. Personal representatives are not entitled to any personal reliefs but other statutory reliefs and deductions may be available, for example loss relief for trading losses. Under *FA 1989, s 151*, the assessment may be raised in the name of one or more of the personal representatives.

9.16 Personal representatives will also be liable to CGT in respect of chargeable gains accruing on disposals of assets (other than to legatees, where there is no chargeable gain and the personal representatives' acquisition is treated as if it had been the legatee's acquisition). [*TCGA 1992, s 62(4)*].

Reporting and self-assessing by personal representatives

9.17 The notification and reporting obligations of individuals as outlined in the following Chapter extend to personal representatives, since they are included within the ambit of 'persons chargeable to income tax and CGT' within *TMA 1970, ss 7* and *8*. Accordingly personal representatives also have the ability to self-assess as outlined in Chapter 11, should they choose.

9.18 Personal representatives also fall within the scope of *TMA 1970, s 13* which enables the Revenue to require returns from a person in receipt of money or value, profits or gains, belonging to another. There are also further specific reporting provisions relating to personal representatives contained in *TA 1988, s 700(4)* which enable an Inspector to require a personal representative to furnish him within a period of not less than 28 days with such particulars as he considers necessary for determining the income tax liability arising from estates in the course of administration.

General position of legatees

9.19   As indicated above, during the course of administration of an estate, the income is in the first place assessable on the personal representatives. But such income may also be taken into account in determining the total income of the persons who are ultimately entitled to it.

9.20   The legislation is contained in *TA 1988, ss 695–702*, and distinguishes between those persons who have an 'absolute interest' and those who have a 'limited interest' in residue. A beneficiary has an absolute interest where the capital of the residue, or part of it, is properly payable to him or for his benefit, or would be so payable if the residue had been ascertained. [*TA 1988, s 701(1)*]. A person has a limited interest where he does not have an absolute interest, but where income of the residue, or part of it, would be payable to him if the residue had been ascertained. [*TA 1988, s 701(3)*].

Absolute interest

9.21   In the case of a person with an absolute interest, provisionally he is taxed on the grossed up equivalent of amounts paid to him as income, or on the actual amounts paid in respect of a foreign estate up to the amount of the residuary income. Once the administration has been completed, there is then an adjustment. The person's share of the residuary income for each tax year is then taxed upon him for that year, and the provisional assessments are adjusted accordingly. Thus the final apportionment is by reference to the years in which the income actually arose. The detailed provisions are contained in *TA 1988, s 696*.

Limited interest

9.22   A person with a limited interest in residue is first taxed on the grossed up equivalent of any actual payments made as income distributions in the administration period. On completion of the administration, the total payments are allocated to the various years of assessment as if they had accrued from day-to-day, and are grossed up at the basic rate (or if dividends, at the lower rate). The income which has been provisionally assessed is then adjusted as necessary to the final figures.

Reporting and self-assessing by legatees

9.23   The position of persons who have income from estates in the course of administration is no different from that of other taxpayers. They have the obligation to file returns and the ability to self-assess.

9.24   As with the position of beneficiaries under settlements, there may be problems in ascertaining information, in which case the same considerations as set out in 9.12 above apply. Again some form of code of Revenue practice may be anticipated here.

Chapter 10

Notices, Returns, Record-keeping, Claims and Elections

Introduction

10.1   The machinery for the administration and collection of tax is contained in *TMA 1970*, which consolidated the provisions in earlier legislation. This book is concerned to explain the changes made under Simplified Assessing, rather than to provide a detailed explanation of the entire system. For this readers are referred to Tolley's *Taxes Management Provisions*. But a brief overview may be helpful prior to a consideration of the changes made by *FA 1994*.

10.2   Taxes are under the care and management of the Commissioners of Inland Revenue. [*TMA 1970, s 1(1)*]. Referred to as 'the Board', they consist of a Chairman, two Deputy Chairmen and presently four other senior civil servants. The representative of the Revenue who generally deals with the taxpayer or his agent is the local district inspector, officially 'HM Inspector of Taxes' and his staff. Their principal functions under the current system are to examine tax returns and the accounts of businesses, compute the profits for tax purposes, and then raise and subsequently agree the tax assessments with the taxpayer or his agent. Tax is collected by a separate Collector of Taxes, also a Revenue Official.

10.3   Later Chapters in this book look more closely at the rules relating to the assessment of tax, particularly the new system of self-assessment, the rights of appeal which remain open to taxpayers, the provisions for payment of tax, and the sanctions of the Revenue against non-compliance. This Chapter examines the machinery for information gathering in the light of *FA 1994*.

10.4   In this regard there are a series of existing provisions in *TMA 1970* which enable Inspectors to obtain information about taxpayers, notably the right of an Inspector to require the taxpayer to make a return of his income, profits and gains. The present system relating to information collection and the requirement of taxpayers to submit tax returns is substantially retained under Simplified Assessing. But a number of changes have been made to reflect the general principle of self-assessment. This Chapter also considers the amended procedures regarding the making of claims and elections by the taxpayer. The new legislation in *FA 1994* generally adopts the neutral expression 'Officer of the Board', in lieu of 'Inspector of Taxes'.

Notification of liability to income tax and CGT

10.5 The provisions regarding notification of chargeability to tax are contained in *TMA 1970, s 7*. Their purpose is to ensure that every person who is chargeable to income tax or CGT is duly 'logged in' with the Revenue, so that he can be sent a tax return. These provisions are slightly amended as from 1995/96 to reflect the new system. [*FA 1994, 19 Sch 1(2)*]. They come into force earlier than the other self-assessment provisions to ensure that the Revenue are informed of all taxpayers likely to be affected by the new rules.

10.6 Thereafter every person who is chargeable to income tax or capital gains tax, and has not received a tax return, must notify the Revenue within six months of the end of the year of assessment. [*TMA 1970, s 7(1) (2)*]. This compares with twelve months under the present system, and is the principal change.

10.7 However there is no reporting obligation if the person has no chargeable gains and all his income falls into one or more of the following categories:

(*a*) it is chargeable under Schedule E and has been taxed or taken into account under PAYE (including benefits in kind);

(*b*) it has already been assessed or taken into account in computing his tax liability; or

(*c*) basic or lower rate income tax has been deducted (or treated as deducted) or the income consists of dividends from UK resident companies, and the person is not liable to higher rate tax.

[*TMA 1970, s 7(3)–(7)*].

10.8 If a person fails to comply with his reporting obligation, he is liable to a penalty of up to the tax which is due and unpaid by the following 31 January [*substituted TMA, s 7(8)*] and see 14.17 below, which is the same penalty as at present. It is to be noted that there is no penalty provided that tax is paid on time even if a taxpayer has been dilatory in notifying the Revenue as to his liability. Otherwise there is a significant potential cost for those who are behind in notifying the Revenue.

Example 1

Mr Blank only notified the Revenue in January 2000 that he had taxable income in 1998/99. He made a payment in January 2000 of £10,000 but the actual tax liability was £15,000. The balance of £5,000 was only paid in

March 2000 after the return had been sent to him and the correct amount of tax calculated. He is potentially liable for a penalty of up to £5,000.

10.9 The reason given by the Revenue for the reduction in the notification period from twelve months to six months was that otherwise notification at the end of the permitted period could lead to returns being issued for two years, followed by estimated assessments if the returns were not submitted properly. This was an example of the wasteful procedures that Simplified Assessing should avoid. Moreover, there could be an advantage in delaying notification to the last possible moment. For example, a twelve-month period would mean that notification for chargeability in 1997/98 would only have to be made by April 1999. The return for 1997/98 would then need to be submitted and the tax paid within three months (see 13.12 below) which would be July 1999 at the earliest. This would be at least six months after the normal final payment date of 31 January 1999, and would be unfair on those who notified the Revenue earlier. Nevertheless the six-month period is quite short and can be a trap for those uninitiated in the tax system, notably non-resident individuals taking up UK residence, or for example taxpayers within PAYE who find themselves in receipt of additional non-Schedule E income.

Tax returns of individuals and trustees

10.10 The provisions in *TMA 1970, ss 8* and *8A*, relating to the submission of tax returns by individuals and trustees, are amended with effect from 1996/97 by *FA 1994, s 178* to reflect the principle of self-assessment, although the information requirements are essentially the same.

10.11 Where a tax return is sent by the Revenue to an individual or trustee, this must be completed and sent back to the Revenue together with any accounts, statements and documents as may reasonably be required. [*TMA 1970, ss 8(1), 8A(1)*]. The requirement for 'documents' is a new one, and may perhaps be linked with the new requirement to keep records (see 10.29) and the Revenue's enquiry powers (see 12.7 *et seq.*). The reporting obligations are also applicable to personal representatives (see 9.17).

Filing deadline – self-assessment

10.12 The general rule under the new provisions is that the return has to be filed by 31 January following the end of the year of assessment. [*TMA 1970, ss (1A)(a), 8A(1A)(a)*]. But this deadline only applies to taxpayers who self-assess. In their case the return must also include the self-assessment (see 11.7). [*TMA 1970, s 9(1); FA 1994, s 179*]. Moreover, where the tax return is only sent to the taxpayer after 31 October following the end of the year of assessment, the time limit for filing (and self-assessment) is three months from the sending of the return. [*TMA 1970, ss 8(1A)(b), 8A(1A)(6)*]. There are penalties for late filing (see 14.18). It is understood that there will be a Revenue practice statement dealing with these issues, and that there will be a 14-day period of grace before a penalty is imposed.

Example 2

Mr Green is sent a tax return on 1 July 1998 in respect of 1997/98. Assuming he wishes to self-assess the deadline for filing is 31 January 1999. However, if the return had been issued on 1 December 1998, the deadline for filing would be 28 February 1999.

Filing deadline – Revenue assessment

10.13 Where a taxpayer does not want to self-assess, but prefers to leave it to the Revenue, generally the return has to be sent back to the Revenue by 30 September following the end of the year of assessment. [*TMA 1970, s 9(2)*]. This is earlier than the current filing date of 31 October, and the date has been brought forward to assist the Revenue in calculating the person's tax liability. In the consultation process the Revenue indicated that since the annual coding exercise was concentrated in October, November and December returns would be needed by the end of September if the information was to be taken into account in the coding.

10.14 However, if the return is only sent to the taxpayer after 31 July he is still permitted to require the Revenue to make the assessment if he sends back the return within two months.

Example 3

Mr White is sent a tax return on 1 July 1999 in respect of 1998/99. If he does not wish to self-assess the return must be filed by 30 September 1999. If the return is only sent to him on 1 September 1999 he must send the return back to the Revenue by 31 October 1999 for them to make the assessment.

10.15 Where the taxpayer is a partner in a profession, trade or partnership, the return is to include his share of any income or loss as reported in the partnership statement referred to in 10.26 and made under *TMA 1970, s 12AB; FA 1994, s 185*. [*TMA 1970, s 8(1B)(1C); FA 1994, s 178(1)*].

Form of return

10.16   The form of the tax return will be substantially amended to reflect the move from the previous year to current year basis and self-assessment. Drafts have been prepared by the Revenue with input from returns used in other countries with self-assessment systems, and these are under consideration with the consultative bodies. Electronic return submission is also a probability. The stated objective is that taxpayers should be able to complete the return correctly within the filing dates without necessarily having to seek assistance from the Revenue or professional advisers. Laudable objective though this is, the authors have a natural scepticism about the return achieving this objective in view of the complexities inherent in the tax system and the form of the legislation.

Tax returns of companies

10.17   The obligation of a company to complete a tax return is contained in *TMA 1970, s 11* as amended by *FA 1994, s 181*, which has already been amended under Pay and File for accounting periods ending after 30 September 1993. The return may call for such information, accounts and reports relevant to the application of the *Corporation Tax Acts* to the company as are stipulated in the notice. [*TMA 1970, s 11(1A)*].

10.18   The only modification under Simplified Assessing is the addition to *TMA 1970, s 11* of new *subsections 2A* and *2B* which apply to a company carrying on a profession, trade or business in partnership with another person or persons. The company must include in the return its share of any income, loss or charge for the period concerned as shown in the partnership statement prepared by the partnership. This reflects the general changes relating to partnerships and reporting discussed next.

Tax returns of partnerships

10.19   The provisions regarding partnership tax returns are presently contained in *TMA 1970, s 9*. For 1996/97 and subsequent years these provisions are replaced by a new *TMA 1970, s 12AA* by *FA 1994, s 184*, which reflects the significant changes in partnership tax set out in Chapter 7, in particular the changes from a joint partnership assessment to a separate assessment for each partner. The changes and information requirements in the legislation are quite extensive. The legislation, however, really only provides a framework, which the Revenue have indicated will be expanded by practice procedures in due course.

10.20   Where a profession, trade or business is carried on by two or more persons in partnership, a Revenue Officer will be empowered to serve a notice either on the partners as a body [*TMA 1970, s 12AA(2)*] or on a particular partner [*TMA 1970, s 12AA(3)*] requiring a return to be made to facilitate an income tax or corporation tax assessment. In the case of a notice on the partners as a body this may be given to such person 'as is identified in accordance with rules given with the notice'. Otherwise it may be given to any or each partner. There is no guidance from the legislation as to how any particular partner is to be identified. But the Revenue have intimated that their ability to issue a return to any partner is a fall back position only, and that if a return is duly made by the partners as a body they will not seek a return from any individual partner. Indeed they will issue the return to a nominated partner if requested. The selected person must deliver the return to the Revenue, together with such accounts and statements as are required. [*TMA 1970, s 12AA(1)– (3)*].

10.21 The notice may require different information, accounts and statements for different periods, or in relation to different descriptions of sources of income. [*TMA 1970, s 12AA(8)*]. Hence all income (not just trading income) is covered. Moreover, the provisions reflect the fact that the partnership period of account may not coincide with the normal basis period for a particular class of income. The return may also require different information, accounts and statements in relation to different descriptions of partnerships. [*TMA 1970, s 12AA(9)*]. The return must also include a 'partnership statement', as explained in 10.26 below.

10.22 If there have been any disposals of partnership property in the period, the return is to contain the details that would be required for a capital gains tax computation if the partnership were chargeable. Details of all acquisitions of partnership property are also to be given. [*TMA 1970, s 12AA(7)*]. However, the Revenue have intimated that information about a reallocation of property within the firm would not fall within this subsection.

10.23 The return is to include a declaration of the names, residence (which, in the case of a company means its registered office and in the case of individuals is to be their address) and tax references of anyone who has been a partner in any part of the period to which the return relates. The purpose of requiring this information is that:

(*a*) an automatic cross check of arithmetic can be made to see that individual partner's returns are consistent with the partnership return;

(*b*) any formal notices relevant to the partnership can if necessary be issued to individual partners if the notice is relevant to their personal tax liability; and

(*c*) when final figures are agreed at the end of an audit, notice of conclusion of the review and amended computations of individual liability to tax can be issued automatically to all partners.

The person making the return also has to make a declaration to the best of his knowledge that it is correct and complete. [*TMA 1970, s 12AA(6)*].

10.24   Where at least one of the partners is an individual, the filing date for the return (as specified in the notice) is to be no later than 31 January following the end of the year of assessment, or if notice is served on the partners after 31 October no later than three months from the date of issue of the return. [*TMA 1970, s 12AA(4)*]. Where at least one of the partners is a company, the filing date is no later than one year after the period in respect of which the return is issued, except that if the notice is served more than nine months after the end of that period the filing date is no later than three months from the issue of the return. [*TMA 1970, s 12AA(5)*]. In the event that the partnership consists of at least one individual and one company the filing date is the latest of the above dates.

10.25   It is to be noted that the requirement to submit a return extends to a 'business' carried on in partnership. This is wider than the current requirements which do not extend to a business which is not a trade. It seems that this is aimed at joint commercial activities falling short of a trade. The Revenue have intimated that not every form of joint ownership will necessarily constitute a business, and that they have not sought to prejudge the issue. Rather they are content to let joint owners file as partners in a business should they wish (see 7.10).

Partnership statement

10.26   As part of the mechanism for self-assessment, a partnership return delivered to the Revenue under the above provisions must now include what is described as a 'partnership statement'. This is a statement of:

(*a*)   the income or loss from each source which has accrued to, or been sustained by, the partnership for each period of account ending in the period covered by the tax return; and

(*b*)   any charges on income for the period.

The statement must also set out the share of each partner in such income, loss or charge so that he can then self-assess. [*TMA 1970, s 12AB(1); FA 1994, s 185*]. In relation to changes in accounting date it is understood that the requirements for a valid change in *TA 1988, s 62A; FA 1994, s 203* apply on the level of the partnership, and not the individual partner (see 2.25 above).

Record-keeping

Background

10.27   Extensive provisions have been introduced laying down particulars as to the records which a taxpayer is now required to maintain. Previously (and unlike VAT) there was no general obligation on the part of the taxpayer to retain records for tax purposes. Some form of record-keeping was indirectly imposed by the ability of the Revenue to raise an estimated assessment of a substantial amount where there was no return, or where they doubted the veracity of the information in a taxpayer's return and accounts. If the taxpayer disputed the assessment, and could not resolve the matter by agreement with the Inspector, his only remedy would be to appeal to the Commissioners. On appeal the onus would be on the taxpayer to provide evidence to satisfy the Commissioners that the assessment was excessive. [*TMA 1970, s 50(6)*]. The most obvious form of evidence would be documentary evidence, specifically records of business transactions. It would, however, be open to the taxpayer to convince the Commissioners of the merits of his case by his own oral testimony and by other forms of evidence other than that contained in the primary documents relating to his trade, profession or vocation.

10.28   The Revenue considered that in the new self-assessment system, enforcement of data retention by means of estimated assessments and setting down cases for appeal was quite inappropriate. Moreover, given that greater responsibility was placed on the taxpayer to determine his own tax liability, checks and balances should be provided by detailed powers of audit. Linked with this was the view that obligations should be imposed upon the taxpayer to maintain full documentary evidence to support the figures used in self-assessment. The Revenue also considered that a simpler procedure for obtaining information than that contained in *TMA 1970, s 20* should be implemented.

Records to be maintained

10.29   The new provisions are to be found in *TMA 1970, s 12B* as inserted by *FA 1994, 19 Sch 3*. Any person who may be required to deliver a tax return under *TMA 1970, ss 8, 8A, 11* or *12AA* (individuals, trustees, companies and partnerships) must keep certain records for the period set out in 10.35 (generally five years from the filing date for those in business, with six years for companies). The records are all those which may be required for the purpose of enabling the taxpayer to make and deliver a correct and complete tax return. [*TMA 1970, s 12B(1)(a)*].

10.30   In the case of a person carrying on a trade, profession or business these records are specifically to include records of all amounts received and expended in the course of the trade, profession or business and the matters in respect of which the receipts and expenditure took place. Furthermore, if the trade involves dealing in goods, the records must also be of all sales and purchases of goods made in the course of the trade. All supporting documents (including accounts, books, deeds, contracts, vouchers and receipts) relating to these various items must be retained. [*TMA 1970, ss 12B(3)(6)*].

10.31   The duty to preserve records may be discharged by the preservation of the information contained in them, and a copy of any document is to be admissible in any proceedings before the Commissioners. [*TMA 1970, s 12B(4)*]. The latter differs from the position at present where, strictly speaking, any documents used in proceedings before the Commissioners have to be proved in accordance with the law of evidence.

10.32   It will be seen that these provisions impose a comprehensive obligation on the part of taxpayers engaged in a trade, profession or business. Virtually all records of the business and all transactions therein, even down to the smallest petty cash document, are apparently to be retained. The Revenue have said that they will issue a Code of Practice indicating what records they would expect to see. There is a sanction against taxpayers who fail to comply with their obligations, taking the form of a penalty up to £3,000. [*TMA 1970, s 12B(5)*]. It will remain to be seen in practice how strictly the Revenue seek to apply these provisions and exact penalties in cases of default, although they have indicated that they will apply the same standards of mitigation in respect of the gravity of the offence as in any other case.

10.33   It is also to be noted that the obligation to retain detailed records is imposed not just upon those engaged in a trade or profession, but also those engaged in a business. The latter would include persons who, although not actually carrying on a trade, within the precise meaning of the term as interpreted by case law, were nevertheless involved in quasi-trading activities. A business could include, for example, an investment activity carried on in a businesslike manner. *Prima facie* it would also extend to certain forms of property letting, but the legislation specifically provides that a person engaged in the letting of property is to be treated as carrying on a trade [*TMA 1970, s 12B(6)(a)*] for the purpose of record-keeping.

10.34   Vocations are apparently excluded from these detailed provisions regarding data retention, but the extension of the obligations to persons engaged in a business may in appropriate cases bring in persons carrying on a vocation, where the vocation is carried on in a businesslike way.

Period for retention of records

10.35   In the case of an individual carrying on a trade, profession or business alone or in partnership all relevant records have to be preserved until the fifth anniversary of the 31 January following the end of the year of assessment. In the case of a company all records have to be preserved until the sixth anniversary of the end of the accounting period in question. [*TMA 1970, s 12B(2)(a)*].

10.36   In any other case records have to be kept until the first anniversary of the 31 January following the end of the year of assessment, except that where a tax return is delivered after 31 January, they must be kept until the quarter day following the first anniversary of the day on which the return is delivered. [*TMA 1970, s 12B(2)(b)*]. This date coincides with the expiry of the period during which the Revenue are empowered to make an enquiry into a taxpayer's affairs. As the legislation is now drafted those persons who carry on a trade, profession or business have to retain non-trading records (e.g. details of investment income) for the full five-year period mentioned in 10.35, but it seems that this was not the intention, and the legislation is to be amended accordingly.

10.37 In all cases where a Revenue enquiry is taking place, the records have to be kept until the completion of the enquiry.

Claims, elections and revisions

10.38 The provisions for making claims are contained in a substituted *TMA 1970, s 42; FA 1994, 19 Sch 13*, which has been revised in the light of the current year basis and self-assessing. They apply in all cases where relief is given, or any other thing is to be done on the making of a claim, election or notice (unless it is specifically provided to the contrary). [*TMA 1970, s 42(1)(10)*]. The general rule under the new system is that all claims should be made by inclusion in the tax return wherever possible. This reflects the move to self-assessing as part of the return and the idea that income and gains, and reliefs and allowances, are brought together to arrive at net taxable income and gains.

10.39 Claims and elections broadly fall into three categories:

(*a*) those relating to income and gains of the year covered by the return;

(*b*) those relating to income and gains of future years which will be made in advance; and

(*c*) those that allow carry back to earlier years, permitting a revision of an assessment or self-assessment.

Most claims will fall into the first category, and these will generally be dealt with retrospectively by inclusion in the return for the year as described in 10.41 *et seq.* For other kinds of claims, separate formal notices will be required.

10.40 A claim may be made on behalf of an incapacitated person by his trustee, guardian, tutor or curator. Moreover a person who is charged with tax on the profits of another under *TMA 1970, Pt VIII, ss 78–85* (persons responsible for tax payable by non-residents) may make a claim for relief by discharge or repayment of that tax. [*TMA 1970, s 42(8)*].

Claims to be included in tax return

10.41 As indicated, the majority of claims and elections will be made with the return, and the form of the return will reflect this. Certain reliefs will be claimed merely by a deduction of the relevant amount (such as personal allowances). Others will be claimed by adoption of a particular treatment such as the use of a 'tick box' in the return, or by set-off of trade losses. Others again will be in a formal claim either on the return or as a separate claim to be submitted with the return. In some circumstances it will be impossible or inappropriate for a claim to be made as part of a return, and the procedure set out in 10.45 *et seq.* will then apply. This separation between the two procedures does not depend on the type of claim, but purely on whether a claim in the return is appropriate or possible.

10.42   The amended legislation accordingly provides that where a taxpayer has been sent a tax return a claim has to be made by being included in the relevant return, or an amended return as the case may be, if it could be made by being so included. [*TMA 1970, s 42(2)(5)*]. In the case of companies, this does not extend to a claim for payment of a tax credit which will continue to be made on Form CT61. [*TMA 1970, s 42(4)*]. Another exception is where the claim relates to Schedule E and is to be taken into account in the application of the PAYE rules. [*TMA 1970, s 42(3)*]. This latter aspect is to be dealt with in *FA 1995*.

10.43   When a tax return can be amended, such as under the repairs procedure outlined in 11.18 below (generally twelve months from the filing date) any claims which would generally be included in a tax return and which are made subsequent to the filing date are to be made by an amendment to the return and the self-assessment. The same applies to an amendment of a return following the resolution of a Revenue enquiry (see 10.49 and 12.27 *et seq.*).

Partnership claims expressly to be included in return

10.44   In the case of partnerships where a return form has been sent to a particular partner, a claim under any of the following *sections* is specifically to be included in the return. (In other cases it is to be made by any person nominated by the partners for the purpose.) [*TMA 1970, s 42(6)*]. *TA 1988, s 84* (gift to educational establishment), *s 91B* (waste disposal; preparation expenditure), *s 101(2)* (value of stock-in-trade on discontinuance), *s 120(2)* (rent for electric line wayleave), *s 401* (pre-trading expenditure), *s 471* (exchange of securities), *s 472* (securities issued in connection with nationalisation), *s 484* (savings banks), *s 504* (letting of furnished holiday accommodation), *s 531* (know-how), *ss 534* and *535* (copyrights), *s 537A* (payments for designs), *s 538* (painters, sculptors and other artists), *ss 570* and *571(4)* (industry rationalisation schemes), *s 723(3)* (foreign securities: delayed remittances), *s 810* (capital allowances and to secure double tax relief), *5 Sch 2, 6* and *11*, (herd basis). *FA 1989, s 43(5)* (Schedule E emoluments and computation of Schedule D liability). *CAA 1990, s 1* (enterprise zones), *s 11* (long lease of industrial building), *s 17* (mining structures), *ss 22* and *23* (first year allowances), *ss 24* and *25* (writing-down allowances), *ss 30, 31* and *33* (ships), *s 37* (short life assets), *ss 48* and *49* (leased plant and machinery), *ss 53* and *55* (fixtures), *s 68(5)* and *(9)* (films, tapes and discs), *ss 77* and *78* (successions), *ss 124A* and *129(2)* (agricultural buildings), *s 140(3)* (allowance in taxing trade), *s 141* (other income tax allowances) and *s 158* (connected persons). *F(No 2)A 1992, ss 41* and *42* (expenditure on films).

Claims not in tax return

10.45   A new *TMA 1970, 1A Sch* inserted by *FA 1994, 19 Sch 35* sets out the procedure which is to apply for the making of a claim where the claim is not included on the taxpayer's return, and does not relate to a matter dealt with by a PAYE adjustment. [*TMA 1970, s 42(11)*]. This procedure therefore applies, for example, to cases where a retrospective claim is made within the two (or six) year period which may be allowed to enable an adjustment to be made to a prior year's liability.

10.46   A claim is to be made to a Revenue Officer, except where there is specific provision requiring the claim to be made to the Board, and it has to be in the prescribed form. [*TMA 1970, 1A Sch 2(1)(3)*]. There has to be a declaration to the effect that all the particulars given are correctly stated to the best of the information and belief of the person making the claim. [*TMA 1970, 1A Sch 2(4)*]. The form of claim may require:

(*a*)   a statement of the tax which is to be discharged or repaid to give effect to the claim;

(*b*)   a return of profits in support; and

(*c*)   any particulars of assets acquired as may be required in a tax return containing information about chargeable gains.

[*TMA 1970, 1A Sch 2(5)*].

10.47   No claim requiring the repayment of tax is to be made unless the claim has documentary proof of payment. [*TMA 1970, 1A Sch 2(2)*]. In the case of a claim by or on behalf of a non-UK resident, or a person claiming to be not resident, not ordinarily resident, or not domiciled in the UK, a statement or declaration in support of the claim may be required by way of affidavit. [*TMA 1970, 1A Sch 2(6)*].

10.48   The Revenue are required to give effect to such a claim by a discharge or repayment of tax as soon as is practicable after the claim is made. In the case of a partnership claim, they are likewise required to give effect to the claim or as respects each partner, by a discharge or repayment of tax. [*TMA 1970, 1A Sch 4(1)(2)*].

Revenue powers of enquiry into claims

10.49   The Revenue are also given the same powers to enquire into claims and call for documents as apply to enquiries into tax returns. [*TMA 1970, 1A Sch 5, 6*]. See 12.8 and 12.27 *et seq.*

Amendments to claims/repairs

10.50 As with the 'repairs' procedure relating to a taxpayer's return and self-assessment outlined in 11.18, the Revenue may repair a claim. They can do so at any time within nine months from the day on which the claim is made, correcting any obvious errors or mistakes, whether errors of principle, arithmetical mistakes or otherwise. [*TMA 1970, 1A Sch 3(1)(a)*]. The taxpayer may likewise amend his claim within twelve months from the day on which the claim is made by the appropriate notice on a Revenue Officer. [*TMA 1970, 1A Sch 3(1)(b)*]. However, where the Revenue initiate a formal enquiry into the claim no amendment of the claim may be made thereafter until the enquiry is completed. [*TMA 1970, 1A Sch 3(2)*]. This follows the similar prohibition on repairs to a return as explained in 11.23.

Error or mistake claims – individuals, trustees and companies

10.51 Under the present system a taxpayer who considers that an assessment was excessive by reason of an error or mistake in a return, may make a claim for a repayment of tax within six years after the end of the year of assessment or, if the assessment is to corporation tax, six years after the end of the accounting period to which the assessment relates. This ability to make a repayment claim is retained under Simplified Assessing and applies also when the taxpayer has made a self-assessment. The time limit for such a claim becomes five years from 31 January following the year of assessment to which the return relates for income tax and CGT, and remains at six years after the end of the accounting period to which the return relates for corporation tax. [*TMA 1970, s 33(1) as amended by FA 1994, 19 Sch 8*].

10.52 On receiving the claim the Board are to enquire into the matter, and give by way of repayment such relief as is reasonable and just. [*TMA 1970, s 33(2)*]. However, there is no relief where the return is made on the basis of or in accordance with the practice generally prevailing at the time when it was made, or where the error or mistake was in a claim which was included in the return. [*TMA 1970, s 33(2A); FA 1994, 19 Sch 8*].

Error or mistake claims – partnerships

10.53 Bearing in mind that partnerships are to submit a partnership statement rather than a partnership return the rules have to be amended to deal with errors or mistakes in a partnership statement. This is done by a new *section; TMA 1970, s 33A*, as inserted by *FA 1994, 19 Sch 9* which follows the format of the revised *TMA 1970, s 33*. Any partner ('the representative partner') or his successor may within five years from the filing date make a claim for relief. [*TMA 1970, s 33A(2)(10)*] .The Board are then to enquire into the matter, and make any amendment to the partnership statement to give such relief as is reasonable or just. [*TMA 1970,* *s 33A(3)*]. Where this is done they are to give notice to each partner so that his self-assessment can be amended. [*TMA 1970, s 33A(4)*].

10.54 The Board are to have regard to all the relevant circumstances of the case and are to consider whether the granting of relief would result in the exclusion from the charge to tax of any part of the profits of any of the partners. They may take into consideration a partner's liability in respect of chargeable periods other than that to which the claim relates. [*TMA 1970, s 33A(6)*]. No relief is permitted where the partnership statement was made on the basis of or in accordance with, the practice generally prevailing when the statement was made. [*TMA 1970, s 33A(5)*].

10.55 There is a right of appeal to the Special Commissioners against the Board's decision. They are to hear and determine the appeal in accordance with the principles laid down for the Board to follow in determining the claim. [*TMA 1970, s 33A(7)*]. If either the Board or the representative partner then subsequently require a case to be stated under *TMA 1970, s 56* (necessary to pursue a further appeal to the High Court) that case stated can only be in respect of a point of law arising in connection with the computation of the partnership profits. [*TMA 1970, s 33A(8)*].

General time limits for claims

10.56 The provisions containing the time limits for the making of claims are contained in *TMA 1970, s 43*. At the present time there is generally a six-year time limit from the end of the period to which a claim relates, unless a particular provision specifies a longer or shorter period (sometimes two years). Under an amended *TMA 1970, s 43(1)*, from 1996/97 the time limit for income tax and CGT becomes five years from 31 January following the year of assessment, unless a longer or shorter period is specifically prescribed. [*FA 1994, 19 Sch 14* The period is thus generally linked with the filing date for self-assessment. In the case of corporation tax, the time limit remains at six years from the end of the accounting period to which it relates.

10.57 Where a claim has been made, whether by inclusion in a return or otherwise, and the claimant subsequently discovers that an error or mistake has been made in the claim, he may make a supplementary claim within the time limit for making the original claim. [*TMA 1970, s 42(9)*].

Time limits: special cases

Farm profits averaging

10.58 There is an amendment to the prescribed time limits for claims relating to farm averaging and the relief for fluctuating profits. Where the first of the two years of assessment to which the claim relates is 1996/97 or any subsequent year, a claim is to be made twelve months from 31 January after the end of the second of the years of assessment to which the claim relates. Any further claim must be made before 31 January following the end of the year of assessment following that in which the adjustment is made. [*TA 1988, s 96(8) as amended*].

Copyrights and designs

10.59 There is an amendment to the spreading relief for payments from copyright sales. A claim is to be made within seven years from 31 January following the year of assessment in which the work was first published. [*TA 1988, s 534(5) as amended*]. There is a like amendment in relation to payment for the sales of designs. [*TA 1988, s 537A(5) as amended*].

Herd basis

10.60 There are a number of minor changes relating to the making of elections for the herd basis to apply under *TA 1988, 5 Sch*. Given the specialist nature of the matter, these are not analysed in detail here, but the principal change is that the time limit for an election for individuals and partnerships becomes twelve months after 31 January in the following year of assessment. The time limit for companies remains at two years after the end of the accounting period.

Chapter 11

Assessments to Tax

Introduction

11.1   Under the present system, the process which generally follows that of information gathering described in Chapter 10 is that of assessing the taxpayer to tax. This covers the process from the examination of the completed tax returns to the issue of notices of assessment, stating the income, profits or gains which have been assessed, and the amount of tax payable.

11.2   Except for certain specific cases where the power of assessment is reserved to the Board, assessments are made by an Inspector based upon the information in the return. [*TMA 1970, s 29(1)(a)*]. In cases where no return has been made by a taxpayer, or where the Inspector is dissatisfied with the return, he may make an assessment to the best of his judgment. [*TMA 1970, s 29(1)(b)*].

11.3   Notice of the assessment must be served on the person assessed and must state the date on which it is issued and the time within which an appeal may be made. [*TMA 1970, s 29(5)*]. Once it has been served it cannot be altered except by express provision. [*TMA 1970, s 29(6)*]. The taxpayer has the right of appeal against the assessment within 30 days of the notice. [*TMA 1970, s 31(1)*]. The issue may then subsequently be resolved by agreement with the Inspector. [*TMA 1970, s 54(1)*]. Otherwise, the appeal is to be determined by the General or Special Commissioners under the provisions outlined in Chapter 15. If there is no appeal the assessment generally becomes final.

11.4   The basis of the new system under Simplified Assessing is for the taxpayer to assess his own tax liability. Hence much of the existing assessment machinery is no longer appropriate. The changes to this machinery, and the instances where parts of the existing system are retained, are examined in this chapter.

Self-assessment for individuals and trustees

11.5   The radical change under Simplified Assessing is the move away from assessment by the Inspector in every case. From 1996/97 the taxpayer is permitted, and indeed encouraged, to make his own assessment to income tax and CGT, based upon the information provided in his tax return. This right to self-assess also extends to trustees.

11.6   As part of this self-assessment procedure, the current system with each source of income the subject of a separate assessment, is to be abolished. Income will still be calculated by reference to the existing sources of income, e.g. Schedule D, Cases I, II and III etc., but there is to be a single tax assessment, incorporating all sources of income and CGT. The various strands of income will be aggregated to give a total figure upon which the tax liability is based.

11.7   The self-assessment is to be included in the person's tax return. [*TMA 1970, s 9(1); FA 1994, s 179*]. Hence it must be filed at the latest by 31 January following the end of the year of assessment, unless the return is sent to the taxpayer after 31 October when the deadline is three months from the sending of the return (see 10.12). The tax liability having been so self-assessed, any remaining tax liability for the year of assessment must then be paid. There are no specific provisions in the legislation requiring the Revenue to acknowledge receipt of a return and self-assessment, but it seems that there will be some form of taxpayer statement which will effectively acknowledge receipt.

11.8   In the event that the taxpayer does not wish to self-assess, he may instead leave it to the Revenue to make the assessment, but the tax return must then generally be submitted by 30 September following the end of the year of assessment (see 11.10). Where a taxpayer does self-assess, any reference in *TA 1988* and *TCGA 1992* to a person being assessed to tax, or being charged to tax by an assessment, is to be construed as a reference to self-assessment. [*FA 1994, s 197*].

11.9   In cases where there has been a self-assessment the Revenue have twelve months within which they have the right to enquire into the assessment, i.e. audit the return and the self-assessment. Otherwise, and subject to any 'repairs' made to the return by the taxpayer or the Revenue under the procedure described later in this Chapter and the possibility of 'discovery' by the Revenue in cases of fraud, neglect, or mistake, the self-assessment becomes final and the Revenue are precluded from reopening it.

Revenue assessment where return but no self-assessment filed

11.10   As indicated in 11.8 self-assessment is not compulsory. The taxpayer is permitted to leave all the relevant calculations and the making of the assessment to the Revenue, as under the present system. However the tax return must then be submitted to the Revenue by 30 September following the end of the year of assessment or, if the return is issued after 31 July, within two months of its issue. [*TMA 1970, s 9(2); FA 1994, 179*].

11.11 Where a tax return has been filed by 30 September (or the two-month extended deadline) and it does not include a self-assessment the Revenue must make an assessment on the taxpayer on the basis of the information in the return. Where the return is filed out of time and without any self-assessment the Revenue may make an assessment, although they are not then obliged to base it on the return figures. In either case the taxpayer is to be sent a copy of the assessment, which is treated for all purposes as a self-assessment. [*TMA 1970, s 9(3); FA 1994, s 179*].

11.12 The legislation contemplates that the Revenue will make the assessment without any verification or checking of the underlying information, which is different from the present system where the underlying data in a return, particularly any accounts, may be scrutinised. The Revenue can subsequently open an enquiry into that information should they wish.

Revenue determination where no return filed

11.13 New provisions in *TMA 1970, s 28C* as introduced by *FA 1994, s 190* deal with cases where the taxpayer has been sent a return, but fails to submit it by the filing date. In such cases the Revenue may make a determination to the best of their information and belief of the taxpayer's liability to income tax, CGT or corporation tax. [*TMA 1970, s 28C(1)*]. This is to be served on the taxpayer, and is to state the date of issue. [*TMA 1970, s 28C(2)*].

11.14 The determination may be superseded by a later self-assessment, whether an actual self-assessment or a 'deemed' self-assessment made by the Revenue, and based upon information provided in a return submitted subsequently. Until then it is to count as a self-assessment. [*TMA 1970, s 28C(3)*]. References in *TA 1988* and *TCGA 1992* to a person being assessed to tax, or charged to tax by an assessment, include such determination. [*FA 1994, s 197(1)(b)*]. However, such a determination is not a self-assessment, and it is automatically displaced by the submission of an outstanding return. For the time limits applicable to such determinations and subsequent self-assessment see 11.37.

11.15 Where recovery proceedings have been commenced following such a determination, and before they are concluded the taxpayer makes a self-assessment, the proceedings may be continued as though they were for tax due according to the self-assessment but unpaid. [*TMA 1970, s 28C(4)*]. This is to avoid the necessity of recovery proceedings having to be recommenced.

Procedure where assessment made by Revenue

11.16 Minor changes are made to the assessing procedure which applies where the Revenue make an assessment. The present provisions in *TMA 1970, s 29* are to be replaced by a new *TMA 1970, s 30A* as inserted by *FA 1994, 19 Sch 5*. All assessments which are not self-assessments are to be made by an officer of the Board except for those which in law can only be made by the Board. [*TMA 1970, s 30A(1)*]. Notice of assessment is to be served on the taxpayer, stating the date of issue and the time limit for appealing. [*TMA 1970, s 30A(3)*].

11.17 Notwithstanding that the taxpayer may have income chargeable under more than one *Schedule* (and might therefore receive several assessments representing the different sources of income) a single assessment covering all sources of income may be made. [*TMA 1970, s 30A(2)*]. Notice having been so served, the assessment is not to be altered, except expressly in accordance with the provisions of the *Taxes Acts*, e.g. by an amended self-assessment or by an appeal to the Commissioners. [*TMA 1970, s 30A(4)*]. These provisions generally take effect for 1996/97, although for partnerships in existence at 5 April 1994 they take effect from 1997/98. [*FA 1994, 19 Sch 5(2)*].

Amendments to self-assessments/repairs

11.18 An important feature of the new system is the ability of a taxpayer to amend his return and self-assessment within twelve months of the filing date, colloquially described as 'repairing' the return. [*TMA 1970, s 9(4)(b)*]. This could cover cases, for example, where a taxpayer, having filed his return, subsequently realises he has made a mistake in the computation, or where the self-assessment was initially based on an estimate, and a final figure has since become available. It seems that where the taxpayer repairs his return in these circumstances, although interest will run on any additional tax which is payable, the Revenue will not generally seek to exact penalties.

11.19 Moreover, certain mistakes in a self-assessment (for example an arithmetic error) may also be picked up by the Revenue without any detailed audit or verification of the self-assessment, say, by computer scanner or by a Revenue Officer giving it a cursory check. Where there have been any 'obvious' errors or mistakes (whether errors of principle, arithmetical mistakes or otherwise) the Revenue may within nine months from the date the return is filed, correct them by an appropriate amendment to the self-assessment. [*TMA 1970, s 9(4)(a)*]. As with amendments by the taxpayer, it seems in such cases that the Revenue would not seek to exact penalties, but that such an amendment would be part of the 'customer service' procedure to ensure the smooth and effective working of the new system.

11.20 As to the meaning of an 'obvious' error or mistake, this might be thought as somewhat loose terminology in a taxing statute. The Revenue's view is that it covers mistakes which are self-evident, such as the transposition of figures, arithmetical mistakes and other matters which are obvious in the every day sense of the word. In practice it may well be evident in most cases that a particular error falls within this description.

11.21 It is not clear how the Revenue will deal with cases where they have information in their possession which casts doubt on the correctness of a self-assessment. An obvious example is when a taxpayer's declaration of bank interest does not correspond with the information received by the Revenue from the bank. Where the amounts are relatively small it would appear to be reasonable for the matter to be dealt with by suggesting to the taxpayer that a repair be made, rather than by opening a formal enquiry into the person's tax return.

11.22 There is no specific right of appeal as such against a Revenue repair to a taxpayer's self-assessment. But if a taxpayer disagrees with the Revenue that a repair was appropriate, the Revenue accept that he may simply amend his return and self-assessment as he sees fit, substituting his own figures. This would then supersede the Revenue's repair. If the Revenue disputed what had been done they could open a formal enquiry into the return. (Otherwise, given that a Revenue repair can only be made to 'correct' an error or mistake, it would in an extreme case be open to an aggrieved taxpayer to seek judicial review if the Revenue refused to accept that their repair could be superseded, on the basis that the Revenue amendment was simply not a correction.)

11.23 No amendment of a self-assessment can be made once the Revenue announce their intention to make a formal enquiry into a taxpayer's return, until the enquiry is concluded. [*TMA 1970, s 9(5)*]. This precludes, for example, a series of repairs during the course of an audit. The apparent reason is to prevent the situation whereby a taxpayer made amendments to which the Revenue had to give immediate effect, with a view to disrupting the Revenue enquiry.

11.24 But the Revenue have intimated that it would be expected that the taxpayer would notify the Revenue during the enquiry period if he became aware of any mistakes in the return. Thus amendments would be notified informally. The cooperation of the taxpayer in this way would then be a factor in his favour in determining penalties, in the event that the return and the self-assessment were found to be incomplete or incorrect. Moreover, further payments of tax could be made to stop interest running if the taxpayer considered that these were due.

11.25 Similar provisions to the above apply to enable repairs to be made to partnership statements within the same time periods and on the same grounds. [*TMA 1970, s 12AB(2)(3)*]. Where a statement is so amended (whether by the Revenue or the partner making the return) the Revenue Officer is required to give notice to the various partners to amend their own self-assessments accordingly. [*TMA 1970, s 12AB(4)*]. There is a similar prohibition on repairs once an enquiry has begun. [*TMA 1970, s 12AB(4)*].

Self-assessment for companies

11.26   The self-assessment provisions relating to individuals and trustees are reflected in similar provisions for companies, contained in a new *TMA 1970, s 11AA* as inserted by *FA 1994, s 182*. The difference is that it is compulsory for the return to include a self-assessment of the corporation tax for which the company is chargeable for the particular period. [*TMA 1970, s 11AA(1)*]. Given that the current form of Pay and File return already amounts to a self-assessment, this is no real change.

11.27   However, a new feature is that when there are any obvious errors or mistakes in the self-assessment there is a 'repairs' procedure on the lines of that for individuals and partners described in 11.18 to 11.25. The Revenue are permitted within nine months from delivery of the return to amend the company's self-assessment. [*TMA 1970, s 11AA(2)(a)*]. The company may also submit an amended self-assessment at any time within twelve months of the filing date. [*TMA 1970, s 11AA(2)(b)*]. No amendment can be made once the Revenue have given notice of their intention to enquire into the return until the enquiry is concluded. [*TMA 1970, s 11AA(3)*].

Estimates

11.28   On the date for filing a tax return and making a self-assessment, the information available to the taxpayer may not be complete. For example, a precise figure may not be available as to income from a particular foreign source. There are no specific provisions in the self-assessment legislation dealing with such cases. But the Revenue have indicated that they will issue a statement setting out their proposed practice regarding estimates used in returns.

11.29   It seems that in the first instance the taxpayer's self-assessment should be based upon a reasonable estimate of the particular item, and this should be highlighted in the return/self-assessment, so that it is brought to the Revenue's attention. The estimate should be corrected if appropriate as soon as the actual figure is known, in accordance with *TMA 1970, s 97* and any further tax paid.

11.30   If the initial use of the estimate resulted in an underpayment of tax this would carry interest from the due date but there would then be no penalty or 'punitive' interest. Moreover, provided that the return was properly completed, the rest of the return would become final on the normal timescale (see Chapter 12).

Valuations

11.31   There are occasions on which a valuation may be required for a self-assessment, for example in a CGT computation relating to the disposal of land owned on 31 March 1982, or a gift of unquoted shares. As with estimates, there are no specific provisions in the legislation dealing with the position; for example, there are no particular powers given to the Revenue to question the valuation during an enquiry. Moreover, the Revenue have indicated that a valuation would not be regarded in itself as an estimate, unless designated as such by the taxpayer.

11.32   But where valuations are required for a computation it would generally be advisable for the taxpayer to include in the return a professional valuation, and to highlight its existence. Provided that the valuer had taken all the relevant issues into account in arriving at the valuation and no information had been withheld from him, the self-assessment based upon that valuation should be in order if the Revenue were later to enquire into the return.

11.33   The Revenue have indicated that they would generally not expect to be able to raise a discovery assessment (see 12.32) with regard to figures based upon a professional valuation, provided that the valuation fell within a reasonable range of valuations which might have been made by a valuer acting *bona fide* and fully instructed on the facts. However, in the event that any of the underlying information proved to be incorrect, and this came to the attention of the taxpayer, he would need to submit an amended assessment, as with the case of an estimate which turned out to be wrong.

Time limits for Revenue assessment or determination

11.34   The time limits for the making of assessments by the Revenue are amended. The previous normal time limit of six years from the end of the year of assessment becomes five years from 31 January following the end of the year for income tax and CGT. [*TMA 1970, s 34(1)(a)*]. It remains at six years after the end of the accounting period for corporation tax. [*TMA 1970, s 34(1)(b)*].

11.35   In the case of fraudulent or negligent conduct, the time limit becomes 20 years from 31 January following the end of the year of assessment for income tax and CGT, and 21 years after the end of the accounting period for corporation tax. [*TMA 1970, s 36(1)*]. Moreover, in the case of a partnership, the assessment can be made not only on the person in default, but also on any partner or partners of his. [*TMA 1970, s 36(2)*].

11.36   In the case of assessments on personal representatives, the time limit is three years from 31 January following the end of the year of assessment in which the deceased died. [*TMA 1970, s 40(1)*]. When there has been fraud or neglect on the part of the deceased, the six years of assessment before the deceased's death may be reopened, again within three years after 31 January following the end of year of assessment in which he died. [*TMA 1970, s 40(2)*].

11.37   Where no tax return has been delivered, so that the Revenue are empowered to make a determination of the tax liability, there is a time limit of five years from the filing date. Moreover no self-assessment can supersede such a determination unless made within twelve months of it. [*TMA 1970, s 28C(5)*].

Assessment to recover overpayment of tax

11.38   In circumstances where tax has been repaid to a taxpayer and the Revenue consider that this ought not to have been done, they may raise an assessment on the taxpayer to recover the tax overpaid. [*TMA 1970, s 30(1)*]. The assessment and appeals procedure set out in the amended *TMA 1970, s 29* relating to discovery by the Revenue (see 12.51) is then to apply.

11.39   The usual six-year time limit for such an assessment in *TMA 1970, s 34* is amended by *FA 1994, 19 Sch 10* permitting the Revenue to raise an assessment to recover the tax before the later of:

(*a*)   the end of the chargeable period following that in which the tax was repaid; and

(*b*)   if there has been a Revenue enquiry into the taxpayer's return, or an amendment to it, the end of the enquiry period.

[*TMA 1970, s 30(5)*].

Post-transaction rulings

11.40   The Revenue are sympathetic to the idea of incorporating in the system of self-assessment a provision for a post-transaction, pre-return, rulings system ('post-transaction rulings'), whereby a taxpayer could ascertain from the Revenue their view as to the consequences of a particular transaction which had been carried out.

11.41   The Revenue see a dual benefit. Some certainty would be given to the taxpayer as to his tax liability, since he should be able to establish the tax consequences of a transaction before the filing date, and he would be assisted in complying with his obligations. So far as the Revenue were concerned, voluntary compliance with the tax laws should thereby be encouraged. Such systems operate in the United States and Australia, both of which have self-assessment.

11.42   The mechanics are presently under consideration by the Revenue, and there is the possibility of some form of initial pilot scheme. An important issue is whether the system should be incorporated in the legislation, or dealt with by a statement of practice.

11.43   There might be, say, a time limit for seeking a post-transaction ruling of six months from the end of the year of assessment or the accounting period. Details of the transactions would have to be provided, with full disclosure, copies of relevant documents, references to relevant statutory provisions, case law, and statements of practice. The Revenue might then require further clarification or documentation. Moreover, there might be instances where the Revenue were not obliged to deal with the questions posed, where the tax was below a *de minimis* figure, where the application was vexatious or frivolous, where tax avoidance was the principal driving force, or where the matter was too complex in the light of available resources.

11.44 It is contemplated that the Revenue would be bound by any favourable ruling, although a taxpayer would not be bound by an unfavourable ruling. He would be entitled to pay tax on his view of the consequences of the transaction, and would have the right of appeal should the Revenue seek to enquire into his return and amend his assessment.

11.45 Such ideas are currently under discussion with the representative bodies, and it seems that a system of rulings on such lines is likely to be introduced, either by a comprehensive statement of practice, or by legislation in a subsequent *Finance Act*.

Chapter 12

Finality and Certainty, Revenue Powers of Enquiry; Discovery

Finality and certainty

12.1   The issues of finality and certainty are most important features of any tax system. In particular the taxpayer should be reasonably sure that, given full disclosure on his part, once his liability for a particular year has been determined, the matter cannot be reopened and reviewed at a later date.

12.2   The method of achieving this under the present system is for a review by the Inspector of every single case, aimed at satisfying himself as to the taxpayer's liability. The procedures involved, namely the submission by the taxpayer of his return, together with any accompanying accounts and other data, followed by subsequent requests by the Inspector for further information if required, correspondence, and negotiations in some cases, generally ensure that any controversial issues have been explored. The usual result is a tax assessment being agreed and becoming final. The matter can only be opened subsequently if there has been fraud or neglect by the taxpayer, or if the Revenue's discovery powers can be invoked.

12.3   The matter becomes more complicated in a system based upon self-assessment, where it is contemplated that in the vast majority of cases a taxpayer will calculate his own liability and the matter will not be reviewed by the Revenue. A balance has to be struck between giving reasonable certainty to taxpayers and the need to ensure that individual taxpayers do not benefit to the detriment of the general body of taxpayers, either by deliberately or carelessly underdeclaring their taxable income, or by taking an unjustifiably 'liberal' interpretation of the law, for example claiming a deduction for expenditure which on any reasonable view is unlikely to be allowable.

12.4   The approach which has been taken in the new system to resolve these issues may be summarised as follows.

(*a*)   For a given period, which is generally twelve months after the filing date for returns and the making of a self-assessment, the Revenue have complete freedom to audit a taxpayer's return and self-assessment.

(*b*)   Once that period has elapsed, a taxpayer's liability becomes final and conclusive, subject to the ability of the Revenue to reopen the matter in cases of fraud or neglect, or where they 'discover' an error or mistake.

12.5   The Revenue's powers of enquiry are considered in 12.7 *et seq*. The rights given to the Revenue in connection therewith, for example to require the taxpayer to produce data, are much greater than those currently available to an Inspector carrying out his normal review of a taxpayer's affairs. But this is perhaps an inevitable outcome of a self-assessment system.

12.6   The Revenue's powers of discovery are considered in 12.37 *et seq*. They are expressed in relatively simple form and generally allow the Revenue to open a matter only if there has not been full disclosure by the taxpayer. Inevitably there may be some doubt as to the proper treatment of certain items in the taxpayer's computation, and questions then arise as to the extent to which these must be drawn to the Revenue's attention. This has led to the proposal for a form of 'rulings' system in respect of transactions carried out by a taxpayer, which has received a sympathetic response from the Revenue as outlined in 11.40 *et seq*. It is presently the subject of detailed consideration between the Revenue and the representative bodies. Taking advantage of the ability to obtain such a ruling may in certain instances be the only safe way in which a taxpayer can be assured of finality and certainty in difficult cases.

Revenue enquiry/audit

Revenue powers of enquiry

12.7   The ability and freedom of the taxpayer to self-assess his liability is balanced by giving to the Revenue detailed powers of enquiry and investigation into his return and his self-assessment. There are like powers to enable the Revenue to enquire into partnership returns. It has been decided that the usual period within which such an enquiry can be commenced is one year from the filing date, namely 31 January for individuals and trustees.

12.8   The Revenue considered that this would give them sufficient time to amass and assimilate other information received about taxpayers' returns from third parties, such as employers, contractors and financial institutions, as well as a reasonable period within which to decide whether to raise an enquiry within their normal work programme. They have stated that they are not prepared to give any taxpayers an earlier assurance or clearance that they would not be audited, as this would be unfair on others who could not be given such an assurance. The nature of any particular enquiry will depend upon the particular case, and could range from a straightforward computational question to a full investigation.

12.9   A Revenue Code of Practice for enquiry work is to be issued together with information for taxpayers who are selected for enquiry. There is also a right of taxpayers to ask the Commissioners to close enquiries when these are unreasonably prolonged (see 12.23). The Revenue envisage that failure to follow up notice of enquiries within a reasonable period would be a justifiable cause of complaint into the Code.

Individuals and trustees

12.10   To implement the new powers of enquiry, there is a new *TMA 1970, s 19A* dealing with individuals and trustees. A formal notice in writing must be served on the taxpayer within specified time limits. [*TMA 1970, s 19A(1) as inserted by FA 1994, s 197*]. In the case of a tax return, or any amendment to it, delivered before the filing date (31 January) the time limit is twelve months from that date. In the case of a return or amendment delivered after the filing date, the time limit is the quarter day following the anniversary of the date of delivery of the return or the amendment. [*TMA 1970, s 19A(2)*]. For these purposes the quarter days are 31 January, 30 April, 31 July and 31 October. So if a return for 1997/98 is submitted to the Revenue on 15 March 1999 the Officer can serve a notice of enquiry on the taxpayer up to 30 April 2000. There is a like provision for companies in *TMA 1970, s 11AB*, and for partnerships in *TMA 1970, s 12AC*. [*FA 1994, ss 183, 186*].

12.11   Where the return and self-assessment are delivered to the Revenue before the filing date, but an amendment is made after the filing date, enquiries can only be raised by the Revenue after the first anniversary of the filing date in respect of items that were the subject of the amendment. Once a return or amendment has been the subject of an enquiry, there can be no further enquiry. [*TMA 1970, s 9A(3)*]. Where an enquiry has been opened, the ability of the taxpayer to amend his return or self-assessment is frozen. However, the Revenue would expect the taxpayer to inform them of any 'repairs' he considered appropriate (see 11.23 and 11.24).

Partnerships

12.12   Essentially the same provisions apply to enable the Revenue to enquire into partnership statements or amendments to such statements, with the same time limits applying. [*TMA 1970, s 12AC*]. Notice is to be given to the person who delivered the return or his successor. For this purpose, 'successor', in a case where the person who delivered the return is no longer a partner or is otherwise not available, means a partner nominated by the majority of the remaining partners. [*TMA 1970, s 12AC(6)*]. (This definition is a little vague and may be amended in *FA 1995*.) It is understood that the Revenue will in practice notify individual partners of the opening of their enquiries.

Companies

12.13 Under new *TMA 1970, s 11AB* the Revenue are given matching powers to enquire into a company's tax return or any amendments to it. The time limit is also twelve months from the filing date if the return was delivered on time, otherwise it is the quarter day following the first anniversary of the date of delivery of the return. [*TMA 1970, s 11AB(2)*].

Production of documents

12.14 The investigating officer may require the taxpayer (on not less than 30 days notice) to produce such documents, accounts or particulars as are in his possession or power as the officer may reasonably require for the purpose of determining whether a return is correct or complete or any amendment to it is correct. [*TMA 1970, s 19A(2)(a)*]. The officer may also require the taxpayer to furnish him with such accounts or particulars as he may reasonably require. [*TMA 1970, s 19A(2)(b)*]. The purpose of this is to obtain information not at the time in existence, for example to obtain written answers to questions. There are penalties for failure to comply (see 14.31). This power to require information ties in with the new obligations imposed on taxpayers with regard to the pre-servation of records (see 10.29). Inevitably questions will arise as to what is 'reasonable' in any particular case, for example, whether reason-ableness relates to materiality (such as a request for petty cash dockets) or to other criteria. These issues are to be covered in the Revenue's Code of Practice on enquiries.

12.15 It is in order for the taxpayer to supply photographic or other facsimile copies of documents, but the Revenue can require (on not less than 30 days notice) to see the originals and take copies or make extracts. [*TMA 1970, s 19A(3)(4)*]. The Revenue already have powers of investigation under *TMA 1970, s 20*, but these are subject to parti-cular safeguards. They evidently considered that they required almost an unfettered right to examine prime records, and that the existing *section 20* powers were too cumbersome for general use in policing self-assessment. But the Revenue did not apparently consider that a right of entry into the taxpayer's premises was required, although a 'field audit' might in practice be the simplest way of confirming the taxpayer's accounts with the original books of accounts, invoices and other original documents.

12.16 A taxpayer is not obliged to produce documents, or furnish accounts or particulars which relate to the conduct of any pending appeal by him. [*TMA 1970, s 19(A)(5)*]. The value to a taxpayer or the relevance of this is debatable since under self-assessment it is unlikely that an appeal will be pending. The Revenue have indicated that they are considering this point and there may be legislation dealing with it in *FA 1995*.

Right of appeal against notice to produce documents

12.17   A taxpayer does however have the right of appeal to the Commissioners against a notice to produce documents, or furnish accounts or particulars. The same appeals procedure then applies as if it were an appeal against an assessment to tax. [*TMA 1970, s 19A(6)(7)(8)*]. The Commissioners are empowered to confirm the notice if it appears to them that the production of the documents etc. was reasonably required, otherwise they are to set it aside. [*TMA 1970, s 19A(9)*]. How this ties in with the limitation on the obligation to produce documents when an appeal is pending or documents containing legal advice is not clear, although there may be some clarification in *FA 1995*. There is no further right of appeal by way of case stated. [*TMA 1970, s 19A(11)*]. It would seem that an aggrieved taxpayer's only remedy would then be by way of judicial review. This right of appeal does provide some element of balance, and is an assurance for the taxpayer against possible abuse of their powers by the Revenue. In the original proposals there was no such right of appeal, and this is therefore a welcome addition to the legislation.

Assessment of tax after opening of enquiry

12.18   Where an enquiry into a taxpayer's return has been opened, if it appears to the Revenue Officer that the tax paid under the self-assessment was too low, and that unless there was an immediate amendment to the assessment there was likely to be a loss of tax to the Crown, he is entitled to amend the assessment by notice served on the taxpayer. [*TMA 1970, s 28A(2); FA 1994, s 188*].

12.19   The purpose of this power is to enable the Revenue to move quickly, well before the enquiries are completed, to try and forestall the loss of tax by, for example, a taxpayer skipping the jurisdiction or contriving a bankruptcy. The taxpayer has the right of appeal against such an amended assessment, as shown by the procedures as set out in 15.5 below. But the appeal is not to be heard until the enquiries are completed. So the taxpayer's only interim remedy to expedite the matter is to apply to the Commissioners to direct the Officer to bring the enquiries to an end (see 12.23).

Conclusion of enquiry and amendment of assessment – individuals, trustees and companies

12.20   Having completed his enquiries, the Revenue Officer is obliged to issue a notice to the taxpayer, informing him he has done so and stating his conclusions as to the proper amount of tax. [*TMA 1970, s 28A(5)*]. The taxpayer is then allowed 30 days to amend his self-assessment to make good any deficiency or eliminate any excess. [*TMA 1970, s 28A(3)*]. The taxpayer thus has the opportunity to amend his assessment upwards or downwards to accord with the views of the Revenue

Officer (or indeed to some other level which the taxpayer considers appropriate).

12.21 Amendment by agreement between the Revenue and the taxpayer is the clearly desired course, as it would result in the enquiry coming to an end without the necessity for any further consideration of the matter. Furthermore, in the event that during the enquiry it became evident that additional tax was due it would be to the benefit of the taxpayer to make further payments on account in order to prevent further interest running. It is contemplated that the agreement would follow a negotiation process, effectively resulting in an arbitrated figure.

12.22 In the event that the taxpayer does not amend his self-assessment to the Officer's satisfaction within the 30-day period, the Officer is permitted, within the next 30 days, to amend the assessment to what he considers is the appropriate figure. The taxpayer has a right of appeal against such amendment (see 15.5 below). This effectively preserves a system similar to the present in cases where agreement cannot be reached between the taxpayer and the Inspector.

Direction to bring enquiry to an end

12.23 At any time during the enquiry period the taxpayer is entitled to apply to the Commissioners to direct the Officer to bring the enquiries to an end. The issue is then heard and determined in the same way as an appeal, and the Commissioners are to give such a direction unless they are satisfied that the Officer has reasonable grounds for continuing his enquiries. [*TMA 1970, s 28A(6)(7)*]. There is thus some protection against the Revenue prolonging their enquiries beyond a reasonable period.

Conclusion of enquiry and amendment of assessment – partnerships

12.24 *TMA 1970, s 28B* as inserted by *FA 1994, s 189* contains the provisions which apply where the Revenue have made an enquiry into a partnership statement. These largely mirror the provisions relating to enquiries made into the tax returns of individuals, trustees and companies outlined above. Thus, having completed his enquiries the Officer is to inform the taxpayer (which includes a reference to any predecessor or successor of his) [*TMA 1970, s 28B(8)*] that he has completed those enquiries, stating his conclusions as to the proper amount of tax. [*TMA 1970, s 28B(5)*].

12.25 The taxpayer is then allowed 30 days to amend the partnership statement to make good any deficiency of tax or eliminate any excess. [*TMA 1970, s 28B(2)*]. Should the taxpayer not do so the Officer is permitted, within the next 30 days, to amend the assessment as appropriate. [*TMA 1970, s 28B(3)*]. In either case the Officer is to give notice to the various partners to amend their self-assessment to give effect to the amendments of the partnership statement. [*TMA 1970, s 28B(4)*].

12.26 The taxpayer has the right of appeal to the Commissioners against such Revenue amendment to the partnership statement (see 15.5). Moreover, at any time in the enquiry period, the taxpayer has like powers to apply to the Commissioners to direct the Officer to bring the enquiries to an end as those set out in 12.23.

Revenue enquiry into claims

General position

12.27 In the same way as the Revenue are empowered to enquire into a taxpayer's return and self-assessment (which will include any claim made in the return) there are like powers to enquire into a claim made by a taxpayer other than in his return, or any amendment made to such a claim. [*TMA 1970, 1A Sch 5(1) as inserted by FA 1994, 19 Sch 35*]. A formal notice in writing must be served on the taxpayer, or in the case of a partnership claim, any successor, within specified time limits. The time limit is the period ending with the quarter day following the first anniversary of the day on which the claim or amendment was made. [*TMA 1970, 1A Sch 5(2)*]. Once such an enquiry has been made into a claim there cannot be a further enquiry. [*TMA 1970, 1A Sch 5(3)*].

12.28 Where an enquiry has been opened, the Revenue may require the taxpayer (on not less than 30 days notice) to produce such documents as are in his possession or power and are reasonably required for the purpose of determining whether the claim or amendment is incorrect. There are like powers to request accounts or particulars. [*TMA 1970, 1A Sch 6(2)*]. All the provisions which apply in a case of a Revenue enquiry into a taxpayers return, as outlined in 12.10 *et seq.* above, are to apply. [*TMA 1970, 1A Sch 6(3)*]. The Revenue have intimated that such enquiry will require the same sort of dialogue between the Inspector and the taxpayer as is seen at the moment. In the progression towards agreement it is anticipated that points would be agreed along the way and that the Inspector's conclusions at the end of the enquiry would summarise the agreed positions and the Inspector's position in any items in dispute. As set out below there would then be 30 days for the taxpayer to deal with the mechanics of any amendments, such as additional or amended claims, in line with the procedure relating to enquiries into tax returns.

Conclusion of enquiry and amendment of claim

12.29 As with Revenue enquiries into a taxpayer's return, once the enquiries have been completed the Revenue Officer must inform the taxpayer and state his conclusions as to the amount which should have been in the claim. [*TMA 1970, 1A Sch 7(4)*]. The taxpayer is then allowed

30 days to amend his claim to eliminate or make good any excess or deficiency, or to give effect to any amendments to the claim which he has notified to the Officer. [*TMA 1970, 1A Sch 7(2)*].

12.30   The taxpayer thus has the opportunity to amend the claim, so as to reflect the conclusions of the Revenue Officer. Should he not do so the Officer is permitted, within the next 30 days, to amend the claim as appropriate. [*TMA 1970, 1A Sch 7(3)*]. The taxpayer has the right of appeal against such amendment by the Revenue Officer [*TMA 1970, 1A Sch 9*] (see 15.7 below). After a claim has been so amended, effect is to be given to the amendment within 30 days either by way of an assessment on the taxpayer, or by a discharge of tax, or a repayment of tax as the case may be. [*TMA 1970, 1A Sch 8(1)*]. Like provisions are included for partners. [*TMA 1970, 1A Sch 8(2)*].

12.31   As with the like provisions relating to enquiries into a taxpayer's return, at any time during the enquiry period the taxpayer may apply to the Commissioners to direct the Officer to bring the enquiries to an end. The provisions set out in 12.23 are to apply as regards the handling of the matter thereafter. [*TMA 1970, 1A Sch 7(5)*].

Discovery

Present position and background

12.32   The present rules relating to discovery have developed from two apparently contradictory provisions in *TMA 1970*, and have been a continuing source of controversy. They are now covered by a combination of statute and case law, Revenue practice and concession.

12.33   Outside the fields of fraud and neglect, *TMA 1970, s 29(3)* gives the Inspector an ostensibly untrammelled right to raise a further assessment, within six years of the end of the year of assessment in question, if he 'discovers' that the original assessment was incorrect. But where an assessment has been determined by agreement under *TMA 1970, s 54*, following an appeal by the taxpayer, the determination is treated as final and conclusive under *TMA 1970, s 46(2)*. Where there is new evidence, the matter can be reopened. But where there is merely a change of mind by the Inspector (or his successor) there is a limitation on the right to make further assessments.

12.34   The issues were considered in two leading cases. The first, *Cenlon Finance Co Ltd v Ellwood 1962 40 TC 176* held, in a case where the Inspector had explicitly agreed the point in issue, that a further assessment was not possible on a point which had been agreed in the course of determining the first appeal. The second case, *Olin Energy Systems Ltd v Scorer* [*1985*] *STC 218* concerned a company's computation in which the point at issue was identified, but was not explicitly addressed by the

Inspector. It was held that the matter could not be reopened, since it was reasonable to accept that the Inspector had *implicitly* considered and accepted the position put forward by the company in a computation.

12.35 After considerable debate the Revenue issued a Statement of Practice, SP 8/91, which set out their interpretation of the position where there has been an appeal and a *TMA 1970, s 54* agreement. The stance taken by the Revenue, in cases where there has been no *explicit* agreement, is to accept that discovery cannot be made if:

(*a*) the point was fundamental to the basis of computation of the taxpayer's liability; and

(*b*) it was so clearly and fully described in the accounts or computations that its significance was clearly apparent and the Inspector was put on notice of the point.

12.36 By concession the Revenue take the same line in cases where there has been no formal appeal and determination. Moreover, in cases where the point is not fundamental, they do not seek to raise a further assessment if the position taken by the original Inspector was a tenable one.

Discovery under Simplified Assessing

12.37 As outlined above, apart from fraud or neglect, the ability under the present system to make a discovery assessment is essentially linked to two questions:

(*a*) whether there has been full disclosure by the taxpayer; and

(*b*) whether the Inspector has agreed the point at issue, which must be fundamental, either explicitly or implicitly.

12.38 In self-assessment, the second question is no longer relevant because there is no requirement for the Inspector to be satisfied as to the information in a taxpayer's return and agree upon a particular point, so that he can raise the requisite assessment. The issue accordingly becomes one of full disclosure by the taxpayer only.

12.39 Given this narrowing down of the position, and the fact that the problem becomes somewhat simpler, the Revenue have chosen to codify the law in appropriate statutory provisions. Their expressed intention has been to follow the tests which they consider emerge from the judgments in the *Olin* case. In particular, for a taxpayer to avoid any possibility of a discovery assessment being raised at a later date, the disclosure of a particular point has to be sufficiently full and clear to put an ordinarily competent Inspector on notice of precisely what issues need to be considered and the stance taken on them.

12.40 A related factor is the extent to which information which has been provided to the Revenue in connection with past returns can be regarded as information in the Revenue's possession for the purposes of the current return and tax liability. The Revenue have taken a rather restrictive approach here, and only regard information as disclosed in the previous two years as in their possession.

12.41 The position for 1996/97 and subsequent years (and in the case of companies for accounting periods ending on or after 1 April 1996) is set out in substituted *TMA 1970, s 29*, as follows. If the Revenue discover that any profits which should have been assessed to tax have not been assessed to tax, or that an assessment has been insufficient, or excess relief has been given, they may make the appropriate assessment to make good the loss of tax only if one of two alternative conditions is satisfied. [*TMA 1970, s 29(1)*].

12.42 The first alternative condition is that the loss of tax is the result of fraudulent or negligent conduct by the taxpayer, or any person acting on his behalf. [*TMA 1970, s 29(4)*]. 'Fraudulent or negligent' conduct would extend to a failure to observe the standards to be expected of a reasonable man in the circumstances. An arithmetical error, a double deduction, or such other obvious error would possibly amount to negligence. (These concepts exist in the current system and are considered in the appropriate text books.)

12.43 The second alternative condition (and the one relevant to the issues raised in 12.38 to 12.40) is that when a Revenue Officer ceased to be entitled to enquire into a return or, in the event of any enquiry, informed the taxpayer that he had completed his enquiries, he could not reasonably have been expected to be aware of the tax deficiency on the basis of the information made available to him. [*TMA 1970, s 25(5)*].

12.44 For the purposes of this second condition information is treated as made available to the Officer if:

(*a*) It is contained in the taxpayer's tax return, or in any accounts, statements or documents accompanying the return (which includes any amended return and accompanying documents). For this purpose the return is that for the chargeable period in question and the two immediately preceding periods. [*TMA 1970, ss 29(6)(a), 7(a)(i)*].

(*b*) It is contained in any claim made by the taxpayer, or in any accounts, statements or documents accompanying the return. [*TMA 1970, s 29(6)(b)*].

(*c*) It is contained in any documents, accounts or particulars which are produced during the course of any Revenue enquiry. [*TMA 1970, s 29(6)(c)*].

(*d*)　It is information the existence and relevance of which could reasonably be expected to be inferred by the Revenue Officer from the
information in (*a*)–(*c*), or which is notified in writing by the taxpayer
to the Revenue. [*TMA 1970, s 29(6)(d)*].

12.45　It follows that provided the information submitted to the Revenue is sufficiently comprehensive, and either any controversial point is
specifically raised, or its relevance can clearly be inferred, discovery will
not be possible.

12.46　Although the test of 'reasonableness' in the opening words of the
second alternative condition in 12.43 is ostensibly linked to the particular
Officer concerned with the taxpayer, it would seem that an objective
standard of reasonableness is appropriate. So, for example, the degree of
reasonableness does not depend on the grade and experience of the
actual Officer concerned. It seems that this is the view of the Revenue and
that the hypothetical Officer will be the 'ordinarily competent' Officer.

12.47　This apart, questions will inevitably arise whether the information, or the form in which it was presented, was sufficient to satisfy the
'reasonableness' test in the second condition or the 'inference' and 'relevance' tests related to that condition and set out in 12.44(*d*). A further
aspect is that a taxpayer is not protected from the kind of case where, for
example, the information given should have put the Officer on enquiry,
but he actually decided not to make such an enquiry.

12.48　An example could be a practice of calculating work-in-progress
which might not strictly be correct, but which had been agreed with the
Officer's predecessor as satisfactory, possibly on the basis that it was
straightforward, applied consistently, and saved time in calculations. If
such approach was applied in future periods, but the accounts and return
did not fully describe the particular method, it would appear that the
successor Officer would not be precluded from reopening the case.

12.49　Another point is the limited extent to which information given to
the Revenue in past periods is to be assumed to be known to them in the
current period (see 12.44(*a*) which only brings in the two prior returns).
In this regard, even a permanent note on the taxpayer's file would not
suffice. The Revenue have observed that it cannot be assumed that a
Revenue Officer will always make systematic permanent notes regarding
a particular taxpayer. It would seem that some form of cross-referencing
to past periods might be in order, but to be sure any potentially controversial areas would have to be dealt with explicitly, at least once every
three years.

12.50　In cases where liability is determined by reference to valuations,
for example, a CGT computation where March 1982 value was relevant,
it seems that if a professional valuation has been included in the return,
which is within a reasonable range, the matter cannot be reopened under

a discovery assessment after the twelve-month period has elapsed (see 11.31). This assumes that the information given to the valuer is sufficiently comprehensive.

12.51   Finally, where a tax return has been filed and the tax shortfall results from an error or mistake as to the basis on which the liability should have been computed, the shortfall is not recoverable if the return was made on the basis of, or in accordance with, the practice generally prevailing at the time when it was made. [*TMA 1970, s 29(2)*]. An objection by a taxpayer to the making of a discovery assessment is to be made by an appeal against the assessment. [*TMA 1970, s 29(8)*]. The usual appeal procedures set out in Chapter 15 then apply.

Discovery and partnership statements

12.52   There are similar discovery provisions relating to partnership statements on the same lines as those described above in 12.37 *et seq*. Subject to one of two alternative conditions, if the Revenue discover that any profits which should have been included in the partnership statement have not been included, or that the profits therein are insufficient, or that any relief given is excessive, they may by notice given to the representative partner (or his successor) amend the statement accordingly. [*TMA 1970, s 30B(1)(4); FA 1994, 19 Sch 6*].

12.53   The Revenue Officer is then, by notice given to each of the relevant partners (being persons who were partners at any time in the period in respect of which the partnership statement was made) [*TMA 1970, s 30B(9)*], required to make the appropriate amendments to their self-assessments. [*TMA 1970, s 30B(2)*].

12.54   The first alternative condition is that the incorrect partnership statement is attributable to fraudulent or negligent conduct of the representative partner or a person acting on his behalf, or a relevant partner or a person acting on his behalf. [*TMA 1970, s 30B(5)*].

12.55   The second alternative condition is that when a Revenue Officer ceased to be entitled to enquire into the representative partner's return (or, in the event of an enquiry, informed him that he had completed his enquiries), the Officer could not reasonably have been expected to be aware of the tax deficiency on the basis of the information made available to him. [*TMA 1970, s 30B(6)*]. In determining the extent of the information which is regarded as made available to the Revenue Officer, the corresponding provisions relating to individuals set out in 12.44 are to apply with appropriate amendments. [*TMA 1970, s 30B(7)*].

12.56   There is provision for appeal against a notice of amendment to a partnership statement served by the Revenue. [*TMA 1970, s 30B(8)*].

Moreover, as with individuals, where the tax deficiency in the partnership statement results from an error or mistake as to the basis of which the statement should have been made, the deficiency is not recoverable if the statement was made on the basis of, or in accordance with, the practice generally prevailing at the time when it was made. [*TMA 1970, s 30B(3)*].

Chapter 13

Payment and Repayment of Tax

Payment of income tax and CGT – system in outline

13.1   In devising the new system for the payment of tax, Exchequer cash flow had to be preserved in the transition from the preceding year to the current year basis, yet the taxpayer had to be able to self-assess several months after the end of the year of assessment. Simplicity was also an important factor. The current system had become far too complex. An individual with different sources of income and capital gains would have several separate payment dates, and indeed more if assessments were issued after the normal due date. All the paperwork involved, with separate assessments and payment slips, complicated the Revenue's administrative tasks and led to errors.

13.2   The system which has been devised to resolve these issues is for income tax to be payable in three instalments. The first two instalments are payments on account, called 'interim payments'. These are due on 31 January in the year of assessment and on 31 July in the next year of assessment. The general rule is that each interim payment is 50 per cent of the income tax liability of the preceding year of assessment, less any tax deducted at source. [*TMA 1970, s 59A(1) as inserted by FA 1994, s 192*]. The third and final instalment discharges the balance of the taxpayer's income tax liability, and the whole of any CGT, and is due the following 31 January.

Example 1

Mr Andrew was assessed to income tax of £24,000 for 1997/98, of which £6,000 was deducted at source. The interim payments for 1998/99 will be £9,000 each, due on 31 January 1999 and 31 July 1999. His self-assessment for 1998/99 in due course indicates a total income tax liability of £32,000. The final payment for 1998/99 will be £8,000 due by 31 January 2000 assuming again £6,000 deducted at source.

Interim payments

13.3   The system of interim payments summarised in 13.2 is to operate in all cases of a continuing trade, vocation or profession, where:

(*a*) the person concerned has been assessed to tax in the preceding year; and

(*b*) the amount so assessed exceeded the income tax deducted at source.

[*TMA 1970, s 59A(1)(2)*].

Tax deducted at source means income tax deducted from any income, or treated as deducted or paid, any PAYE deduction which is in respect of the year but is to be made in a subsequent year, or a tax credit attaching to dividends. [*TMA 1970, s 59A(8)*]. It includes tax credits on dividends, foreign tax credits and amounts relating to previous years which have been 'coded out' and therefore paid through PAYE. For recovery purposes any amount payable on account by way of interim payment is treated as income tax. [*TMA 1970, s 59A(7)*].

13.4 The Board have the power to make regulations to establish minimum limits, below which interim payments will not be required. These have not yet been announced, but they can either set an absolute minimum level, or they can establish a percentage of total income not taxed at source that must apply before interim payments are required. [*TMA 1970, s 59A(1)(c)(d)*]. So a taxpayer may be excused from making payments on account if a significant proportion of his tax liability is met by deduction at source. The effect may be to allow taxpayers who receive the greater part of their income under deduction of tax to pay their higher rate liability after the end of the year.

13.5 In other cases, in particular where the year of assessment is the year in which a trade is commenced there will be no interim payments, all the tax being due under the final payment procedure. Moreover, the interim payments may be eliminated or reduced in certain cases, for example, where a trade has ceased or where profits are falling.

13.6 If the taxpayer believes that he will not be assessed to tax for a particular year of assessment, or that the amount assessed will not exceed the tax deducted at source, he may submit a claim to this effect before 31 January following the year of assessment, giving the reasons for his belief. Interim payments will then not be required [*TMA 1970, s 59A(3)*], and all necessary and consequential adjustments are to be made; whether by repayment of tax, or otherwise. [*TMA 1970, s 59A(5)*].

Example 2 (continuing)

Mr Brown is a property developer and is considering the interim payments for 1998/99. His profits for the year to 31 December 1997 were £60,000 (being the profits assessable for 1997/98). He has no other sources of income and his actual tax liability for 1997/98 is £18,000. His management accounts prepared towards the end of the following year to 31 December 1998 indicate that a loss will be likely. Accordingly he submits a claim that there should be no interim payments for 1998/99, the first of which in the amount of £9,000 would otherwise fall due on 31 January 1999.

13.7   If the taxpayer believes that he will have some tax liability for a particular year, but the difference between the tax deducted at source and his anticipated total liability will be less than the equivalent difference for the previous year, he may submit a claim for the interim payment to be calculated by reference to his estimate of the difference in the current year. The claim must again be made by 31 January of the following year and must state the reasons. [*TMA 1970, s 59A(4)*]. Likewise any appropriate adjustments or repayments are to be made to give effect to the claim.

Example 2

Continuing the previous example, assume that Mr Brown's management accounts for the year to 31 December 1998 indicated a profit of £40,000, rather than a loss. The anticipated tax liability on this figure would be say £10,000. The claim would then be for interim payments of £5,000 each, rather than £9,000.

13.8   This example illustrates the difficulty in which a taxpayer might find himself when his accounting year end is close to the end of the year of assessment. Indeed when the year end falls after 31 January in the year of assessment he will not know what his profits are yet he will still be obliged to make an interim payment before the year end. The legislation does not specifically provide for any amended claims to be made if circumstances change between the due dates for the interim payments. It is understood, however, that the Revenue's intention is for the second interim payment to be amended, upwards or downwards, to reflect any underpayment or overpayment of the first interim payment, in recognition of the fact that Simplified Assessing is a taxpayer driven system.

13.9   Where an incorrect statement is made in such a claim, whether fraudulently or negligently, the taxpayer will be liable to a penalty. The maximum is the difference between the correct amount and the actual interim payment made. [*TMA 1970, s 59A(6)*]. The severity of the potential penalty highlights the dilemma of the taxpayer who believes that his profits are falling, but does not know his precise position. However, the Revenue have stated that the intention of this penalty is to prevent gross or persistent abuse of the provisions, and that a penalty would be applied in cases either of large reductions made without foundation or where the taxpayer year on year claims to pay tax less than he should. The

Revenue will not seek to apply hindsight or penalise someone who acted in good faith but got his sums wrong.

Final payment

13.10   The balance of the taxpayer's liability, calculated under the self-assessment to be submitted by the taxpayer by 31 January (or by the Revenue where the return is submitted by 30 September) is then normally also due on 31 January. This also includes the whole of any CGT liability for the year in question. Thus CGT is not subject to payment by instalments, and is not taken into account in computing any of the interim payments of income tax. The amount payable reflects any tax which has been deducted at source and tax credits on dividends. In the event that the assessment indicates that tax has been overpaid, this is then repayable. [*TMA 1970, s 59B(1)(4) as inserted by FA 1994, s 193*].

13.11   In the case of tax deducted under the PAYE procedure, the tax deduction from the final payment is to reflect the liability of the year in question, rather than the actual year of payment. Take the case of an employee paid at the end of each calendar month. PAYE for 1 to 5 April 1999 will be accounted for on 30 April 1999, i.e. in the following year of assessment 1999/2000. An appropriate adjustment would be required in determining the final payment on 31 January 2000 for 1998/99, giving credit for the tax paid in April 1999 (and where appropriate making a compensating adjustment for any overpayment in April 1998). The position is similar for tax credits attaching to dividends. [*TMA 1970, s 59B(2)*].

13.12   In cases where the taxpayer has notified the Revenue of his chargeability to income tax within six months of the end of the year of assessment [*as required by TMA 1970, s 7*], but was not sent a tax return until after 31 October, the final payment is not due (or repayment is not to be made as the case may be) until three months after the day on which the return was issued. [*TMA 1970, s 59B(3)*]. So take the case where a person (not previously chargeable to tax) commences a trade in 1997/98 and notifies the Revenue in August 1998 that he has done so. If he is not issued a return until 15 December 1998 he is not required to pay any tax until 15 March 1999.

Payment after amendment of self-assessment/discovery

13.13   Where a self-assessment is amended, special rules apply. Such an amendment may be made by the taxpayer or the Revenue under the 'repairs' procedure (see 11.18 above) or after a Revenue enquiry has been carried out (see 12.20 above) or under the 'discovery' procedure in the case of partnership statements (see 12.52 above). If the amended self-assessment is made more than 30 days before the normal due date for the final payment, or the extended due date as set out above, the tax consequential to the amendment is payable (or repayable) on that due date. Otherwise it is payable, or repayable, within 30 days of notice of the amendment. [*TMA 1970, s 59B(5)*].

13.14   In the case when the Revenue make a discovery assessment under the revised procedures set out in *TMA 1970, s 29*, tax is due within 30 days of the issue of the discovery assessment. [*TMA 1970, s 59B(6)*]. But these rules relating to amended self-assessments and discovery assessments do not displace the right of the taxpayer to postpone tax under *TMA 1970, s 55* where there is an appeal.

Corporation tax

13.15   The basic rule that corporation tax is payable nine months after the company's accounting period is not changed. [*TMA 1970, s 59(1)*]. In particular there are to be no interim payments on account. However, certain specific provisions are introduced regarding overpayments of tax. If tax has been paid which the company considers is excessive because of a change in circumstances since the tax was paid, a claim can be made for the recovery of the excess at any time before the corporation tax assessment for the period has become final. [*TMA 1970, s 59D(2) as inserted by FA 1994, s 195*]. Such a claim can only be made after the due date and must spell out the reasons why it is justified. [*TMA 1970, s 59D(3)*].

13.16   In any case where a company has appealed against an assessment, and it has not been finally determined, the company may apply to the Commissioners for a repayment of tax pending determination of the actual liability if it believes that there has been an overpayment of tax due to changed circumstances. [*TMA 1970, s 59D(4)*]. An application for repayment, whether to the Revenue Officer or to the Commissioners, is to be determined in the same way as an appeal. [*TMA 1970, s 59D(5)*]. An application for repayment may be combined with a postponement application under *TMA 1970, s 55*. [*TMA 1970, s 59D(6)*].

13.17   It is understood that in cases where tax paid in excess of a company's liability on Form CT 200 is left with the Revenue 'on deposit' to cover any extra tax liability which may arise (so performing a similar function to certificates of deposit, a facility now withdrawn for companies) a Revenue Officer will not repay the extra tax, in the absence of the company's formal request, until such time as the assessment for the period has been fully determined.

Interim payments in 1996/97

13.18   The calculation of the interim payments in *TMA, s 59A*, as set out in 13.2, is amended by *FA 1994, s 198* for the transitional year 1996/97. The calculation is extremely complicated, and it appears that the amount of the payments could be affected by the allocation of personal allowances and rate bands between different assessments and sources of income. Detailed guidance will no doubt be forthcoming from the Revenue in due course. The provisions of *FA 1994, s 198* are best explained by means of an example, of which the following sets out the authors' rather tentative views of the position.

Example 3

In 1995/96 Mr Jacobs had the following income, and deductions of tax at source.

Source of income	Amount £	Tax deducted £
Schedule A	12,000	–
Schedule D, Case I	40,000	–
Bank interest	10,000	2,500
Schedule F	8,000	2,000
	£70,000	£4,500

His assessments, and the allocation of allowances and lower rate bands, all against Schedule D, Case I income, were as follows (making certain assumptions and 1994/95 rates of tax).

	Total £	Sch A £	Case I £	Bank Interest £	Sch F £
Income	70,000	12,000	40,000	10,000	8,000
Personal allowances	(3,445)		(3,445)		
Income after allowances	66,555	12,000	36,555	10,000	8,000
Tax calculation					
20% (£3,000)	600		600		
25% (next £20,700)	5,175		5,175		
40% (balance £42,855)	17,142	4,800	5,142	4,000	3,200
Total tax	22,917	4,800	10,917	4,000	3,200
Less deducted at source	(4,500)	–	–	(2,500)	(2,000)
Tax due	18,417	4,800	10,917	1,500	1,200

The two interim payments which would normally be required for 1996/97, if it were not the transitional year, would be half the difference between the total tax liability for the previous year (known as the 'assessed amount'), namely £22,917, and the tax deducted at source of £4,500, i.e. 50% × (£22,917 − £4,500) = £9,208 each. But because it is the transitional year a different calculation is required.

First the assessed amount is recalculated, by deducting from what it would otherwise have been the amount of income tax charged at a rate other than the basic rate on any income:

(i)   from which tax has been deducted, otherwise than under *TA 1988, s 203*;

(ii) from or on which income tax is treated as having been deducted or paid; or

(iii) which is chargeable under Schedule F.

[*FA 1994, s 198(1)(b)*].

The assessed amount for 1996/97 then becomes:

	£
Amount before recalculation	22,917
Less higher rate tax on bank interest (£4,000 − £2,500)	(1,500)
Less higher rate tax on Schedule F (£3,200 − £2,000)	(1,200)
	£20,217

The first interim payment is then the aggregate of the relevant proportion of the relevant amount and 50 per cent of the difference between the relevant amount and that proportion of that amount. [*FA 1994, s 198(1)(c)(i)*].

(*a*)   The relevant amount is the difference between the assessed amount (£20,217) and the amount of tax deducted at source (£4,500); i.e. £15,717. [*TMA, s 59A(1)(c); FA 1994, s 192*].

(*b*)   The relevant proportion is the proportion which the amount of tax charged under Schedule A or Schedule D, Cases III to VI for 1995/96 bears to the assessed amount. [*FA 1994, s 198(2)*].

	£
Tax charged under Schedule A	4,800

Relevant proportion of relevant amount =

$$\frac{4,800}{15,717} \times £15,717 = £4,800$$

Hence the first interim payment is £4,800 + 50% (£15,717 − £4,800) = £10,259.

The second interim payment is to be 50 per cent of the difference between the relevant amount and the relevant proportion of the relevant amount, namely:

$$50\% \times (£15,717 - £4,800) = £5,459.$$

13.19 In the event that a taxpayer considers that he will have no additional tax to pay in the transitional year, taking into account tax deducted at source, he may make a claim to make no interim payments, as set out in 13.6.

13.20 In the event that the taxpayer considers that he will have some tax to pay in the transitional year, but that it will be less than the amounts under the above formulae, then he will likewise be entitled to pay tax by reference to his estimate of what the tax liability will be (see 13.7). In this case the calculation of the two payments as set out above still must be made, but it is to be done on the basis that the amount which is stated by the taxpayer as his estimate is used in the calculation rather than the assessed amount. [*FA 1994, s 198(1)(d)*].

Payment by cheque

13.21 A new *TMA 1970, s 70A* is introduced by *FA 1994, 19 Sch 22*, to clarify the date on which payment by cheque is made. For the purpose of *TMA 1970* and for the repayment supplement, where any payment to the Revenue is made by cheque, and the cheque is paid on its first presentation to the bank on which it is drawn, the payment is treated as made on the day it was received by the Revenue. This applies in respect of cheques received on or after 6 April 1996.

Chapter 14

Surcharges, Interest, Penalties and Repayment Supplement

Surcharges on late payment

14.1 A contentious aspect of the new system is the imposition of an automatic 5 per cent surcharge on late payment of CGT or the final income tax instalment. It is not imposed on late interim payments. This has been prompted by the deficiencies of the present somewhat laissez faire system of unclear time limits, estimated assessments, appeals, postponements and hearings. The objective has been to move to a simpler and more streamlined system having clear time limits, with surcharges and penalties for delays.

14.2 From the Revenue's point of view, the surcharge is aimed at achieving a high degree of voluntary compliance; keeping the costs of running the tax system as low as possible, yet without over penalising defaulters. The amount of surcharge originally proposed was 10 per cent of the tax paid late, but this has been reduced to an initial 5 per cent in the light of serious concern about its steepness and its arbitrary automatic imposition for payment made even one day after the due date. Arguments that in the absence of culpability interest was the appropriate cost to the taxpayer were not accepted by the Revenue.

14.3 The liability to the surcharge arises where payment is 28 days in arrears, i.e. 28 days from the due date, generally 31 January following the year of assessment (see 13.10 and 13.12 above). [*TMA 1970, s 59C(1)(2) as inserted by FA 1994, s 194*]. If any tax still remains unpaid six months later there is a further 5 per cent surcharge. [*TMA 1970, s 59C(3)*]. It is understood that where a taxpayer has not self-assessed, but has filed his return by 30 September to enable the Revenue to make the assessment, and the Revenue are late in assessing, the trigger date for the surcharge will be 30 days after issue of the tax bill, if this is later than 31 January. In the Standing Committee debates on the *Finance Bill* the Financial Secretary gave an assurance that if a taxpayer paid tax late as a result of a *bona fide* mistake in his self-assessment, interest would be charged but not a surcharge, provided that the taxpayer volunteered the information and paid promptly.

Example 1

Mr Green's final liability for 1998/99 is £40,000. Tax deducted at source was £5,000 and interim payments totalling £20,000 were made in the correct amounts. The balancing payment of £15,000 would thus fall due on 31 January 2000. If this was only paid on 15 March 2000 there would be a surcharge of £15,000 × 5% = £750. Assume that the only amount paid then was £5,000. There would then be a further surcharge of £10,000 × 5% = £500 on 1 August 2000.

14.4   However, where a tax geared penalty is imposed on the taxpayer under *TMA 1970, ss 7* (failure to notify Revenue of chargeability), *93(5)* (failure to complete a return) or *95* (fraud or neglect), he is excused from these surcharges. [*TMA 1970, s 59C(4)*]. The rationale is that the penalty is likely to be rather greater than any surcharge, and the amount will reflect the fact that payment is in arrears.

14.5   Notice of any surcharge is to be served formally on the taxpayer, stating the day on which it is issued and the time within which an appeal may be brought. [*TMA 1970, s 59C(5)*]. The taxpayer has a right of appeal against the surcharge to the Commissioners within 30 days of its imposition. [*TMA 1970, s 59C(7)*]. Such an appeal is dealt with as though it was an appeal against an assessment. [*TMA 1970, s 59C(8)*]. If the taxpayer had a reasonable excuse for not paying the tax the Commissioners may set aside the surcharge, otherwise they are to confirm it. [*TMA 1970, s 59C(9)*]. They have no power to reduce it. Inability to pay the tax is not a reasonable excuse for this purpose. [*TMA 1970, s 59C(10)*]. As with VAT, this is likely to be a fertile area for litigation before the Commissioners.

14.6   A surcharge which is more than 30 days in arrears itself carries interest. [*TMA 1970, s 59C(6)*]. The Board have the discretion to mitigate any surcharge, or stay or compound any proceedings for the recovery of any surcharge. [*TMA 1970, s 59C(11)*]. This power can be exercised after judgment has been given in the Revenue's favour for non-payment.

Interest on unpaid tax

14.7   A substituted *TMA 1970, s 86; FA 1994, 19 Sch 23* sets out new rules regarding interest on overdue tax. These are necessitated by the unified payment dates for tax on income from all sources and CGT, and by the system of interim payments. Any arrears of interim or final payments of income tax and CGT carry interest from the due date until the date of payment at the rate specified in *FA 1989, s 78*. [*TMA 1970, s 86(1)*]. The due date for interim payments is 31 January in the year of assessment and 31 July in the next year of assessment respectively (see 13.2). The due date for the final payment is normally the following 31 January although it may be three months after the issue of the tax return if later (see 13.10 and 13.12). As with surcharges, if the taxpayer has opted for Revenue assessment and the assessment is late, the trigger date for interest will be 30 days after issue of the tax bill (see 14.3).

14.8   Tax which has been postponed under an appeal or tax which is charged under an amended self-assessment or discovery carries interest from the 'relevant date' to the date of payment. The relevant date is the date for final payment of tax, as set out in the previous paragraph. [*TMA 1970, s 86(3)*]. The fact that a date for payment may be a non-business day is disregarded. [*TMA 1970, s 86(3)*].

14.9   Where a taxpayer has made a claim to reduce his interim payments (see 13.6 and 13.7) and it transpires that these are less than they should have been, interest is charged on any underpayment. The rules are rather complicated but the principle is that interest is calculated by reference to the lesser of the actual tax liability for the year and what it would have been on a preceding year basis. They ensure that interest will only be payable if the amount of each of the two interim payments is less than 50 per cent of the actual total tax liability for the year. But there is a cap at 50 per cent of the previous year's liability.

14.10   The amount underpaid on an instalment is calculated by deducting the actual payment from the lesser of:

(*a*)   the sum of the actual interim payment and 50 per cent of the final payment, excluding CGT [*TMA 1970, s 86(10)*]; and

(*b*)   what the payment would have been under 13.2 if based on the preceding year liability. [*TMA 1970, s 86(4)*].

Example 2

Mr Robert's tax liability for 1997/98 was £15,000, none of which represented tax deducted at source. For 1998/99 he estimates that his tax liability will be reduced to £10,000. Therefore, instead of making interim payments of £7,500 each (by reference to the 1997/98 liability) he claims that the payments should be reduced to £5,000 each, and duly makes the payments on this basis. It transpires that his actual tax liability is £12,000, so he makes the final payment of £2,000 on 31 January 2000.

Applying the method of calculation prescribed in 14.10, (*a*) in the calculation is the sum of the actual interim payment (£5,000) and 50 per cent of the final payment (£1,000), namely £6,000; while (*b*) is the amount of the interim payment based on the preceding year's tax liability, namely £7,500. The lesser amount is £6,000. So the underpayment, on which interest is payable until the date of the final payment, is £6,000 − £5,000 = £1,000.

In the event that Mr Robert's tax liability for 1998/99 had turned out to be £20,000, so that the final payment was £10,000, the lesser amount in the calculation would have been £7,500, i.e. the amount calculated by reference to the preceding year. So the underpayment on each interim payment, liable to interest, would have been £2,500.

14.11   The interest calculation is amended by *TMA 1970, s 86(5)* where the interim payments are of unequal amounts and the application of the above calculation would ostensibly give the taxpayer a benefit. The amendment applies where adding 50 per cent of the final payment to the interim payment, as in (*a*) in the calculation in 14.10 would result in one of the interim payments exceeding the liability based on the preceding year's tax, and the other interim payment being less. *TMA 1970, s 86(5)* provides that so much of 50 per cent of the final payment as does not affect the amount of interest payable on one of the interim payments is added to (*a*) in the calculation of the interest payable on the other interim payment. The purpose is to ensure that in appropriate cases interest is payable on the lesser instalment by reference to the tax liability of the preceding year in any event. The *subsection* is difficult to understand at first reading. It is probably best explained by means of an example.

Example 3

Mr White's liability for the previous year (1997/98) is £12,000. He makes a claim for the first interim payment for 1998/99 to be reduced to £5,500 and for the second interim payment to be reduced to £4,000. His actual liability turns out to be £13,000, so he makes a final payment in January 2000 of £3,500. Applying the calculation in 14.10 to the first interim payment, the amount in (*a*) would be £7,250, being the sum of the interim payment (£5,500) and 50 per cent of the final payment (£1,750), whilst the amount in (*b*) would be £6,000 (50 per cent of the preceding year liability). Since (*b*) is the lesser amount, the underpayment, on which interest is due, would be £6,000 − £5,500 = £500. If the same calculation were applied to the second interim payment of £4,000, the amount in (*a*) would be £5,750, namely £4,000 plus £1,750, whilst the amount in (*b*) would again be £6,000. Since £5,750 is the lesser amount, the underpayment on which interest would *prima facie* be due is £5,750 − £4,000 = £1,750. The calculation would thus result in an interest liability based on a figure of £5,750, i.e. less than the preceding year figure of £6,000, notwithstanding that 50 per cent of the actual liability was £6,500.

This is counteracted as follows. 50 per cent of the final payment is £1,750. Taking this figure in the calculation of the first interim payment (*a*) was increased to £7,250. But this was capped at £6,000, being the amount in (*b*). Hence £1,250 of the £1,750 did not affect the interest payable on the first interim payment. It is then added to (*a*) in the calculation of interest on the second and lower interim payment. The amount in (*a*) then becomes £4,000 + £1,750 + £1,250 = £7,000. The revised amount in (*a*) then exceeds the preceding year liability figure of £6,000 as calculated in (*b*). The upshot is that the underpayment is instead calculated by reference to the preceding year liability of £6,000, being £6,000 − £4,000 = £2,000.

14.12   In the event that a taxpayer claims to reduce only one of his interim payments, and this results in an underpayment, interest is payable on the difference between the actual payment and the correct amount. [*TMA 1970, s 86(6)*]. The correct amount is the lesser of (*a*) 50 per cent of the taxpayer's preceding year liability and (*b*) the actual payment plus the balancing payment.

14.13   In the event that interim payments are made late, thus incurring an interest charge, there will be a partial remission of interest if there is an eventual repayment of tax. In effect interest on the overpayment element of the interim payment is remitted. [*TMA 1970, s 86(7)*].

Example 4

Interim payments of £15,000 each were made, both of which were paid three months late so that interest was payable. The actual tax liability turned out to be £25,000, so £5,000 is repaid, representing £2,500 for each interim payment. Hence the interest which has been charged on £2,500 of the late interim payment is remitted.

14.14   In the event that the taxpayer makes a claim to reduce only one of the interim payments, which is then paid late, and there is a final repayment of tax, there is a like remission of interest on that interim payment, so that interest is only finally charged on the amount which should have been paid. [*TMA 1970, s 86(9)*]. In the case where there are two interim payments of differing amounts, which are paid late, there is an adjustment which parallels the position set out in 14.10. [*TMA 1970, s 86(8)*].

Penalties

Introduction

14.15   The penalty regime was subject to substantial changes and consolidation in *FA 1989* in the light of the deliberations of the Keith Committee. The present provisions and the historical background are examined in depth in Tolley's *Interest and Penalty Provisions*, to which the reader is referred for a detailed review. It is an area of considerable importance, with a steady increase in the number of investigations, and a substantial and growing yield from such compliance and investigation work. See also Tolley's *Tax Compliance and Investigations.*

14.16   The power to impose penalties of one kind or another, and the accompanying provisions relating to penalty determinations and proceedings are contained in over 30 *sections* of *TMA 1970.* Penalties are generally to be determined by a Revenue Officer under *TMA 1970, s 100*, with the taxpayer having the right of appeal to the Commissioners under *TMA 1970, s 100B.* But in certain cases the Officer has to apply to the Commissioners for the imposition of a penalty, notably for daily penalties. The rest of this Chapter reviews the principal penalties under Simplified Assessing and the changes which have been made.

Failure to notify Revenue of chargeability

14.17   Where a person who is chargeable to income tax or CGT, but who is not on the records of the Revenue and hence has not received a tax return, fails to notify the Revenue as to his chargeability within six months of the end of the year of assessment as required by *TMA 1970, s 7(1)* (see 10.5 above) he is liable to a penalty. [*TMA 1970, s 7(8)*]. It is not to exceed the tax to which he is assessed, whether under a self-assessment or a Revenue assessment [*under TMA 1970, s 9 or 29*] for the period. Moreover, the imposition of the penalty is subject to the tax itself not having been paid before 31 January following the end of the year of assessment. This is the same penalty as under the present system, although the notification period has been shortened from twelve to six months.

Failure to make a return by individuals or trustees

14.18   There are significant changes to the penalty provisions for failure to complete and deliver a tax return by the required filing date (generally 31 January following the end of the year of assessment (see 10.12)). At present there is a penalty up to £300. Under the new system there is to be an automatic flat rate penalty of £100. [*TMA 1970, s 93(1)(2) as inserted by FA 1994, 19 Sch 25*]. There is a further automatic penalty also of £100 if the failure continues after six months from the filing date. [*TMA 1970, s 93(4)*]. But this second penalty is not exigible if an application is made to the Commissioners for daily penalties under the provisions set out in 14.21. It is understood that in practice there will be a 14-day period of grace before a penalty is imposed.

14.19   If the taxpayer establishes that his actual tax would have been less, these fixed £100 penalties are to be reduced to the amount of tax. [*TMA 1970, s 93(7)*]. So if a taxpayer's actual liability turns out to be only £50, the penalties are likewise limited to £50 in total. On an appeal to the Commissioners against the imposition of these flat rate penalties, they can be set aside if it appears to the Commissioners that the taxpayer had a reasonable excuse for not delivering the return. Otherwise, the Commissioners are to confirm the penalties. [*TMA 1970, s 93(8)*].

14.20 If the failure to deliver the return continues after the anniversary of the filing date, and the taxpayer would have been liable to tax had the return been duly submitted, he is liable to a further penalty of up to the amount of tax. [*TMA 1970, s 93(5)*]. This penalty, the same as under the present system, is to be imposed by a Revenue Officer, and is subject to appeal by the taxpayer.

14.21 A Revenue Officer can also apply to the General or Special Commissioners for the imposition of daily penalties, a feature of the present system. On such an application the Commissioners can direct that the taxpayer is liable to a further penalty or penalties up to £60 for each day on which the failure to deliver the return continues. [*TMA 1970, s 93(3)*]. No such penalty is to be imposed after the failure has been remedied. [*TMA 1970, s 93(6)*].

Failure to make partnership return

14.22 Similar penalties to those set out above in relation to individuals and trustees are imposed in respect of partnerships. The provisions apply where a representative partner has been required by notice to deliver a partnership return and has failed to comply. [*TMA 1970, s 93A(1) as inserted by FA 1994, 19 Sch 26*]. Each person who was a partner at any time during the period in respect of which the return was required (defined as a 'relevant' partner) is liable to an automatic penalty of £100. [*TMA 1970, s 93A(2)(8)*]. There is a further automatic penalty, also of £100, on each relevant partner after a default longer than six months. [*TMA 1970, s 93A(4)*]. Again, this second penalty is not exigible if the Revenue Officer applies for daily penalties.

14.23 A Revenue Officer can apply to the General or Special Commissioners for further daily penalties. The Commissioners can then direct that each relevant partner is liable to a further penalty or penalties up to £60 for each day on which the failure continues after the day on which the representative partner is notified of the direction. No such penalty is to be imposed after the failure has been remedied. [*TMA 1970, s 93A(3)(5)*].

14.24 Where more than one partner appeals against the imposition of any of these penalties the appeals shall be treated as a single, composite appeal by the representative partner. On an appeal against the £100 flat rate penalties the Commissioners can set them aside if it appears to them that the representative partner had a reasonable excuse for not delivering the return. Otherwise they are to confirm the determination.

14.25 It is to be stressed that the fixed and daily penalties apply to each partner and not the partnership as a whole. Hence in a large partnership the total penalties can be significant. It is also to be noted that there is no procedure to impose tax-related penalties for failure to deliver a return, the partnership return not forming the basis of an assessment.

Failure to make return – European economic interest groupings

14.26 The existing provisions in *TMA 1970, s 98B*, regarding EEIG's are amended by *FA 1994, 19 Sch 30*. Where an EEIG or a member fails to deliver a tax return or other required documents the EEIG or member thereof will be liable to a penalty of up to £300 multiplied by the then number of members. [*TMA 1970, s 98B(2A)*]. An application can also be made by a Revenue Officer to the General or Special Commissioners for further daily penalties of £60 per day multiplied by the number of members at the end of each day. [*TMA 1970, s 98B(2B)*]. Under the present provisions the penalties are £300 and £60 respectively, regardless of the number of members.

Incorrect returns by individuals or trustees

14.27 Penalty provisions for failure to deliver a correct return are contained in *TMA 1970, s 95* as amended by *FA 1994, 19 Sch 27*. No fundamental changes have been made to these provisions, which apply where an individual or trustee fraudulently or negligently:

(*a*) delivers an incorrect tax return; or

(*b*) makes any incorrect return, statement or declaration in connection with any claims for any allowance, deduction or relief in respect of income tax or CGT; or

(*c*) submits any incorrect accounts in connection with the ascertainment of his liability to income tax or CGT.

The penalty is of an amount up to the difference between the tax actually payable, and that which was shown as due.

14.28 Where any of the above returns, statements, declarations etc. have not been made fraudulently or negligently, and it comes to the person's notice (or the notice of his personal representatives if he has died) that they were incorrect, the error must be remedied without unreasonable delay. Otherwise the returns etc. are to be treated as made negligently. [*TMA 1970, s 97*]. This provision remains unaltered.

Incorrect partnership return

14.29 New penalty provisions are included as *TMA 1970, s 95A* [*as introduced by FA 1994, 19 Sch 28*] dealing with incorrect partnership returns or accounts. They apply where a partner (the representative partner) fraudulently or negligently:

(*a*)   delivers an incorrect return;

(*b*)   makes any incorrect statement or declaration in connection with the return; or

(*c*)   submits incorrect accounts in connection with the return.

They also apply where the making of the incorrect return etc. is attributable to the fraudulent or negligent conduct of another partner who was a partner at any time during the period in respect of which the return was made. [*TMA 1970, s 95A(1)(4)*].

14.30   Each partner is then liable to a penalty up to the difference between the tax actually payable (including corporation tax) and the amount shown as payable. In determining each penalty regard is to be had only to the fraudulent or negligent conduct mentioned in the *section*. [*TMA 1970, s 95A(2)*]. Where two or more partners wish to appeal they have to do so via an appeal brought by the representative partner. The appeal is then treated as a composite appeal against the determination of each penalty. [*TMA 1970, s 95A(3)*].

Failure to produce documents

14.31   New provisions are included as *TMA 1970, s 97AA* [*as introduced by FA 1994, 19 Sch 29*] for failure to provide documents requested during a Revenue enquiry under the new *section 19A* (see 12.13 above). Where a person fails to comply with a notice to provide the documents or other information he is liable to an initial penalty of £50.

14.32   If the failure continues, a Revenue Officer may directly impose a further penalty of up to £30 per day for each day on which the failure continues under the determination provisions of *TMA 1970, s 100*. [*TMA 1970, s 97AA(1)(b)(2)(a)*]. In the alternative, the Officer may commence penalty proceedings before the General or Special Commissioners, in which case the Commissioners may, if satisfied, impose a penalty of up to £150 per day. [*TMA 1970, s 97AA(2)(b)*]. In either event no penalty is to be imposed after the failure has been remedied.

Failure to retain and preserve records

14.33   The new *TMA 1970, s 12* imposes an obligation on a taxpayer to retain and preserve his records (see 10.29 above). Generally these have to be kept for five years after 31 January following the end of the year of assessment for individuals, and six years after the end of the accounting period for companies. A penalty of up to £3,000 is exigible for any taxpayer who fails so to do. [*TMA 1970, s 12B(5); FA 1994, 19 Sch 3*].

Claim to reduce interim payments – fraud or neglect

14.34 A taxpayer subject to income tax may make a claim to make either nil or reduced interim payments (see 13.6 and 13.7 above). If in doing so he fraudulently or negligently makes any incorrect statement he is liable to a penalty up to an amount equal to the difference between what he should have paid and what he did pay.

Time limit for tax-related penalties

14.35 At present a penalty determination must generally be made or proceedings commenced within six years of the date on which the penalty was incurred, or at any later time within three years of the final determination of the tax liability. [*TMA 1970, s 103(1)*]. This is not altered. However, in the case of a deceased taxpayer the later date is not permissible under Simplified Assessing if the tax was charged in an assessment made later than six years after 31 January following the year for which it is charged. [*TMA 1970, s 103(2)*].

Repayment supplement – income tax

14.36 Where a taxpayer has overpaid tax, so that a tax repayment is made to him, he is entitled to a repayment supplement under *TA 1988, s 824* if the repayment is made after a certain period, effectively representing interest on the overpayment. The repayment supplement is calculated as simple interest on the amount of tax repaid but is itself completely free of tax. [*TA 1988, s 824(8)*].

14.37 At the present time entitlement to the supplement generally only runs from the later of the end of the year of assessment following that for which the repayment was made and the end of the year in which the overpayment was made. So if the year of assessment was 1992/93 and the tax was paid on, say, 1 October 1993, repayment supplement runs from 5 April 1994. But if the tax was paid on 1 October 1994, repayment supplement runs from 5 April 1995.

14.38 The provisions in *TA 1988, s 824* are substantially amended by *FA 1994, 19 Sch 41* under Simplified Assessing from 1996/97 (and from 1997/98 for partnerships commencing before 6 April 1994) particularly regarding the dates used for calculation of the supplement. Repayment supplement will apply to repayments of any of the following:

(*a*)   interim payments on account of income tax;

(*b*)   income tax paid by an individual;

(*c*)   surcharges on late payment of tax; and

(*d*)   any penalties imposed.

14.39   The repayment supplement on such amounts will be equal to interest at the rate specified from time to time under *FA 1989, s 178* for the period between the 'relevant time' and the date on which the order for repayment is issued. *[TA 1988, s 824(1) as amended]*. For payments of income tax the relevant time is the later of the date on which the payments were due (namely 31 January in the year of assessment and the following 31 July for interim payments, and generally the following 31 January for the final payment) and the date of payment. So under the new system there is a substantial acceleration of the date from which repayment supplement runs on overpaid tax. If the repayment was of a surcharge or penalty the relevant time is the later of 30 days from the date when the penalty or surcharge was imposed or repaid, and the date when it was actually paid. *[TA 1988, s 824(3) as amended]*.

14.40   The previous requirement that the taxpayer had to be UK-resident is removed. This follows the judgment of the European Court in *R v CIR ex parte Commerzbank AG [1993] STC 605* where it was held that the restriction of repayments to residents of the UK was an unlawful discrimination against residents of other member states of the European Community.

14.41   Under the present *TA 1988, s 824(5)* where there is an overpayment of Schedule E tax for several years, the Revenue are empowered to make regulations to attribute repayments of Schedule E tax to particular years. This power under *TA 1988, s 824(5)* is to be abolished, reflecting the new regulations which will be given to the Revenue to make regulations on repayment supplement for Schedule E, using the payment date as the starting point for the calculation of a supplement. These regulations have at the time of writing not been published.

Repayment supplement – CGT

14.42   The rules for repayment supplement for CGT in *TCGA 1992, s 283* are brought into line with the new income tax rules set out above. *[FA 1994, 19 Sch 46]*. It will no longer be a requirement for the taxpayer to be UK-resident. Moreover, repayment supplement is to run from 31 January in the year following that in which the repayment relates, or the date on which the tax paid if later, until the date on which the repayment is made.

Chapter 15

Appeals: Collection and Recovery

Introduction

15.1 Under the present system, once an assessment has been raised the taxpayer has a general right of appeal under *TMA 1970, s 31*. After a notice of appeal has been lodged, unless the taxpayer and the Inspector determine the matter by agreement under *TMA 1970, s 54*, the assessment has to be determined by proceedings before the General or Special Commissioners.

15.2 The General Commissioners are laymen who have local jurisdiction. They are persons of standing in their area who provide their services without remuneration. In England and Wales they are appointed by the Lord Chancellor, in Scotland by the Secretary of State. They are assisted by a clerk, who can advise them on legal issues. The Special Commissioners are remunerated, and are appointed by the Lord Chancellor from persons with relevant legal experience of tax matters, gained either in private practice or within the Revenue.

15.3 Certain appeals, generally involving technical matters, must be heard by the Special Commissioners. But generally the appeals are to be heard by the General Commissioners, subject to the right of the taxpayer to elect to bring the appeal before the Special Commissioners instead. For more details on the role of the Commissioners, the conduct of appeals before them, and the rights of appeal to the High Court against their determinations, see Tolley's *Taxes Management Provisions*. Also of interest will be Tolley's *Tax Appeals to the Commissioners*.

Appeals under Simplified Assessing

15.4 With a system of self-assessment, the taxpayer no longer needs a general right of appeal against an assessment to tax as is provided by the present *TMA 1970, s 31*. However, there are still cases where a right of appeal is required, in particular where the taxpayer does not self-assess, and the assessment is raised by the Revenue.

15.5 The provisions of *TMA 1970, s 31(1)* are amended accordingly by *FA 1994, 19 Sch 7*, preserving the taxpayer's rights of appeal in the following cases:

(*a*) Where a self-assessment is amended by a Revenue Officer under *TMA 1970, s 28A(2)*, which permits an immediate assessment to be raised after a Revenue enquiry has been opened, with a view to avoiding a loss of tax (see 12.18). But the appeal is not to be heard until the enquiry has been completed. [*TMA 1970, s 31(1A)*].

(*b*) Where a self-assessment is amended by a Revenue Officer under *TMA 1970, s 28A(4)* after a Revenue enquiry has been completed (see 12.22).

(*c*) Where a partnership statement is amended under *TMA 1970, s 28B(3)* as the result of a Revenue enquiry (see 12.25) or under *TMA 1970, s 30B(1)* as the result of a 'discovery' by the Revenue (see 12.56).

(*d*) In all other cases where a tax assessment is made which is not a self-assessment. This covers such cases as:

    (i)   assessments by the Revenue where there has been no self-assessment (see 11.11); and

    (ii) a 'discovery' assessment by the Revenue (see 12.41).

15.6   The notice of appeal is to be given to the Officer by whom the notice of amendment or assessment was given, within 30 days of the issue of notice of amendment or assessment. [*TMA 1970, s 31(1)(2)*]. Amended *TMA 1970, s 31(3)* provides that the appeal must be heard before the Special Commissioners if:

(*a*) it relates to the provisions relating to Settlements [*TA 1988, ss 660–685*] or Estates in the course of administration [*TA 1988, ss 695–702*]; or

(*b*) it relates to an assessment to tax made by the Board.

Appeals against amendments to claims

15.7   The procedure relating to claims for relief, and the review of such claims by the Revenue, has been substantially changed under Simplified Assessing as outlined in Chapter 10. The procedure permits the Revenue to enquire into a claim made otherwise than in a tax return under the provisions of *TMA 1970, 1A Sch*, in the same way that they have the right of enquiry into a tax return and a claim made therein. There are like powers given to the Revenue to amend claims made under *TMA 1970, 1A Sch* if they consider it appropriate (see 12.30).

15.8   Where a Revenue Officer amends such a claim under *TMA 1970, 1A Sch 7(3)* the claimant taxpayer has the right of appeal by written notice to the Officer within 30 days of the amendment. [*TMA 1970, 1A Sch 9(3)*]. This time limit is extended to three months where the issues arising include:

(*a*)   any question under *TA 1988, s 278* (personal reliefs for non-residents);

(*b*)   any question of residence, ordinary residence or domicile; or

(*c*)   the question whether a fund is one to which *TA 1988, s 615(3)* applies (pension funds for service abroad).

[*TMA 1970, 1A Sch 9(2)*].

The Commissioners may then vary the amendment appealed against, whether or not it is to the advantage of the appellant. [*TMA 1970, 1A Sch 9(3)*]. Due effect is then to be given to such variation, either by an assessment on a claimant, or by a repayment of tax. [*TMA 1970, 1A Sch 9(4)*]. The appeal lies to the General Commissioners, but the taxpayer may elect to go before the Special Commissioners instead. [*TMA 1970, 2 Sch 1*]. However, where the decision comes from the Board, rather than a Revenue Officer, the appeal must go to the Special Commissioners. [*TMA 1970, 2 Sch 3*].

Appeals against surcharge and penalties

15.9   As set out in 14.1 above there is a 5 per cent surcharge for late payment of CGT and the final income tax instalment. There is a limited right of appeal against the surcharge, namely on the grounds of reasonable excuse, as set out in 14.5.

15.10   As regards penalties, although there has been some change to the provisions relating to penalties as outlined in 14.15 *et seq.* there has not been any fundamental changes in the system itself. The taxpayer's existing right of appeal to the Commissioners under *TMA 1970, s 100B* generally remains.

15.11   Flat rate penalties for failure to make a return can be set aside by the Commissioners if there has been a reasonable excuse (see 14.19 and 14.24).

Procedure on appeal

15.12   The procedure for appeals to the Commissioners is contained in *TMA 1970, s 50*. The basic provisions have not been changed. The appellant is to be given notice of the day for hearing the appeal. [*TMA 1970, s 50(1)*]. A Revenue Officer may attend every appeal, and is entitled to be present during the entire hearing and to give reasons in support of the assessment. [*TMA 1970, s 50(3)*]. The Commissioners are empowered to postpone the appeal for absence, sickness or other reasonable cause. [*TMA 1970, s 50(4)*]. The taxpayer may be represented by a barrister, solicitor or accountant.

15.13 There are then some consequential amendments in *TMA 1970, s 50(6)(7)* made by *FA 1994, 19 Sch 17*, reflecting the procedure for assessments under Simplified Assessing, notably the right of the Revenue to amend self-assessments and partnership statements. The Commissioners are directed to make the appropriate adjustments to any assessments, or any amendment to a self-assessment, whether upwards or downwards as the case may be, or to hold that the assessment etc. should stand good.

Postponement of tax pending appeal

15.14 Provisions are contained in *TMA 1970, s 55* dealing with the postponement of tax pending an appeal by the taxpayer to the Commissioners. For a summary of these provisions and the procedure see Tolley's *Taxes Management Provisions* (6.37–6.43). *TMA 1970, s 55(1)* is amended by *FA 1994, 19 Sch 18* to ensure that these rules for postponement of tax and the collection of tax which has not been postponed apply to appeals to the Commissioners under Simplified Assessing.

Collection and recovery

15.15 The proceedings relating to the collection and recovery of tax are presently contained in *TMA 1970, ss 60–70*, which are described in Tolley's *Taxes Management Provisions*. The first of these deals with the Collector's powers to distrain upon the goods and chattels of a taxpayer in default, and the Revenue's prior claims over other creditors, and the separate recovery and priority procedures in Scotland. These provisions are unchanged under Simplified Assessing.

15.16 Under *TMA 1970, s 65* small amounts of tax can be recovered summarily in the Magistrates Court. *TMA 1970, s 65(1)* is amended by *FA 1994, 19 Sch 19* to increase the amount which can be so collected from £1,000 to £2,000, which will include interim payments. Proceedings are to be brought within twelve months from the time of default. [*TMA 1970, s 65(3)*]. The provisions in *TMA 1970, s 66* regarding recovery in the county courts remain unchanged.

15.17 At present, interest which is due on unpaid tax is treated as tax for recovery purposes under *TMA 1970, s 69*. Under amended *TMA 1970, s 69*, penalties and surcharges will also be regarded as tax. [*FA 1994, 19 Sch 20*]. A certificate from a Collector that such interest, penalties and surcharges are payable is sufficient evidence of that fact for recovery purposes. [*TMA 1970, s 70(2)*].

Chapter 16

Tax Planning and Anti-Avoidance

New businesses – choice of accounting date

16.1   Where a new business is being set up after after 6 April 1994, the date to which accounts are prepared will obviously affect the basis period and therefore the assessable profits for the fiscal year. An accounting period ending on 5 April is the simplest under the new rules and will avoid any overlap on commencement and hence any overlap relief on cessation. Accounts will be made up for the fiscal year and the profits as adjusted for tax purposes will be those taxed.

16.2   Attractive as this may appear it may not be the best solution. The self-assessment rules require the return and accounts to be submitted by 31 January following the end of the fiscal year, or if the Revenue are to compute the tax payable, by 30 September following the fiscal year. In the latter case this would give less than six months for the preparation and agreement of the accounts. If the accounting date year end is 30 April and self-assessment is being applied, there will be 21 months from the end of the year to allow for the filing date of the accounts.

16.3   There is also the question of a timing delay in that the longer the period between earning the profits and the payment of the tax on them, the easier it may be to meet the tax charge. If, therefore, as under the existing rules, an accounting date is chosen early in the fiscal year, and the profits for the first twelve months are kept to an absolute minimum, the overlap profits over the overlap period which are doubly taxed will be kept to a minimum. If inflation were to return at a material level, it would obviously increase the advantage of the delay between the end of the accounting period and the payment of tax.

Minimising profits in initial period

16.4   Legitimate means of keeping profits as low as possible in the opening period would include renting rather than buying premises and leasing rather than buying equipment, if it makes economic sense to lease short term. However because capital allowances are given as an expense under Simplified Assessing, the advantage of leasing equipment is not nearly so marked as under the old rules where capital allowances were given once only for expenditure on plant and machinery, but lease payments (treated as a trading expense) were effectively allowed up to three times in the opening period.

16.5   Techniques used under the old system such as engaging potential partners as employees in the first period in order that their salaries should be a deduction from profits, do not achieve quite the advantage that they did under the old system. Although this would reduce the base line profit for the equity partners in the opening period, when the employee became a partner he would himself have an overlap resulting from his share of profits in the year in which he joined the partnership.

Change of accounting date

16.6   Whether a change of accounting date would be beneficial in 1993/94, 1994/95 or 1995/96 under the existing rules, or whether there should be a change of accounting date in the transitional year of assessment 1996/97, or under the new rules in 1997/98 or later, will depend on the figures in each case. It is impossible to generalise.

16.7   Under the existing rules, if the profits of a period omitted on the change of accounting date were relatively low, or the profits of the period coming in twice were relatively high, the Revenue would gain: conversely, if the profits of a period omitted were relatively high, or the profits of the period coming in twice were relatively low, the taxpayer would gain. The averaging provisions set out in IR 26 (Appendix D) are designed to prevent this happening to any material extent, although a slight advantage may be possible under the existing rules.

16.8   Under the transitional rules, a change of accounting date to a date later in the fiscal year, or even to 5 April, would maximise the profits falling out of assessment on averaging. It would however result in loss of overlap relief on cessation as the period from the end of the accounting period to 5 April would be reduced. Conversely, if the accounting date in the transitional period were brought forward, the profits falling out on averaging would be reduced, but the transitional overlap would be increased.

16.9   As explained in Chapter 2, a change of accounting date under the new rules to a date earlier in the fiscal year results in a further overlap and the change to a date later in the fiscal year involves the profits of in excess of twelve months being charged, subject to possible overlap relief.

Change of accounting date under existing law

16.10   The preceding year basis of assessment can only be applied where the business consistently makes up profits to the same date in each year. It is normally permissible to make up accounts on a 52- or 53-week accounting period provided that the year end remains within four days either side of a particular date.

16.11   If no accounts for a suitable period are available, the Revenue decide what period of twelve months ending on a date within the year preceding the year of assessment shall be deemed to be the 'year' the profits or gains of which are to be taken to be the profits or gains of the 'year preceding the year of assessment' under *TA 1988, s 60(4)* as originally enacted. The Revenue apply an averaging procedure on a change of accounting date. On such a change the profits of the twelve-month period ending on the new accounting date form the basis of the assessment on the normal preceding year basis. If the new accounting date is later than the old accounting date, some profits will fall out of assessment and if it is earlier some profits will be assessed twice. The averaging procedure then applied is as explained below. The Revenue procedure has been approved in *CIR v Helical Bar Ltd 1972 48 TC 221*.

Averaging procedure

16.12   First, it is necessary to adjust the profits for the year to the new accounting date, making any necessary apportionments on a time basis. It is then necessary to compute adjusted profits for the previous twelve months (the corresponding period). The assessments originally based on the profits included in these computations should be examined. If the earliest of those years of assessment cannot be based on the original accounting date on the normal preceding year basis, it is necessary to go back a further year and introduce another corresponding period. The total period of the accounts affected is compared with the total period of the fiscal years affected and the profits are expanded or contracted proportionately to arrive at the total notional adjusted profits. From this is deducted the assessments which are final leaving an adjusted figure for the intermediate period. If the intermediate period figure falls between the corresponding period figure and the original unadjusted assessment for that fiscal year, the intermediate figure will be substituted provided that the difference is at least 10 per cent of the average profits or £1,000, whichever is lower.

16.13   This change of accounting date computation can best be illustrated by an example and further details will be found in the Revenue leaflet IR 26, reproduced in Appendix D. This averaging basis is not used by the Revenue where it would produce an unfair result, for example, where the intermediate figure does not fall between the original and corresponding figures or where the profits of the business are seasonal or where some of the periods involved were loss-making, or during the opening or closing years of a business.

Example 1

On 30 April 1994 Mr Yermolayev changed his accounting date. The results were:

		£
30 April 1994	– 4 months	10,000
31 December 1993	– 12 months	28,000
31 December 1992	– 12 months	24,000
	28 months	£62,000

Accounts will be made up to 30 April in future:

	£
Assessment 1995/96	
Year ended 30.4.94	
4 months to 30.4.94	10,000
8/12 × £28,000 (y/e 31.12.93)	18,667
	£28,667

	£
Assessment 1994/95	
Year ended 30.4.93	
4/12 × £28,000 (y/e 31.12.93)	9,333
8/12 × £24,000 (y/e 31.12.92)	16,000
	£25,333

	£
Original assessment 1994/95	
Year ended 31.12.93	£28,000

	£
Original assessment 1993/94	
Year ended 31.12.92	£24,000

Fiscal years originally based on these profits 1993/94, 1994/95 and 1995/96
3 years = 36 months
Average profits

	£	£
$\frac{36 \text{ months}}{28 \text{ months}}$ × £62,000		79,714
Less Assessed 1995/96	28,667	
1993/94	24,000	52,667
Intermediate period		£27,047

This £27,047 falls between the original assessment (£28,000) and the corresponding period assessment (£25,333), but is within £1,000 of the original assessment. As the difference is also less than 10 per cent of the average profits for the current (1995/96 £28,667) and preceding years' assessments (1994/95 £28,000) i.e. £2,833, the average basis for 1994/95 is not used and the original assessment of £28,000 remains.

16.14 The capital allowances basis periods will be recalculated in accordance with *CAA 1990, s 160* only if the taxpayer so requires. By unpublished concession, the Revenue only adjust the capital allowances basis periods if the taxpayer so insists.

Transitional year planning and anti-avoidance

16.15 The Revenue are well aware that the averaging of profits in the transitional year 1996/97 gives the taxpayer the incentive to maximise the profit for the basis period concerned, as normally only half this profit would be charged to tax. Similarly, the transitional overlap relief would encourage the maximisation of the profit for the 1997/98 basis period because that part of the basis period which falls before 6 April 1997 is ultimately relieved from tax by way of overlap relief.

16.16 Detailed anti-avoidance measures will be introduced in *FA 1995*, but to give taxpayers some forewarning of the provisions the Revenue issued a Press Release on 31 March 1994 (Appendix C). In order to discourage attempts at avoidance, the result of falling foul of the anti-avoidance measures will put the taxpayer in a materially worse position than he would have been had he not attempted to take undue advantage of the transitional measures.

Transitional averaging anti-avoidance

16.17 The anti-avoidance measures relating to trades, professions or vocations taxed under Schedule D, Cases I, II or V apply where one or more triggering events apply. These are:

(*a*)   A change of one accounting policy for another, or a modification within one policy. Accounting policies are defined similarly to Statement of Standard Accounting Practice No 2 (Appendix B) which states 'accounting policies are the specific accounting bases judged by business enterprises to be most appropriate to their circumstances and adopted by them for the purpose of preparing their financial accounts'.

(*b*)   Transactions with a connected person, or with connected persons including partnerships. Connected persons are defined by *TA 1988, s 839*. A connected person is a spouse, brother or brother-in-law, sister or sister-in-law, parent or parent-in-law, grandparent or grandparent-in-law, son or son-in-law, daughter or daughter-in-law, grandson or grandson-in-law, granddaughter or granddaughter-in-law. In addition, a trustee of a settlement is connected with a settlor, or with a company connected with a settlement under *TA 1988, s 681*. Except in connection with *bona fide* commercial partnership arrangements, a partner is connected with his other partners and their spouses or relatives. Companies are connected if they are under common control and two or more persons acting together to exercise control of a company are connected with each other.

(*c*)   Arrangements with unconnected persons which are wholly or partly reciprocal or self-cancelling. This would include stock sold immediately before the end of a transitional basis period and repurchased immediately afterwards.

(*d*)   Any major change in the procedure followed for the issue of bills to customers which would include arrangements for payments on account, procedures for the collection of debts, or procedures for the payment of bills for business expenses including salaries or bonuses. This would be particularly relevant for businesses preparing accounts on a conventional basis such as cash receipts and payments, or bills delivered.

16.18   The existence of a trigger point is not itself fatal if the taxpayer can show that the transactions or changes in accounting or commercial practice were for *bona fide* commercial reasons and not to obtain a tax advantage.

16.19   If the triggering event results in a triggering consequence, the profits so identified would be charged to tax as additional profits in 1996/97, which would not qualify for any averaging reduction. The taxpayer is therefore in a worse position than if the profits had not been shifted into the transitional basis period because half (or the appropriate proportion) of the profits shifted into the transitional period are already taxed under the averaging provisions. The anti-avoidance assessment on the profits diverted is an additional charge in 1996/97, so that the profits shifted are in effect taxed one and a half times, or more.

Triggering consequences

16.20   The triggering consequences are where the main benefit that can reasonably be expected from the triggering event is one or more of the following.

(*a*)   A reduction in the profits which would otherwise have been assessable for 1995/96 and/or 1997/98, which results in a corresponding increase in the profits in the basis period for 1996/97, only the appropriate percentage of which is taxed. In making this comparison it is necessary to aggregate the profits of partners for 1997/98.

(*b*)   An increase in the losses which would otherwise have been allowable for 1995/96, 1996/97 and/or 1997/98, as a result of an increase in the profits moved to the basis period for 1996/97, where only the appropriate percentage is charged. For the purpose of this test the losses of partners are aggregated.

(*c*) An increase in the profits of a business subject to the transitional provisions where only an appropriate percentage is charged in 1996/97, resulting in a corresponding reduction in the profits of a business not subject to transitional averaging, or an increase in the losses of any other business.

(*d*) Any similar tax benefits to those in (*a*)–(*c*) above, i.e. an increase in the profits subject to transitional averaging in 1996/97 as a result of some action or lack of action which leads to a corresponding reduction in profit or increase in loss for any period which is taxed or relieved in full.

De minimis provisions

16.21 The transitional anti-avoidance provisions do not apply where:

(*a*) the turnover is less than £X per annum during the 1996/97 basis period, or the 1997/98 transitional overlap period; or

(*b*) the triggering consequence i.e. the profit diverted as a result of the triggering event, is less than Y per cent of the base line profit. The base line profit is the profit that would have arisen had the triggering event not taken place; or

(*c*) the increased profit in 1996/97, or the increase in the transitional overlap credit is less than £Z.

Partnerships

16.22 The *de minimis* provisions for partnerships are applied as if X and Z were multiplied by the average number of partners throughout the basis period for 1996/97, subject to averaging. In the case of the transitional overlap, the turnover of the whole firm is divided among the partners. The Press Release also refers to the turnover of the firm being divided among partners in the transitional relief period in proportion to the way the profit of the transitional relief period is divided among them and the exception test applied to each partner separately, but this does not appear to make sense if the turnover limit multiplied by the number of partners is to be applied to the firm as a whole.

16.23 It appears that the *de minimis* amounts and percentage i.e. X, Y and Z above, will only be announced immediately prior to the issue of the tax returns for the year. Presumably, therefore, the 1996/97 figures would not be announced until April 1997 and the 1997/98 figures until April 1998. The intention is to discourage taxpayers from activities which would divert profits into the transitional period in order to try and obtain a tax advantage. Accordingly they will not be told the 'safe harbour' rules until it is too late to take any action.

16.24   This probably means that the *de minimis* figures will be fairly high unless in due course it appears to the Revenue that taxpayers generally have been shunting excessive profits into the transitional period. This could have the negative effect of the imposition of low *de minimis* figures, thereby allowing the Revenue to collect substantial additional tax under this penalty element in the anti-avoidance provisions. The *de minimis* exemptions will be fixed by Statutory Instrument under the enabling powers in the *Finance Act 1995*.

Payment of interest

16.25   The Revenue are also well aware that a partner could obtain an advantage by procuring the repayment of partnership borrowings and substituting personal loans to provide capital for the firm, rather appropriately described as 'privatisation'. Interest on a partnership borrowing would be relieved as a trading expense and under the averaging provisions normally only half of this expense would be so relieved. On the other hand if the partners were to borrow personally, the interest would be claimed under *TA 1988, s 353* as payable in respect of a loan to the partnership and there would be no loss of interest relief.

16.26   To counter this, *TA 1988, s 362(1)(b)* will be amended in the *Finance Act 1995* to reduce relief under *TA 1988, s 353* for the years 1994/95 to 1996/97 inclusive. Relief will be prohibited for interest on a loan where the amount borrowed has been used directly or indirectly by the partnership to repay any of the partnership loans in order to reduce the partnership interest which would have been claimed as a deduction in computing the profits taxable under Schedule D, Cases I or II and which falls into the basis period for 1996/97. The relief given to the individual partners [*under TA 1988, s 353*] will be reduced proportionately to the reduction in profits as a result of averaging in 1996/97. This restriction will not apply where the refinancing has taken place prior to the publication of the *Finance Bill 1994* on 11 January 1994.

Interest received

16.27   Interest received from a new source starting on or after 6 April 1994 is on a current year basis under Schedule D, Cases III, IV or V. So it is not possible to set up new accounts specifically designed to avoid the transitional rules, which average the interest arising in 1995/96 and 1996/97 to form the basis of the transitional year assessment in 1996/97. If the Revenue identify any accounts designed to take advantage of the new rule set up prior to 5 April 1994, they will, as new accounts, be assessed on the actual interest arising in 1993/94 and 1994/95. Moreover the Revenue will in the *Finance Act 1995* legislate to assess such accounts for 1995/96 on an actual basis also, which means that they will be assessed on an actual basis throughout. The object is to prevent the creation of accounts with artificial interest arrangements which will concentrate income into the transitional period reduced by averaging.

Existing accounts

16.28 The strict legal situation is that any new deposit in an existing account charged on a preceding year basis is a new source of income (*Hart v Sangster 1957 37 TC 231*). In practice, the Revenue have not treated additional deposits as a new source, but have taxed new accounts on a preceding year basis where there was already in existence a preceding year basis source. From 6 April 1994, any new source of income will be charged on a current year basis under the new provisions even where there are existing 'preceding year basis' sources.

16.29 Where a taxpayer has accounts where the interest is paid gross and which are assessed on a preceding year basis, and accounts where the interest is subject to the deduction of tax and dealt with on a current year basis, the Revenue will reserve the right to assess any new deposit to an existing account as if it were a new source on the current year basis, to prevent taxpayers obtaining a transitional year averaging advantage by moving funds from an account dealt with on a current year basis to an account dealt with on a preceding year basis.

16.30 There is obviously a temptation for banks to alter the terms of interest payable on existing accounts to concentrate the interest into the fiscal years 1995/96 and 1996/97 in order to maximise the amount subject to averaging. The anti-avoidance provision will enable the Revenue to reallocate interest on a day-to-day basis to prevent such bunching.

16.31 It would also be possible to achieve the same effect by adjusting the rate at which interest is paid while leaving unchanged the normal dates of payment of interest, i.e. increasing the interest received in the transitional period subject to averaging and reducing the interest payable that is fully taxed in 1994/95 or 1997/98. In such cases the interest will be recalculated on the average rate of interest for the whole period of the deposit and tax recalculated accordingly. The 1995 legislation will provide for *de minimis* limits below which such anti-avoidance provisions will not be used, but the safe harbour levels will be fixed by Statutory Instrument immediately after the end of the relevant fiscal year.

Schedule D, Cases IV and V

16.32 Non-trading income assessable under Schedule D, Cases IV and V is also brought within a transitional averaging arrangement giving similar opportunities for exploitation. Anti-avoidance measures adopting a similar approach to that applied for trades are likely. How this will apply in the case of remittances bunched into the transitional period remains to be seen.

Schedule D, Case VI

16.33 Miscellaneous income assessed under Schedule D, Case VI is often in practice assessed on a preceding year basis, in particular furnished lettings. Transitional relief will be given on the non-statutory basis by way of averaging in a similar manner to trades under Schedule D, Cases I and II. But for anti-avoidance purposes the Revenue will rely on the powers in *TA 1988, s 69* which allow them to fix the basis period.

Deterrence

16.34 The whole approach of the anti-avoidance measures is not merely to recover tax lost by the Revenue as a result of artificially shifting profits into the transitional averaging period, or the transitional overlap period. It is to deter taxpayers from attempting such manoeuvres by making the anti-avoidance provisions penal in their effect, so that the taxpayer is worse off if caught by the anti-avoidance provisions than he would have been had no attempt been made to divert profits in order to maximise the transitional relief.

Example 2

Mr Chetverikov makes up his accounts to 30 April each year. At 30 April 1994 he thinks it would be a smart move to reduce his stock value by £8,000 which reduces his profit for that year and increases the profits for the year ended 30 April 1995, when stock is valued on a normal basis, by a similar amount.

His profits as adjusted for tax purposes are as follows:

Year ended 30 April 1994		£22,000
Year ended 30 April 1995		£38,000
Year ended 30 April 1996		£30,000
Year ended 30 April 1997		£32,000

Taxable			
1995/96	y/e 30.4.94		£22,000
1996/97	y/e 30.4.95	£38,000	
	y/e 30.4.96	£30,000	
		£68,000	
Average			£34,000
1997/98	y/e 30.4.97		£32,000
Total			£88,000

Had he not reduced his stock value, his profits would have been:

Year ended 30 April 1994	£30,000	
Year ended 30 April 1995	£30,000	
Year ended 30 April 1996	£30,000	
Year ended 30 April 1997	£32,000	

Taxable
1995/96	y/e 30.4.94		£30,000
1996/97	y/e 30.4.95	£30,000	
	y/e 30.4.96	£30,000	
		£60,000	

Average		£30,000
1997/98	y/e 30.4.97	£32,000
Total		£92,000
Saving (£92,000 − £88,000)		£4,000

However, the Revenue invoke the anti-avoidance provisions and assess the diverted profits of £8,000 in 1996/97 increasing the assessment for that year to £42,000 (£34,000 + £8,000) and the total to £96,000 (£22,000 + £42,000 + £32,000) resulting in an additional tax charge or penalty on £4,000 (£96,000 − £92,000).

Example 3

If, in the previous example Mr Chetverikov having learnt the technique, reduces his stock value at 30 April 1997 by £10,000, he would increase the taxable profit for 1997/98 to £42,000. His transitional overlap relief would be based on the proportion of the year ended 30 April 1997 which falls before 5 April 1997 i.e. 340 days. His transitional overlap available for relief is therefore £42,000 × 340/365 = £39,123.

His transitional overlap available for relief would otherwise have been £32,000 × 340/365 = £29,808.

The Revenue invoke the transitional overlap anti-avoidance provisions and reduce the overlap by the artificial increase of £10,000 i.e. from £39,123 to £29,123 leaving him worse off than if he had not diverted profits by £685 (£29,808 − £29,123).

Appendix A

Hunt the Basis Period

Fiscal year in which business commences or is deemed to commence on or after 6 April 1994

Figure A

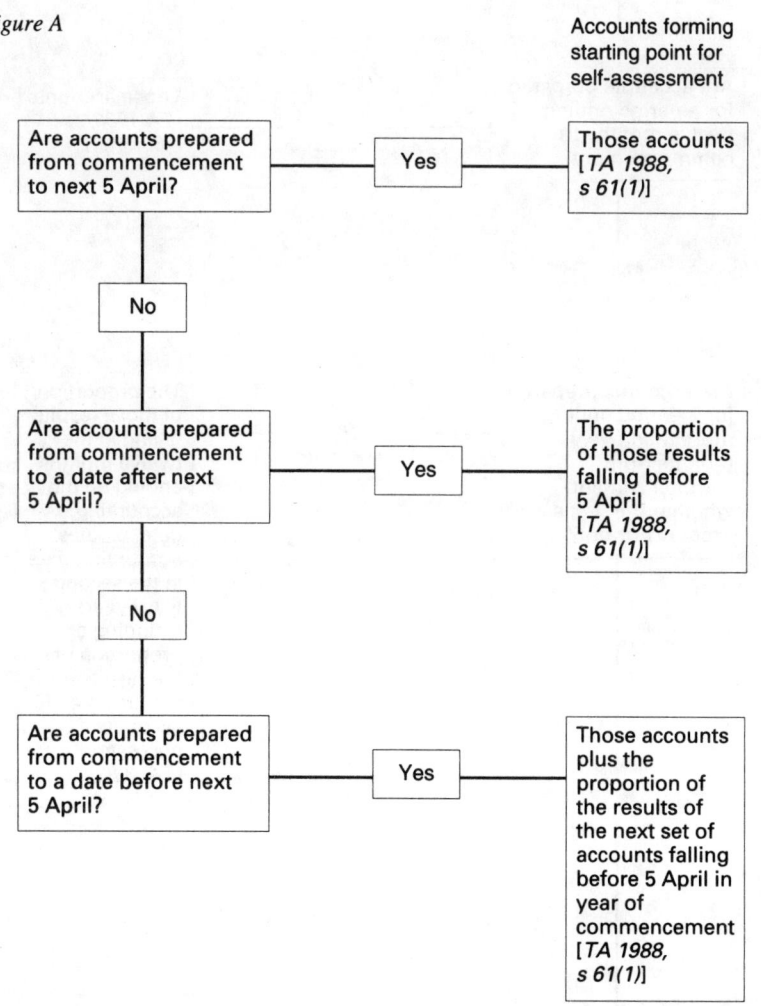

Appendix A

Second fiscal year—year following year of commencement

Figure B

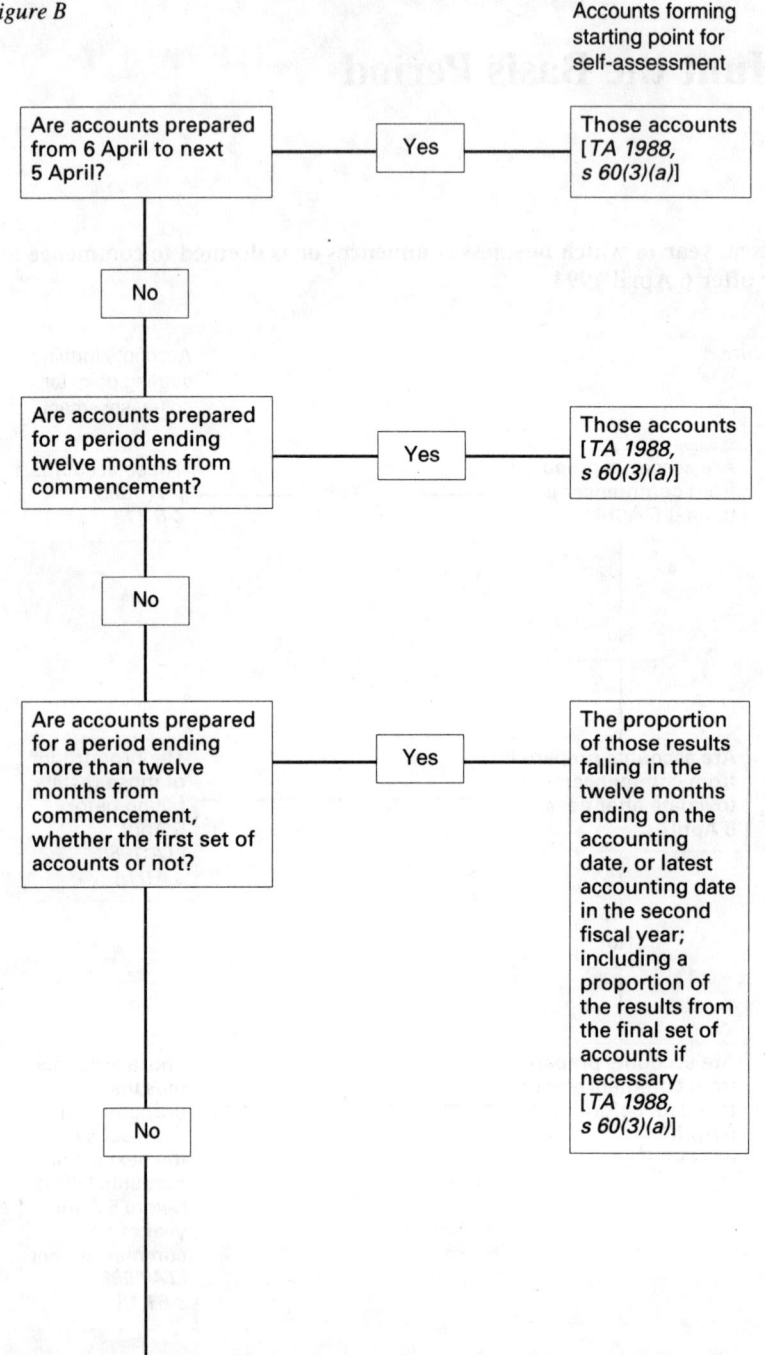

Are accounts prepared from 6 April to next 5 April?	→ Yes →	Those accounts [*TA 1988, s 60(3)(a)*]

No

Are accounts prepared for a period ending twelve months from commencement?	→ Yes →	Those accounts [*TA 1988, s 60(3)(a)*]

No

Are accounts prepared for a period ending more than twelve months from commencement, whether the first set of accounts or not?	→ Yes →	The proportion of those results falling in the twelve months ending on the accounting date, or latest accounting date in the second fiscal year; including a proportion of the results from the final set of accounts if necessary [*TA 1988, s 60(3)(a)*]

No

216

Figure B – contd.

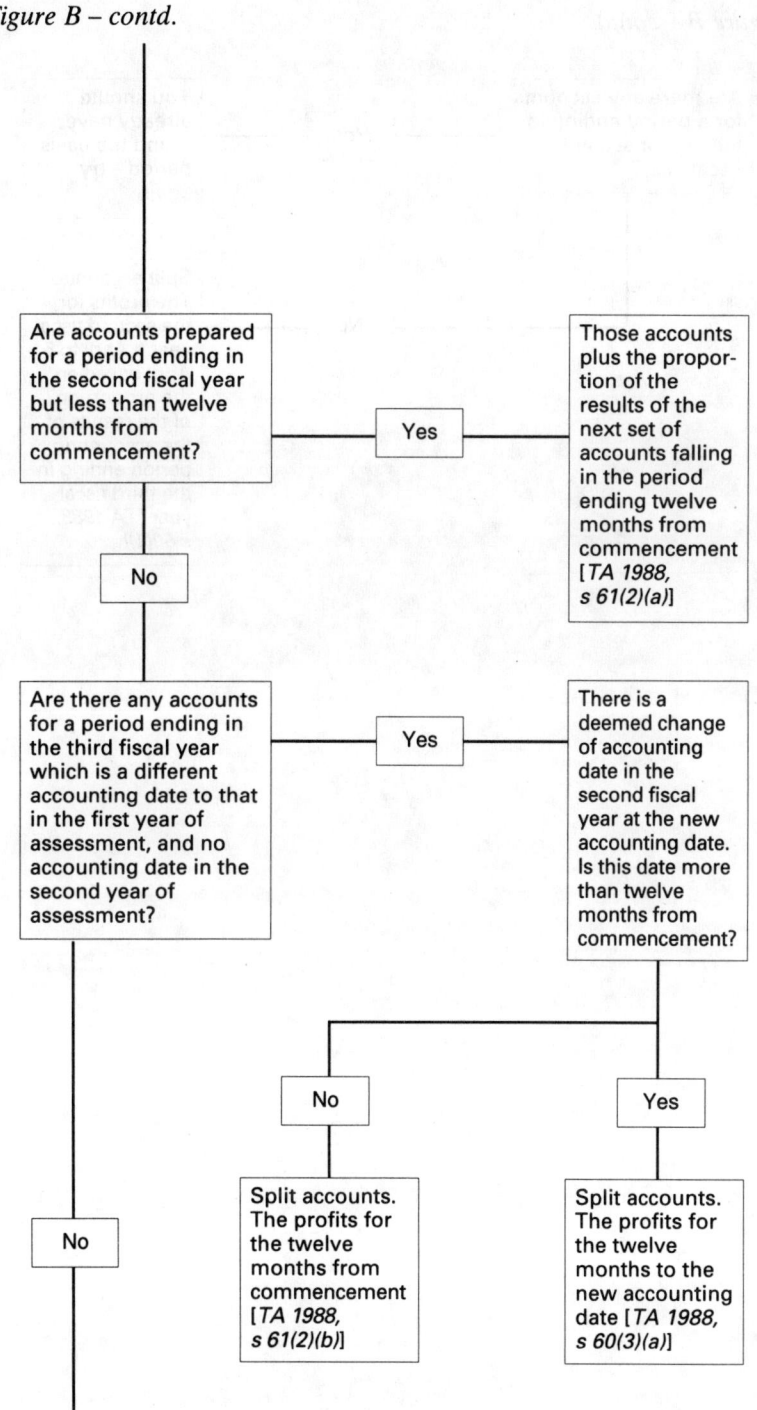

Figure B – contd.

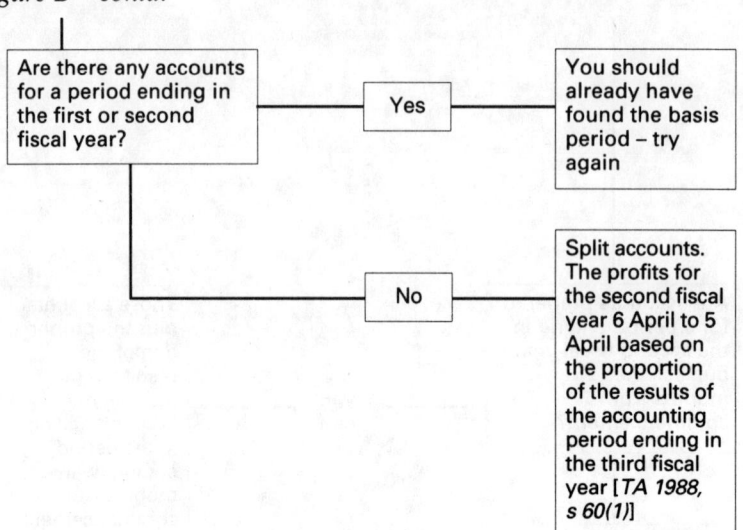

Third fiscal year in which business commenced

Figure C

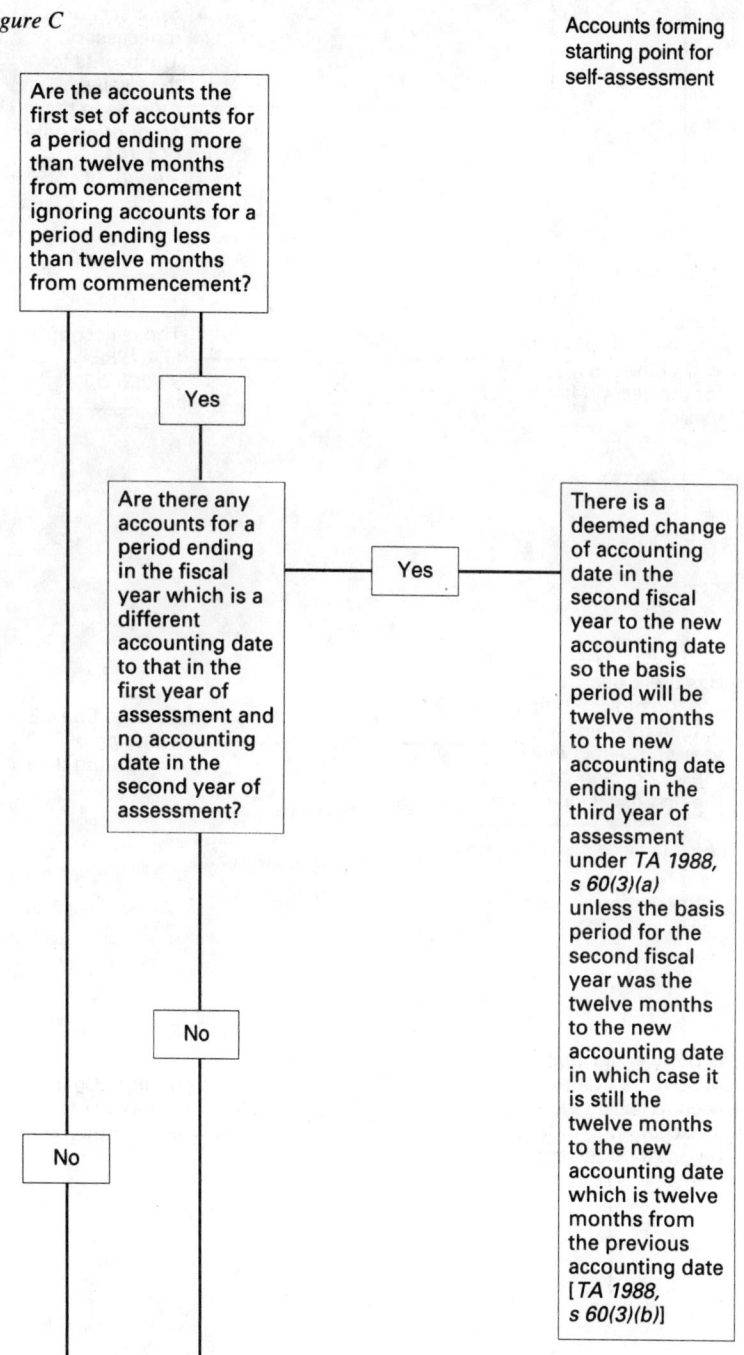

Figure C – contd.

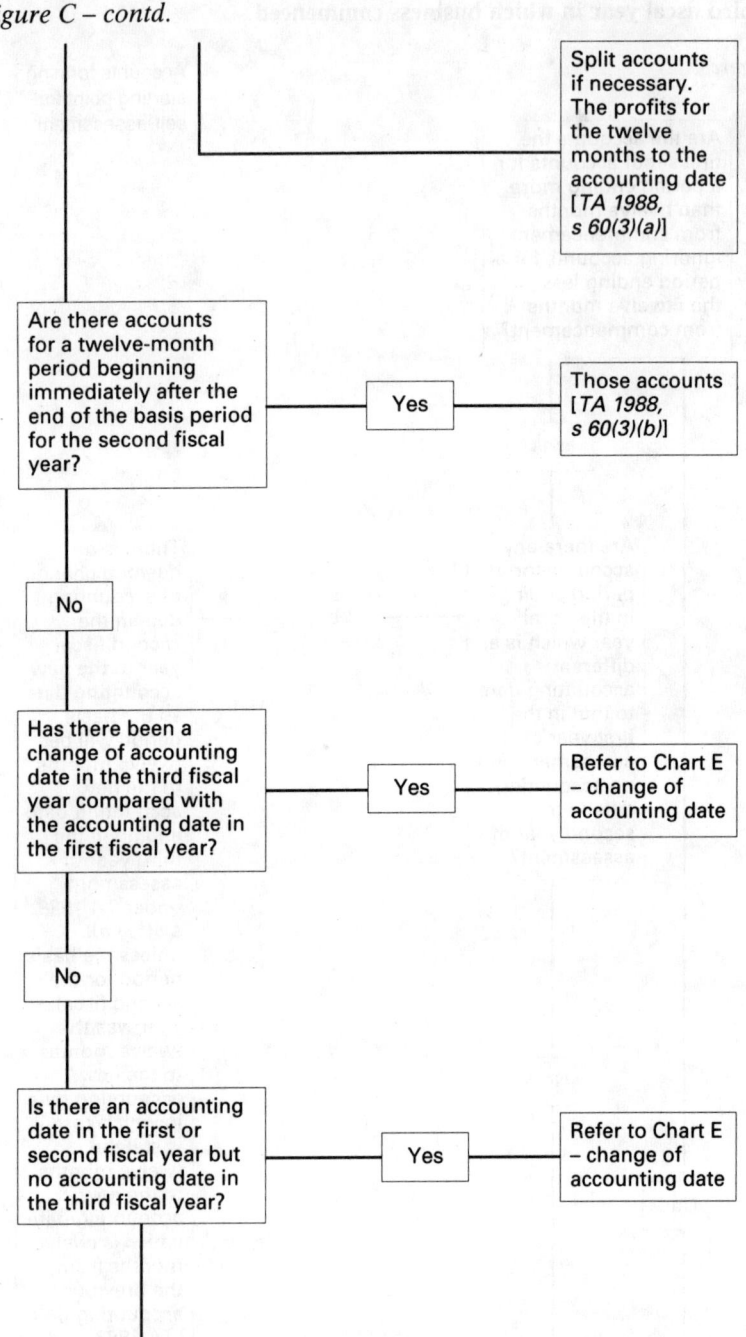

Figure C – contd.

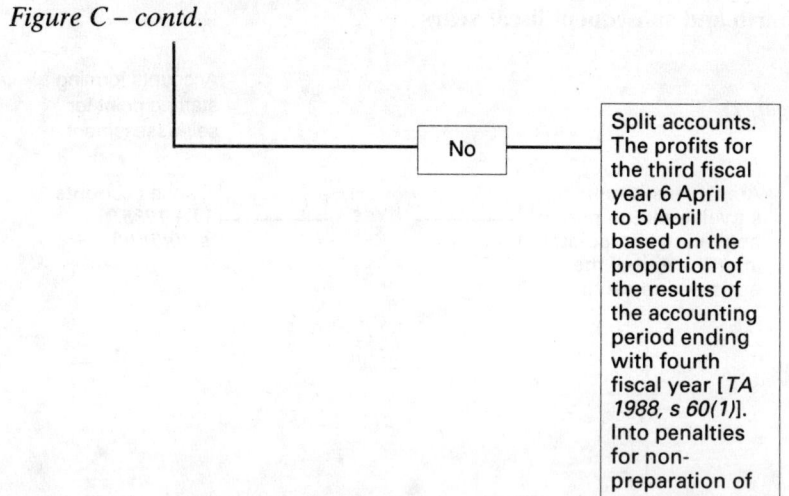

Appendix A

Fourth and subsequent fiscal years

Figure D

Accounts forming
starting point for
self-assessment

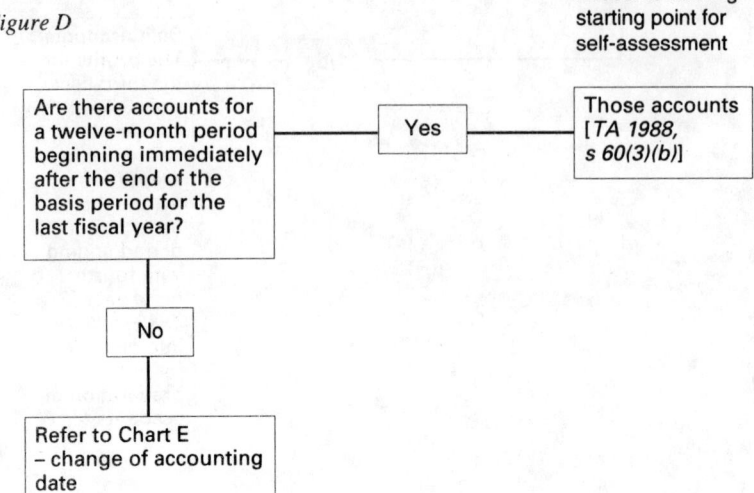

Change of accounting date (change of basis period)

Figure E

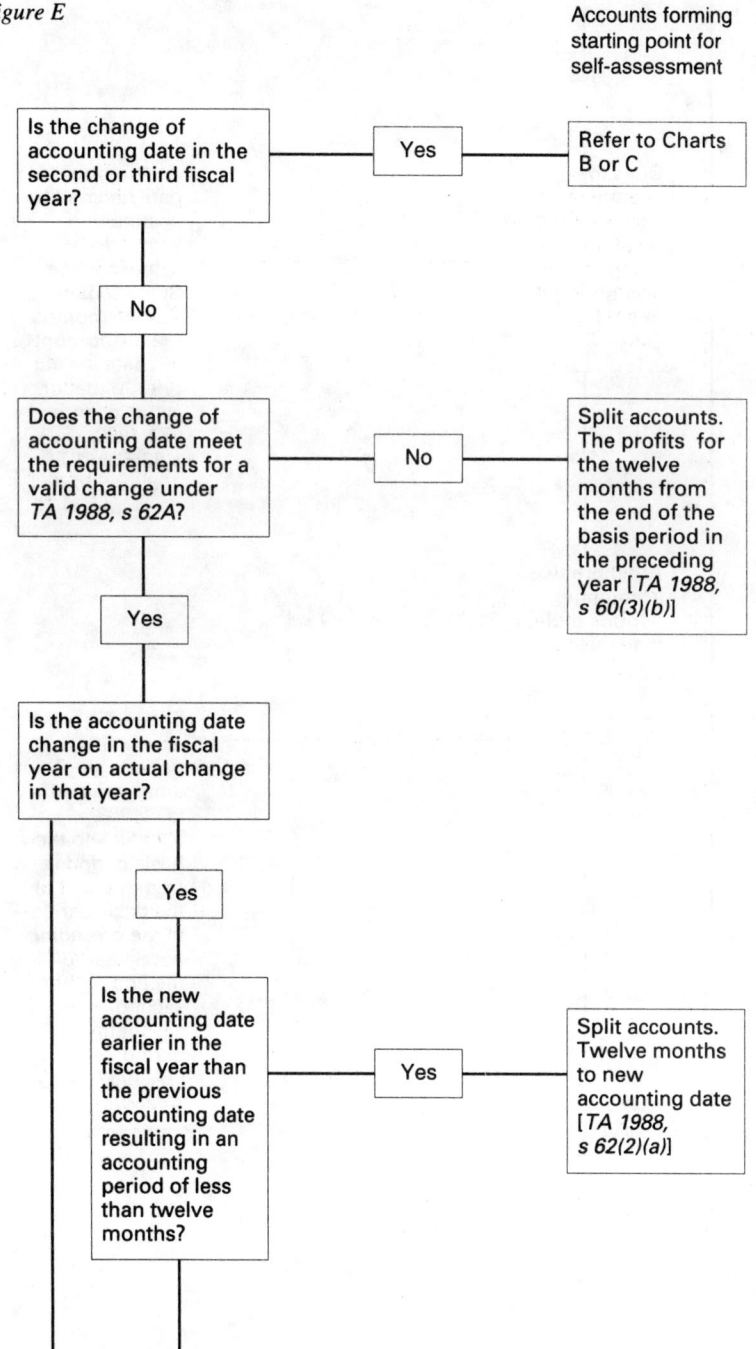

Accounts forming
starting point for
self-assessment

Is the change of accounting date in the second or third fiscal year?

Yes → **Refer to Charts B or C**

No ↓

Does the change of accounting date meet the requirements for a valid change under *TA 1988, s 62A*?

No → **Split accounts. The profits for the twelve months from the end of the basis period in the preceding year [*TA 1988, s 60(3)(b)*]**

Yes ↓

Is the accounting date change in the fiscal year on actual change in that year?

Yes ↓

Is the new accounting date earlier in the fiscal year than the previous accounting date resulting in an accounting period of less than twelve months?

Yes → **Split accounts. Twelve months to new accounting date [*TA 1988, s 62(2)(a)*]**

Figure E – contd.

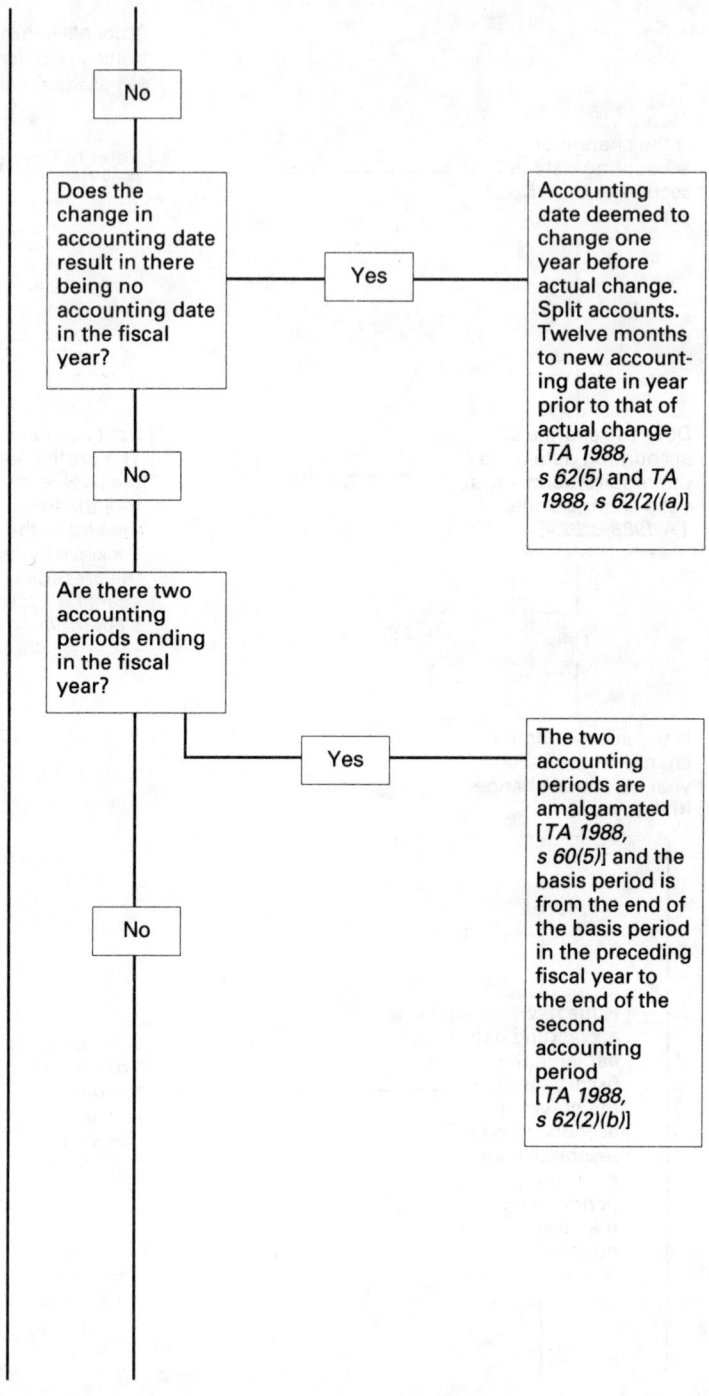

Figure E – contd.

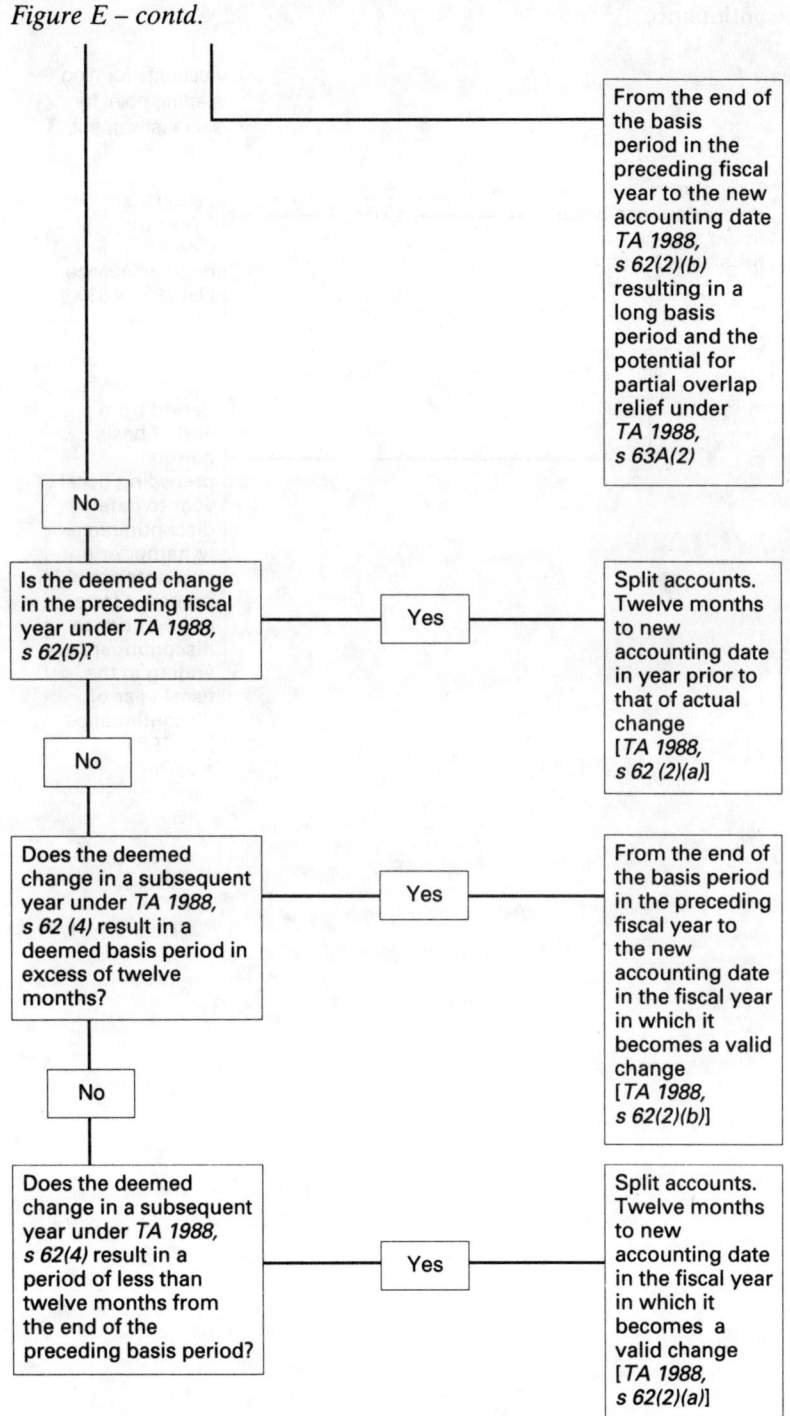

Appendix A

Discontinuance

Figure F

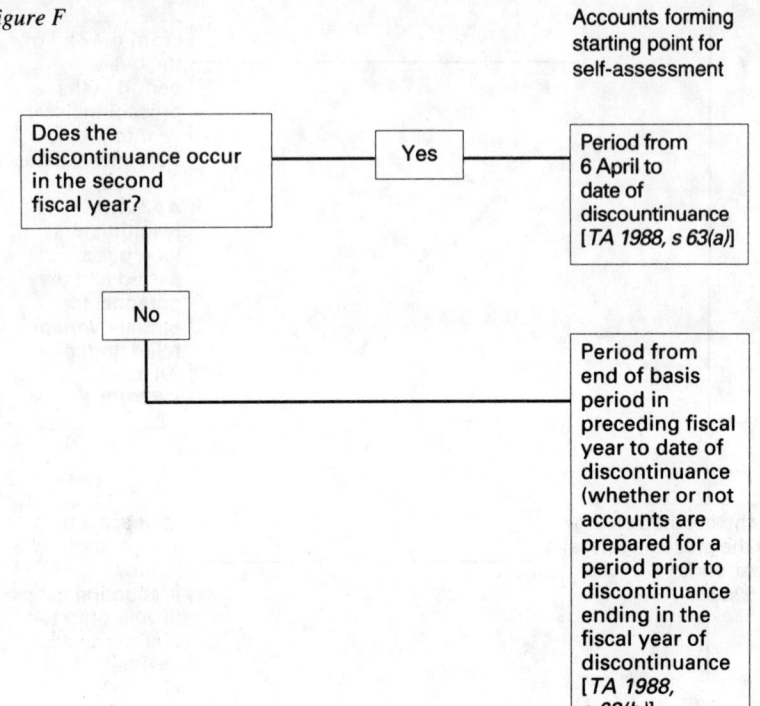

Accounts forming starting point for self-assessment

Does the discontinuance occur in the second fiscal year?

Yes — Period from 6 April to date of discountinuance [*TA 1988, s 63(a)*]

No

Period from end of basis period in preceding fiscal year to date of discontinuance (whether or not accounts are prepared for a period prior to discontinuance ending in the fiscal year of discontinuance [*TA 1988, s 63(b)*]

Transition—from old system to new. Basis period for 1996/97

Figure G

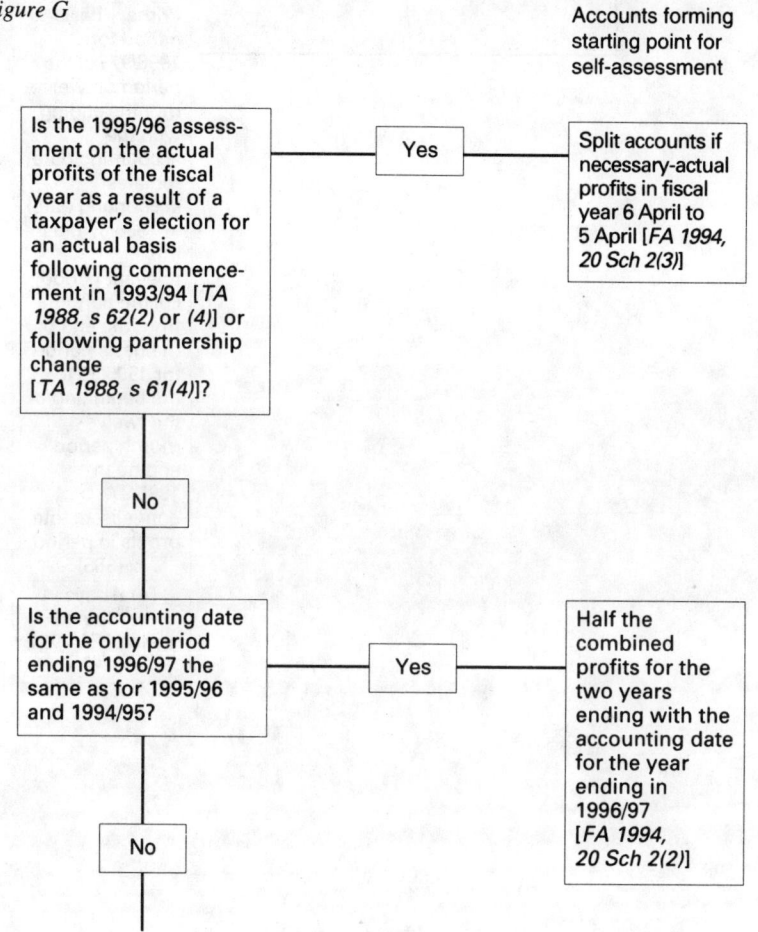

Accounts forming
starting point for
self-assessment

Is the 1995/96 assessment on the actual profits of the fiscal year as a result of a taxpayer's election for an actual basis following commencement in 1993/94 [*TA 1988, s 62(2)* or *(4)*] or following partnership change [*TA 1988, s 61(4)*]?

Yes

Split accounts if necessary-actual profits in fiscal year 6 April to 5 April [*FA 1994, 20 Sch 2(3)*]

No

Is the accounting date for the only period ending 1996/97 the same as for 1995/96 and 1994/95?

Yes

Half the combined profits for the two years ending with the accounting date for the year ending in 1996/97 [*FA 1994, 20 Sch 2(2)*]

No

Figure G – contd.

Primary basis period for 1996/97 i.e. the period of twelve months ending with the accounting date (or latest accounting date) in 1996/97 plus the

relevant period, i.e. the period from the end of the basis period for 1995/96 to the beginning of the twelve-month period ending in 1996/97, annualised; total profits in period x [365]

Total days in combined period [*FA 1994, 20 Sch 2*]

Transitional overlap

Figure H

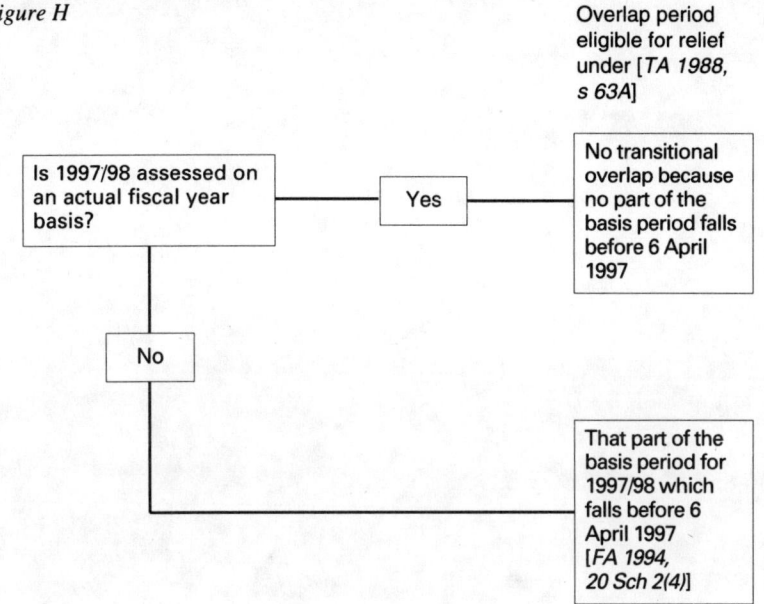

Overlap period
eligible for relief
under [*TA 1988,
s 63A*]

Is 1997/98 assessed on an actual fiscal year basis?

Yes

No

No transitional
overlap because
no part of the
basis period falls
before 6 April
1997

That part of the
basis period for
1997/98 which
falls before 6
April 1997
[*FA 1994,
20 Sch 2(4)*]

SSAP2 – Disclosure of Accounting Policies

Statement of Standard Accounting Practice (SSAP) No 2 'Disclosure of Accounting Policies' was issued by the Institute of Chartered Accountants in England and Wales and other governing bodies of the Accounting Standards Committee in November 1971.

It is fundamental to the understanding and interpretation of financial accounts that those who use them should be aware of the main assumptions on which they are based. The purpose of the statement which follows is to assist such understanding by promoting improvements in the quality of information disclosed. It seeks to achieve this by establishing as standard accounting practice the disclosure in financial accounts of clear explanations of the accounting policies followed in so far as these are significant for the purpose of giving a true and fair view. The statement does not seek to establish accounting standards for individual items; these will be dealt with in separate statements of standard accounting practice issued from time to time.

Part I – Explanatory Note

Fundamental accounting concepts, accounting bases and accounting policies

1   In accounting usage terms such as 'accounting principles,' 'practices,' 'rules,' 'conventions,' 'methods' or 'procedures' have often been treated as interchangeable.* For the purpose of this statement it is convenient to distinguish between fundamental accounting concepts, accounting bases and accounting polices.

2   Fundamental accounting concepts are hence defined as broad basic assumptions which underlie the periodic financial accounts of business enterprises. It is expedient to single out for special mention four in particular:

(*a*)   the 'going concern' concept;

(*b*)   the 'accruals' concept;

231

(*c*)   the 'consistency' concept; and

(*d*)   the 'prudence' concept.**

The use of these concepts is not necessarily self-evident from an examination of accounts, but they have such general acceptance that they call for no explanation in published accounts and their observance is presumed unless stated otherwise. They are practical rules rather than theoretical ideals and are capable of variation and evolution as accounting thought and practice develop, but their present generally accepted meanings are restated in paragraph 14 below.

*   In this series 'accounting practices' has been adopted as a generic term to encompass all aspects of financial accounting methods and presentation.

**   It is emphasised that it is not the purpose of this statement to develop a basic theory of accounting. An exhaustive theoretical approach would take an entirely different form and would include, for instance, many more propositions than the four fundamental concepts referred to here. It is, however, expedient to recognise them as working assumptions having general acceptance at the present time.

3   Accounting bases are the methods which have been developed for expressing or applying fundamental accounting concepts to financial transactions and items. By their nature accounting bases are more diverse and numerous than fundamental concepts, since they have evolved in response to the variety and complexity of types of business and business transactions, and for this reason there may justifiably exist more than on recognised accounting basis for dealing with particular items.

4   Accounting policies are the specific accounting bases judged by business enterprises to be most appropriate to their circumstances and adopted by them for the purpose of preparing their financial accounts.

Particular problems in application of the fundamental concepts

5   The main difficulty in applying the fundamental accounting concepts arises from the fact that many business transactions have financial effects spreading over a number of years. Decisions have to be made on the extent to which expenditure incurred in one year can reasonably be expected to produce benefits in the form of revenue in other years and should therefore be carried forward in whole or in part; that is, should be dealt with in the closing balance sheet, as distinct from being dealt with as an expense of the current year in the profit and loss account because the benefit has been exhausted in that year.

6   In some cases revenue is received for goods or services the production or supply of which will involve some later expenditure. In this

case a decision must be made regarding how much of the revenue should be carried forward, to be dealt with in subsequent profit and loss accounts when the relevant costs are incurred.

7 All such decisions require consideration of future events of uncertain financial effect, and to this extent an element of commercial judgement is unavoidable in the assessment.

8 Examples of matters which give rise to particular difficulty are: the future benefits to be derived from stocks and all types of work in progress at the end of the year; the future benefits to be derived from fixed assets, and the period of years over which these will be fruitful; the extent to which expenditure on research and development can be expected to produce future benefits.

Purpose and limitations of accounting bases

9 In the course of practice there have developed a variety of accounting bases designed to provide consistent, fair and as nearly as possible objective solutions to these problems in particular circumstances; for instance bases for calculating such items as depreciation, the amounts at which stocks and work in progress are to be stated, and deferred taxation.

10 Accounting bases provide an orderly and consistent framework for periodic reporting of a concern's results and financial position, but they do not, and are not intended to, substitute for the exercise of commercial judgement in the preparation of financial reports. Where a choice of acceptable accounting bases is available judgement must be exercised in choosing those which are appropriate to the circumstances and are best suited to present fairly the concern's results and financial position; the bases thus adopted then become the concern's accounting policies. The significance of accounting bases is that they provide limits to the area subject to the exercise of judgement, and a check against arbitrary, excessive or unjustifiable adjustments where no other objective yardstick is available. By definition it is not possible to develop generalised rules for the exercise of judgement, though practical working rules may be evolved on a pragmatic basis for limited use in particular circumstances. Broadly, the longer a concern's normal business cycle – the period between initiation of business transactions and their completion – the greater the area subject to judgement and its effect on periodic financial accounts, and the less its susceptibility to close regulation by accounting bases. These limitations to the regulating powers of accounting bases must be recognised.

Significance of disclosure of accounting policies

11 In circumstances where more than one accounting basis is acceptable in principle, the accounting policy followed can significantly affect a concern's reported results and financial position and the view presented can be properly appreciated only if the policies followed in dealing with material items are also explained. For this reason adequate disclosure of the accounting policies is essential to the fair presentation of financial accounts. As accounting standards become established through publication of statements of standard accounting practice, the choice of accounting bases regarded as generally available will diminish, but it has to be recognised that the complexity and diversity of business renders total and rigid uniformity of bases impracticable.

12   The items with which this statement is mainly concerned are those which are subject to the exercise of judgement as to how far they should be dealt with in the profit and loss account for the period under review or how far all or part should be carried forward in the balance sheet as attributable to the operations of future periods. The determination of the annual profit or loss of nearly every business substantially depends on a systematic approach to a few material items of this type. For the better appreciation of the view they give, annual accounts should include a clear explanation of the accounting policies followed for dealing with these few key items (some examples of which are given in paragraph 13 below). The intention and spirit of this statement are that management should identify those items of the type described which are judged material or critical for the purpose of determining and fully appreciating the company's profit or loss and its financial position, and should make clear the accounting policies followed for dealing with them.

Examples of matters for which different accounting bases are recognised

13   Significant matters for which different accounting bases are recognised and which may have a material effect on reported results and financial position include:

- depreciation of fixed assets
- treatment and amortisation of intangibles such as research
- and development expenditure, patents and trademarks
- stocks and work in progress
- long-term contracts
- deferred taxation
- hire-purchase or instalment transactions
- leasing and rental transactions
- conversion of foreign currencies
- repairs and renewals
- consolidation policies
- property development transactions
- warranties for products or services.

This list is not exhaustive, and may vary according to the nature of the operations conducted.

Part 2 – Definition of Terms

14   Fundamental accounting concepts are the broad basic assumptions which underlie the periodic financial accounts of business enterprises. At the present time the four following fundamental concepts (the relative importance of which will vary according to the circumstances of the particular case) are regarded as having general acceptability.

(*a*)   The 'going concern'concept: the enterprise will continue in operational existence for the foreseeable future. This means in particular that the profit and loss account and balance sheet assume no intention or necessity to liquidate or curtail significantly the scale of operation.

(*b*)   The 'accruals' concept; revenue and costs are accrued (that is, recognised as they are earned or incurred, not as money is received or paid), matched with one another so far as their relationship can be established or justifiably assumed, and dealt with in the profit and loss account of the period to which they relate; provided that where the accruals concept is inconsistent with the 'prudence' concept (paragraph (*d*) below), the latter prevails. The accruals concept implies that the profit and loss account reflects changes in the amount of net assets that arise out of the transactions of the relevant period (other than distributions or subscriptions of capital and unrealised surpluses arising on revaluation of fixed assets). Revenue and profits dealt with in the profit and loss account are matched with associated costs and expenses by including in the same account the costs incurred in earning them (so far as these are material and identifiable).

(*c*)   The 'consistency' concept: there is consistency of accounting treatment of like items within each accounting period and from one period to the next.

(*d*)   The concept of 'prudence': revenue and profits are not anticipated but are recognised by inclusion in the profit and loss account only when realised in the form either of cash or of other assets the ultimate cash realisation of which can be assessed with reasonable certainty; provision is made for all known liabilities (expenses and losses) whether the amount of these is known with certainty or is a best estimate in the light of the information available.

15   Accounting bases are the methods developed for applying fundamental accounting concepts to financial transactions and items, for the purpose of financial accounts, and in particular:

(*a*)   for determining the accounting period in which revenue and costs should be recognised in the profit and loss account; and

(*b*)   for determining the amounts at which material items should be stated in the balance sheet.

16   Accounting policies are the specific accounting bases selected and consistently followed by a business enterprise as being, in the opinion of the management, appropriate to its circumstances and best suited to present fairly its results and financial position.

Part 3 – Standard Accounting Practice

Disclosure of adoption of concepts which differ from those generally accepted

17   If accounts are prepared on the basis of assumptions which differ in material respects from any of the generally accepted fundamental concepts defined above, the facts should be explained. In the absence of a clear statement to the contrary, there is a presumption that the four fundamental concepts have been observed.

Disclosure of accounting policies

18   The accounting policies (as defined above) followed for dealing with items which are judged material or critical in determining profit or loss for the year and in stating the financial position should be disclosed by way of note to the accounts. The explanations should be clear, fair, and as brief as possible.

Date from which effective

19   The accounting practices set out in this statement should be adopted as soon as possible and regarded as standard in respect of reports relating to accounting periods starting on or after 1 January 1972.

Inland Revenue Press Release 31 March 1994

Self-assessment – Transition to Current Year Basis Anti-avoidance Provisions

The Financial Secretary to the Treasury, Stephen Dorrell MP, today announced the broad scope of provisions that the Government intends to introduce in the next Finance Bill. These are intended to counter avoidance of tax through manipulation of the rules for the transition from the preceding year basis to the current year basis of income tax.

In reply to a written Parliamentary question today, the Financial Secretary said:

'The Inland Revenue have today published, in a Press Release, details of the rules that the Government intends to introduce in the next Finance Bill concerning the anti-avoidance provisions for the transition from the preceding year basis to the current year basis.

The transitional rules are set out in Schedule 19 to the 1994 Finance Bill. They apply to businesses that commence before 6 April 1994 and to other sources from which income first arises before that date. Broadly for the year 1996–97 they allow a catching up process by averaging the profits for the two years ending in that year. Income in that period is therefore effectively taxed (in most cases) at half of the normal marginal rate for that year. And business profits arising in the period from the latest accounting date in 1996–97 to 5 April 1997 ultimately drop out of account altogether.

The purpose of the transitional rules is broadly to ensure that there is no double taxation of business profits and other income, presently taxed on the preceding year basis under Schedule D, which the change to the current year basis of assessment might otherwise cause. But because of the way that the rules work, and the certainty that profits of income arising in a particular period will be taxed at a reduced rate (and in some cases will drop out of account altogether), it is necessary to counteract the effect of artificially moving profits or income into these periods. The Government's intention is to deter such avoidance.

The proposals also deal with the treatment of other income, including interest, assessed on the preceding year basis, and with the treatment of interest paid on borrowings to finance trades, profession and businesses carried on in partnership.

The proposed legislation will have effect in respect of all periods which affect the amount of income assessed in 1996–97. For businesses taxed under Cases I or II of Schedule D this could commence as early as 7 April 1994. The legislation will also affect the period before 6 April 1997 which is taxed in 1997–98. The new rules do not affect limited companies.

The Inland Revenue have consulted on the proposals and will publish draft legislation this year.'

Details

Self-employed trades, professions and vocations (including partnerships)

1. At present income taxed under Schedule D is assessed on a preceding year basis except in the first and last years of trading. Under the rules in Finance Bill 1994, such income will from 1997–98 be taxed on a current year basis. Businesses commencing after 5 April 1994 – or deemed to commence under Section 113(1) ICTA 1988 following a change after that date in the membership of a partnership – will be immediately taxed on the new current year basis.

2. 1996–97 will be a transitional year for which the rules for computation are set out in Schedule 19 to the Finance Bill 1994. Tax for this year will normally be assessed on the profits from the end of the 1995–96 basis period (the accounting date ending in 1994–95) to the latest accounting date ending in 1996–97 (the 'transitional basis period'). In the normal case that will be a 24-month period, and one half of the profits will be taxed. In cases where the accounting date is changed, the period may be longer or shorter.

3. Under the new rules, the 1997–98 assessment will normally be based on the 12 months accounts ending in that year. That proportion of the profits which arises before 5 April 1997 will be available – as transitional relief – for deduction from the profits of the final period of trading, or, if earlier, when the accounting date of the business moves to 5 April. This means that eventually the profits arising in the period immediately preceding 5 April 1997 (the 'transitional relief period') will drop out of account.

4. The proposed provisions will cancel any tax advantage that might accrue from artificial movement of profits into periods of account that form the transitional basis period or the transitional relief period. In certain circumstances such counteraction will extend to taxing in full, as well as in a proportionate amount, profits which are artifically moved into the 1996–97 period. Similarly the amount of transitional relief may be reduced by the full amount of the profits shifted into the basis period for 1997–98 of which the transitional relief period forms a part.

5.   In some circumstances, businesses will be taxed for 1996–97 on the actual profits arising in the year to 5 April 1997. Such businesses will not be affected by the proposed provisions set out in this Press Release.

Proposals identifying the avoidance and cancelling the benefit

6.   The legislation will take a four step approach. The first step is to identify the type of transaction, event or change in practice – referred to collectively as 'triggers' – which may bring taxpayers within the scope of the anti-avoidance rules. Those triggers are:

- a change of one accounting policy for another or a modification within one policy;

- transactions with persons with whom the taxpayer has some family or proprietorial link (typically 'connected' persons) including part-nerships;

- arrangements with unconnected persons which are wholly or partly reciprocal or self-cancelling, for example the sale of stock immediately before the end of the transitional basis period and re-purchase immediately afterwards;

- changes in business behaviour, which need not involve any changes in accounting policy. This would mean any change in a settled practice of a trade, profession or vocation as to the timing of any of the following:

  on the incoming side of a business – the supply of goods or services, the invoicing of customers or clients and the collection of debts (including payments on account);
  on the expenditure side of a business – the obtaining of goods or services, the incurring of business expenses and the settlement of outstanding debts (including making payments on account).

7.   Any case that falls into one of these four categories will be regarded as raising a prima facie case for challenge that avoidance has taken place unless either:

(*a*)   the obtaining of a tax advantage arising from an increase in the profits of the transitional basis period, or as the case may be of the transitional relief period, is not the main benefit or one of the main benefits that can reasonably be expected to arise from the trigger; or

(*b*)   the business can show that the triggering transaction was under-taken solely for bona fide commercial reasons. Obtaining a tax advantage will not be such a reason; or

(c)   the absolute and relative amounts of profits shifted into particular periods fall below a prescribed limit, or the turnover of the business is less than a prescribed amount. The legislation will provide powers to make Regulations to set these amounts which will be announced by 5 April 1997. The Government's intention is to deter people from undertaking triggering transactions; it is therefore not appropriate at this stage to indicate the level at which these limits will be set.

8.   If the business is not excluded by any one of the tests in paragraph 7 above, the increase in profits identified for the transitional basis period will be charged in full in addition to the profits averaged down, without any adjustments to the profits for any other year of assessment. For the transitional relief period, the transitional relief will be reduced by the full amount of the profits moved into the basis period for 1997–98. The effect is demonstrated in Examples 1 and 2 respectively in the Annex.

Other income taxed on the preceding year basis

9.   Income taxed under Cases III–V of Schedule D on the preceding year basis will, under the transitional rules, be assessed for 1996–97 on half of the income arising in the two years to 5 April 1997. Broadly similar rules to those applying for trades, professions and vocations will apply to income – other than interest – which is artificially moved into these periods. Such income is not subject to transitional relief.

Interest received

10.   Where an account exists on which interest is paid gross, the law requires that new deposits and withdrawals should strictly be treated on the current year basis under the commencement and cessation provisions respectively. In practice all deposits into bank accounts are usually treated as a single source, unless the taxpayer asks for the strict basis to apply. Additions to existing holdings of National Savings Income Bonds are also usually treated as a single source.

11.   New accounts are at present put directly onto the preceding year basis where there is an existing account taxed on that basis. With the move to the current year basis for new sources of income arising after 5 April 1994, such income will be taxed in accordance with the new basis period rules contained in Finance Bill 1994, even where there already exists one or more accounts assessed on the preceding year basis.

12.   Deposits into or withdrawals from accounts, or additions to or withdrawals from existing holdings of National Savings Income Bonds on which interest first arose before 6 April 1994 that are made in the period from 6 April 1994 to 5 April 1997, will as now generally be treated on the preceding year basis. However the Inland Revenue reserve the right to apply the strict basis (current year) where it appears that pre-existing sources of interest taxed on the current year basis have been depleted and such a source taxed on the preceding year basis has been correspondingly increased in such a way as to avoid tax that would otherwise be due by taking advantage of the transitional provisions. This practice will apply only to deposits made on or after 31 March 1994.

13.   Legislation wil be brought forward in the next Finance Bill to deal with variations made on or after 31 March 1994 in the terms of an account taxed on the preceding year basis. Where such variations provide for interest to arise at irregular intervals or at rates that do not reflect the underlying accrual rate in the period from 31 March 1994 to 5 April 1998 in such a way that a tax advantage might be expected to arise, the interest will be treated as arising on each day during the period of the deposit in the amount accruing to that day.

Interest paid

14.   Payments of interest on borrowings to finance a trade or profession carried on in partnership may presently be relieved in one of two ways. Either there can be a deduction in the partnership accounts, if the interest is paid by the partnership on a partnership loan, or individual partners can get a deduction under Section 353 ICTA 1988 for their own borrowings used to finance the partnership. For the transitional year 1996–97 partnerships choosing the first method would get relief only on a proportion of the interest paid, corresponding to the fraction applied to the basis period for that year. But if they claimed relief under Section 353 the partners would be eligible for relief on the full amount of interest paid on a fiscal year basis. The Inland Revenue are aware that partnerships are being advised to obtain new personal loans to ensure they get relief under Section 353.

15.   The Government intends to legislate to ensure that, unless there are bona fide commercial reasons for the re-financing, and the main or one of the main purposes is not to obtain a tax advantage, Section 353 relief will be reduced proportionately. Any interest which qualifies for relief under Section 353 and is paid in the period between the end of the 1995–96 basis period and 6 April 1997 (exclusive) will be reduced to the fraction of which the numerator is 12 and the denominator the number of months in that period. The effect of these proposals is shown in Example 3 in the Annex. They will not apply to any re-financing arrangements completed before 31 March 1994.

241

Appendix C

Annex

Example 1

Transitional basis period avoidance (Paragraph 8)

Geoffrey returns profits as follows:

Year ended 5 April 1995	£10,000
2 years ended 5 April 1997	£30,000

The assessments are
1995–96	£10,000
1996–97	£30,000 × 12/24 = £15,000

Profits of £5,000 were shifted from the year ended 5 April 1995 to the following period by means of one of the triggers. If Geoffrey is unable to demonstrate that either of the exclusions in paragraph 7(*a*) or (*b*) applies, £5,000 will be added to the returned assessment for 1996–97, making £20,000 in all. The assessment for 1995–96 will remain unchanged.

Example 2

Transitional relief period avoidance (Paragraph 8)

Helen returns profits as follows:

Year ended 5 October 1997	£36,000
Year ended 5 October 1998	£24,000

The assessments are
1997–98	£36,000
1998–99	£24,000

Transitional relief in respect of the apportioned profits for the period from 6 October 1996 to 5 April 1997 would be £36,000 × 6/12 = £18,000.

Profits of £6,000 were shifted from the year ended 5 October 1998 to the previous year by means of one of the triggers. If Helen is unable to demonstrate that either of the exclusions in paragraph 7(*a*) or (*b*) applies, the transitional relief will be reduced by £6,000 to £12,000. There will be no further adjustments.

Example 3

Refinancing of partnership borrowing (Paragraph 15)

Ian is a partner in ABC & Co which draws up accounts to 5 April. In 1994–95, he borrows £100,000 and introduces it into the partnership to reduce the partnership overdraft. In each of the years 1995–96 and 1996–97, he pays interest of £7,500, for which he claims relief under Section 353

ICTA 1988. He is unable to demonstrate that the re-financing is under-taken for bona fide commercial reasons. The relief is reduced in the ratio 12/24: he is given relief of £3,750 in each of these years.

Janet is a partner in DE & Co which draws up accounts to 5 May. On 6 May 1994, she borrows £240,000 and introduces it into DE & Co to enable a term loan to be paid off early. In 1994–95 she pays interest of £16,500, and in each of the years 1995–96 and 1996–97 interest of £18,000. She claims relief each year under Section 353. She is unable to demon-strate that the refinancing is undertaken for bona fide commercial reasons. The relief is reduced in the ratio 12/35 i.e. an average 12-month measure of interest paid is spread over the entire period from the start of the transitional period (6 May 1994) to the end of the transitional relief period (5 April 1997). This is to ensure that some relief is given for 1996–97. She is given relief of £5,658 in 1994–95 and £6,172 in both 1995–96 and 1996–97.

Change of Accounting Date

Revenue leaflet IR 26 is reproduced below (with dates in examples updated). References are to sections as originally enacted.

1. This leaflet sets out briefly the practice of the Board of Inland Revenue in cases where a trader permanently changes his accounting date.

Statutory provisions

2. The relevant statutory provisions are contained in *TA 1988, s 60*. The effect of these provisions is briefly as follows.

(i) In the normal case where there is only one account ending in the year preceding the year of assessment and that account is for a period of one year, the assessment is to be based on the profit of that account. [*TA 1988, s 60(3)*].

(ii) In other cases, the Board of Inland Revenue are to decide what period of 12 months ending on a date in the preceding income tax year is to be the basis year. [*TA 1988, s 60(4)*]. There is no appeal against that decision.

(iii) Where the Board have determined the basis year for any income tax year under (ii), they may direct that the assessment for the preceding income tax year is to be adjusted to the profits of the corresponding period, i.e. the year ending on the same date in the previous year [*TA 1988, s 60(5)*]; an appeal against the Board's decision to make or not to make any such direction lies to the General or Special Commissioners, who are empowered to grant 'such relief, if any, as is just'.

Board's normal practice

3. Under *TA 1988, s 60(4)* the Board normally decide that the assessment is to be based on the profits of the period of 12 months ending on the new accounts date in the preceding income tax year, i.e. the date to which the trader proposes to make up his accounts in future.

4.   The question then arises whether there is to be any adjustment of the assessment for the preceding income tax year under *TA 1988, s 60(5)* to the profits of the 'corresponding' period. Such an adjustment may increase or decrease the liability, according to the trend of profits.

5.   The considerations which the Board have in mind in determining this question are as follows. Where there is a permanent change of accounting date then, whether or not revision under *TA 1988, s 60(5)* is ordered, one of two things must, in the ordinary course, happen:

(*a*)   If the new date is later in the income tax year than the old, the profits of some period will not come into assessment at all.

(*b*)   If the new date is earlier in the income tax year than the old, the profits of some period will come into assessment twice.

If the profits of the period omitted were relatively low, or the profits of the period coming in twice were relatively high, the Revenue would gain: conversely, if the profits of the period omitted were relatively high, or the profits coming in twice were relatively low, the taxpayer would gain. The Board attempt to secure that the profits to be assessed twice, or to be omitted from assessment, as the case may be, are 'average' profits. As a rule this object can be secured neither by straightforward revision nor by non-revision, but only by taking for the year to which *TA 1988, s 60(5)* applies some figure intermediate between the revised and unrevised figures, and it is the Board's normal practice to propose, subject to the concurrence of the Commissioners of Income Tax having jurisdiction in the particular case, the adoption of such an intermediate figure. That intermediate figure is computed by reference to a consideration of:

(i)   the profits of all the accounting periods of which any part enters into either the basis year (or, in some cases, years) under *TA 1988, s 60(4)* or the 'corresponding period' under *TA 1988, s 60(5)* (referred to subsequently as the 'relevant accounting periods'), and

(ii)   the number of years for which the assessments are based in whole or in part on any of the profits of the 'relevant accounting periods' are expanded or reduced on a time basis so as to give a proportionate figure (referred to subsequently as the 'aggregate profit') for the 'relevant years', and the assessment for the year to which *TA 1988, s 60(5)* applies is adjusted, up or down as the case may be, so that the total of the assessments for all the 'relevant years' is precisely equal to the 'aggregate profit'.

The working of this practice can best be illustrated by an example – see *Example 1*.

Right of appeal

6.   It is open to the taxpayer, if he does not accept the Board's proposal to appeal to the General or Special Commissioners against any direction by the Board that may be made under *TA 1988, s 60(5)* or against a decision not to issue a direction, and the Commissioners are empowered on appeal to give such relief, if any, as is just. The Board's proposal represents the solution which they consider would be likely to commend itself to the Commissioners and where it is accepted there is in effect an agreed recommendation as to what is thought to be just.

Special cases

7.   The practice outlined above is suitable for the majority of cases. There are, however, certain classes of case which are incapable of solution along these lines for which modifications are necessary, e.g.:

(a)   cases where the 'aggregate profit' is not intermediate between the sum of the assessments for the 'relevant years' without revision under *TA 1988, s 60(5)* and the sum of the assessments for those years after revision under that section;

(b)   cases where there is a marked seasonal fluctuation in the rate of profit (e.g. in the case of the seaside hotel);

(c)   cases where in some or all of the periods concerned losses were incurred;

(d)   cases where any one of the years concerned is affected by the commencement or cessation provisions.

The modifications that are introduced to deal with these special types of case cannot be described in detail within the limits of this leaflet, but the general method followed throughout is that of equating the average rate of assessments over the years affected to the average rate of profits in the accounting periods that form the basis of those assessments. In cases falling within head (a) it may be necessary in order to secure this result to depart from the general rule mentioned in paragraph 3 and to determine a basis year under *TA 1988, s 60(4)* which, when regard is had to the profits of that year and existing assessments, will enable effect to be given to the 'average' adjustment. Again in cases falling within head (b) it may be necessary to modify the 'average' adjustment so that the assessments reflect a true annual rate of profit and not a rate that is inflated or depressed by seasonal results.

Small differences

8.   Where the 'average' computation brings out an 'aggregate profit' which exceeds, or falls short of, the sum of the unrevised assessment for the preceding year and the assessments for the other 'relevant years' by a relatively small amount, it is not the Board's normal practice to take any action by way of 'average' adjustment. For this purpose, the Board would normally regard as relatively small a difference that was less than 10 per

cent of the average of the current and preceding years' assessments and also less than £1,000 – see *Example 2*.

Example 1: Normal practice – paragraphs 3–5

The accounts of a business have been made up annually to 30 September for, up to and including 30 September 1991. The next account is for the nine months to 30 June 1992, and it is intended that subsequent accounts will be made up annually to 30 June.

The trading profits are as follows:

		£
12 months to 30 September 1990		36,000
12 months to 30 September 1991		18,000
9 months to 30 June 1992		12,000
33		66,000

The 1992–93 assessment has been made on £18,000, the profit of the year to 30 September 1991.
The 1993–94 assessment based on the year to 30 June 1992, under *TA 1988, s 60(4)* will be

	£
(3/12) × £18,000	4,500
	12,000
	16,500

The following review is made to see whether the 1992–93 assessment of £18,000 should be revised.

(i) *'Aggregate profit'*
The profit for the 'relevant accounting periods' is £66,000 for the 33 months to 30 June 1992.
The relevant years are 1991–92, 1992–93 and 1993–94, a period of 36 months.
The aggregate profit is therefore the profit for 36 months at the rate of £66,000 for 33 months, i.e.
(36/33) × £66,000 = £72,000

(ii) *Sum of assessments for 'relevant years' without revision under s 115(3).*

	'Relevant Years'	Assessments £
	1991–92	36,000
	1992–93	18,000
	1993–94	16,500
Sum of assessments for 'relevant years'		70,500

Since the difference between (i) £72,000 and (ii) £70,500 is greater than £1,000 (see paragraph 8) the calculation proceeds as follows:

(iii) *Sum of assessments for 'relevant years' after revision under TA 1988, s 60(5).*

'Relevant years'		*Assessments*
		£
1991–92		36,000
1992–93 (3/12) × £36,000 = £9,000		
(9/12) × £18,000 = £13,500		22,500
1993–94		16,500
Sum of assessments for 'relevant years'		75,000

The figure at (i) £72,000 is intermediate between (ii) £70,500 and (iii) £75,000. The assessment for 1992–93 is therefore revised to such an amount that the total of the assessments for the relevant years equal the figure at (i) as follows:

		£
Figure at (i)		72,000
Assessed 1991–92	£36,000	
Assessed 1993–94	£16,500	52,500
Balance to be assessed for 1992–93		19,500

The assessment for 1992–93 is therefore revised to £19,500 by means of a further assessment of £1,500 (£19,500–£18,000).

Example 2: Small difference – paragraph 8

The accounts of a business have been made up annually to 31 March for years up to and including 31 March 1991. The next account is for the 18 months to 30 September 1992, and it is intended that subsequent accounts will be made up annually to 30 September.

The trading profits are as follows:	£
12 months to 31 March 1990	2,400
12 months to 31 March 1991	3,000
18 months to 30 September 1992	6,000
42	11,400

The 1991–92 assessment has been made on £3,000, the profit of the year to 31 March 1991.

The basis of assessment for each of the years 1992–93 and 1993–94 requires to be determined under *TA 1988, s 60(4)*. In accordance with paragraph 3 the years to 30 September 1991, and 30 September 1992, will be taken as the basis years and the assessments will be

		£
1992–93	(6/12) × £3,000 =	1,500
	(6/18) × £6,000 =	2,000
		3,500
1993–94	(12/18) × £6,000 =	4,000

The following review is made to see whether the 1991–92 assessment of £3,000 should be revised.

(i) *'Aggregate profit'*
The profit for the relevant accounting periods is £11,400 for the 42 months to 30 September 1992.
The relevant years are 1990–91, 1991–92, 1992–93 and 1993–94 a period of 48 months.
The aggregate profit is therefore the profit for 48 months at the rate of £11,400 for 42 months, i.e.
$(48/42) \times £11,400 = £13,028$

(ii) *Sum of assessments for 'relevant years' without revision under TA 1988, s 60(5)*

'Relevant Years'	Assessments £
1990–91	2,400
1991–92	3,000
1992–93	3,500
1993–94	4,000
Sum of assessments for 'relevant years'	12,900

The difference between (i) £13,028 and (ii) £12,900 is £128. This is less than £1,000 and 10 per cent of mean of £3,500 for 1992–93 and £3,000 for 1991–92 i.e. 10 per cent of ½ of (£3,500 + £3,000) = £325.

The case accordingly falls within paragraph 8 and no action is therefore necessary under *TA 1988, s 60(5)*.

Effect of New Rules on Partnership Agreements

Removal of joint and several liability

A fundamental change is that partnerships will not be assessed jointly in the partnership name [*substituted TA 1988, s 111*]. Rather, each partner will be separately assessable. The consequences for partnerships and partnership agreements can be summarised as follows.

(*a*)   There will no longer be a requirement for tax reserves to be made with a view to protecting the partners as a body. In this regard, it has been usual for a provision in partnership agreements that profits are not to be drawn out unless and until there is a surplus available after providing for all amounts of tax which it is anticipated may become payable. Nevertheless, a retention may still be thought desirable, as a means of forced saving to ensure that each partner can discharge his tax liabilities in due course, and does not cause embarrassment to his fellow partners.

(*b*)   There will be no need for a partner to indemnify the other partners jointly and severally for his proportion of any tax payable by the partnership.

(*c*)   Since tax will no longer be a partnership debt, on the retirement of a partner any provision that the continuing partners will take over all the partnership liabilities will not extend to any tax liability of the retiring partner.

Financial reporting and partnership returns

With the new filing deadlines under Simplified Assessing, namely 30 September for assessment by the Revenue and 31 January for self-assessment, it will be necessary for each partner to be in receipt of the appropriate financial information to enable him to file his own return on a timely basis. The legislation also imposes upon the partnership certain reporting requirements relating to the partnership return and the partnership statement. These will also need to be complied with to avoid penalties (see 10.19 *et seq.*).

Various points arise in connection with the drafting of the partnership agreement.

251

(*a*)   A fairly standard clause in a partnership agreement requires a partnership accountant to prepare accounts for the firm for the financial year. It will be advisable for such clause specifically to provide that the accounts are prepared well before the 30 September initial deadline for Revenue assessment.

(*b*)   The partnership agreement should likewise provide for the preparation of the partnership return and the partnership statement in the form required by *TMA 1970, s 12AA* and *12AB*, also well before 30 September if possible. Otherwise, if these are only made available to the partners and filed shortly before the 31 January second deadline, each partner will be forced to self-assess. Provision should be made in the partnership agreement for the filing of such return and partnership statement in any event by the 31 January deadline (see 10.24).

(*c*)   There should be further provision in the partnership agreement to ensure that any requisite claims for relief are made, a number of which have to be included in the partnership return (see 10.44).

These latter aspects are perhaps most appropriately dealt with under a separate clause relating to the precedent partner, dealt with below.

Record-keeping

It is again a usual term of a partnership agreement that proper books of account are kept by the partnership, showing all receipts and payments on behalf of the firm. But now that *TMA 1970, s 12B* contains specific provisions relating to data retention by businesses, both as regards the precise data to be retained and the period for keeping records, it would be advisable as an *aide-mémoire* for the relevant book and record-keeping provisions in the partnership agreement to mirror the requirements of *section 12B* (see 10.19 *et seq*.). There should also be provision for keeping records of acquisitions and disposals of partnerships assets, this being a specific requirement of *TMA 1970, s 12AA(7)* (see 10.22).

The relevant clause might take the following form:

'Proper books of accounts and records shall be kept of all matters transactions and things that are usually entered in such accounts by those engaged in a business similar to the partnership business (including details of acquisitions and disposals of chargeable assets) and such accounts together with all letters, bills, vouchers, papers and other documents relating to the partnership business (including for the avoidance of doubt all such records as are specified in *TMA 1970, s 12B*) shall be kept in a place agreed upon the partners for at least [6] years and shall be open at all times to inspection by any of the partners.'

Change of partners

On a change of partners there will no longer be a cessation, subject to the possibility of making a continuation election. Instead, provided that there is at least one person engaged in the trade, profession or vocation after the change, there is an automatic continuation. Accordingly:

(*a*) There will be no necessity for the usual provision whereby an outgoing partner is required to join with the continuing partners or any new partner in making the continuation election.

(*b*) There will likewise be no necessity for any indemnity to be given to the outgoing partner or his estate in respect of any additional tax which he would not have suffered if he had not joined in such continuation election.

Precedent partner

Given the obligations imposed upon the partnership as a body, and in default on individual partners, to supply the Revenue with information, it would be advisable for the partnership agreement to provide for the appointment of a precedent partner who had the specific authority and obligation to deal with the making of the partnership return and partnership statement.

A clause on the following lines might be appropriate:

(i) The partners shall [on or before . . . [date] and in every subsequent [third] year] elect one of their number to be the precedent partner of the firm for the purposes of the provisions of the *Taxes Management Act 1970* ('TMA') to take office on [1 January] of the following year for the term of [three] years.

(ii) If during his term of office the precedent partner shall resign his appointment by notice in writing to the other partners or be removed from office then the other partners shall as soon as possible after any such event elect a successor who shall immediately take office for the remainder of the term of office of the partner who has been replaced.

(iii) The precedent partner shall ensure that the partnership return and statement is prepared and that a copy thereof is delivered to each partner by [31 August] in any financial year and is duly filed with the Inland Revenue in accordance with *TMA 1970, ss 12AA* and *12AB* and the precedent partner will further ensure that all claims for relief required by *TMA 1970, s 42(6)* and all such other matters as are appropriate to such return are included in the return.

Equitable adjustments

Most partnership agreements are silent about the imbalance that can arise under the existing preceding year system as a result of the tax for a year of assessment being calculated by reference to profits of the preceding year, but allocated in accordance with the profit-sharing arrangements of the current year. However, sometimes there are equitable adjustment clauses. These will generally no longer be required under Simplified Assessing. One exception perhaps is where there are prior salaries to certain partners which exceed the profits of the period (see *Example 2* in 7.7).

A clause on the following lines might be appropriate to cover such a possibility:

(i)   [Name] shall [in addition to the share of profits to which he is entitled under Clause . . .] be paid by way of salary as a prior charge the sum of £. . . per annum which shall be treated as an expense of the partnership in computing the partnership profits.

(ii) In the event that the payment of the said salary results in any of the other partners incurring a loss for the financial year which in computing the income of [name] for tax purposes results in a corresponding reduction in his taxable income, an amount equal to the consequent reduction in his tax liability shall be paid by [name] to the other partner or partners pro-rata to their profit-sharing ratio.

Index

Index